APPLICATIONS OF PSYCHOLOGY
TO THE AVIATION SYSTEM

Applications of Psychology to the Aviation System

Proceedings of the 21st Conference of the European Association for Aviation Psychology (EAAP)
Volume 1

edited by
NICK McDONALD
NEIL JOHNSTON
RAY FULLER

© Nick McDonald, Neil Johnston and Ray Fuller 1995

All rights reserved. No part of this publication may be reproduced, stored in a retrieval system, or transmitted in any form or by any means, electronic, mechanical, photocopying, recording or otherwise without the prior permission of the publisher.

Published by
Avebury Aviation
Ashgate Publishing Limited
Gower House
Croft Road
Aldershot
Hants GU11 3HR
England

Ashgate Publishing Company
Old Post Road
Brookfield
Vermont 05036
USA

British Library Cataloguing in Publication Data

Applications of Psychology to the Aviation System:
Proceedings of the 21st Conference of the European
Association for Aviation Psychology (EAAP)
  I. McDonald, Nicholas
  629.13252019
ISBN 0-291-39818-9

Library of Congress Catalog Card Number: 94-72786

Printed in Great Britain at the University Press, Cambridge

Contents

Introduction   1
Nick McDonald, Neil Johnston and Ray Fuller

Opening speech to the 1994 WEAAP conference   3
Brian Cowen, TD

Part 1 Policy for Human Factors in Aviation

1 The future of Human Factors and psychology in aviation from the ICAO's perspective   9
Capt. Daniel Maurino

2 Human Factors, the next technological advance? Issues and needs: a view from the CEC   16
P.C. Cacciabue and C.J. North

3 Change in European civil aviation: challenges to safety and perspectives   23
Jean Pariès

4 The national plan for aviation Human Factors: Federal Aviation Administration implementation   32
Mark A. Hofmann

5 'How science really works': cultural influences on aviation psychology   38
Allan D. English

Part 2 Systems and Organisation

6 Organisational safety culture and aviation practice   47
Nick Pidgeon and Mike O'Leary

7   Transport Canada's System Analysis and Functional Evaluation   53
    (SAFE) Program
    James P. Stewart

8   Safety and learning: safety services in British Airways   57
    Heather Höpfl and Callum MacGregor

9   Organisational change: the human factor   63
    Brent Hayward

10 Achieving organisational attachment through resource management   69
    Capt. Graham Beaumont

11 Organisational dynamics and safety   75
    Professor Ron Westrum

12 Organisational culture, job satisfaction and work stress: the case   81
    of Irish women pilots
    Eunice McCarthy and Angela McGinn

13 Psychology and Air Traffic Control: who cares?   91
    Bert Ruitenberg

Part 3   Accidents/Incidents and their Aftermath

Section A   Accident Investigation

14 Investigation of Human Factors: the link to accident prevention   101
    Peter G. Harle

15 The contribution of aviation psychology to the investigation of   108
    aircraft accidents of German Armed Forces
    Burkhart Falckenberg

16 Report on air traffic accident on 27 December 1991 at Gottröra,   113
    AB County
    Kristina Pollack

Section B   Voluntary Incident Reporting

17 The quantitative analysis of qualitative data: methodological   117
    issues in the derivation of trends from incident reports
    Don Harris

18	'Too bad we have to have confidential reporting programmes!': some observations on safety culture *Mike J. O'Leary*	123
19	Self-report means under-report? *R.S. Elwell*	129

Section C Accidents in Ground Handling

20	Towards an integrated approach for ramp safety management *Hans Oude Egberink*	139
21	The use of international data in the analysis of accidents *George White and Nick McDonald*	145

Section D Crisis Management

22	'It's not over yet': mitigating the effects of disasters and traumatic accidents *Gerard P.S. Jackson*	153
23	Training for trauma: a real life study *John A. Connolly and Margaret Connolly*	158
24	The ripple-off effect of aviation disasters on families and children *Margaret Connolly and John A. Connolly*	163

Part 4 Cross-cultural Factors

25	Cross-cultural aspects of Human Factors in a multi-national multi-cultural airline *Capt. Majid Kabbani*	169
26	Applying the critical incident management model to intercultural cockpit/ATC communication: a case study *Dr Jan Meyer*	173
27	The multi-national crew: verbal and non-verbal communication, with special reference to safety *Capt. Arild Smith-Christensen and Dr Fanny Duckert*	180

28 Culture and the cockpit in context: a situational perspective of   185
    behaviour in the cockpit
    Roger Lambo and Richard Lambo

29 Cultural differences: flight deck reality and problems   191
    David Johnson

30 Cross-cultural assessment of flight crew behavior styles   195
    Dr Neil A. Johnson and Dennis J. Sullivan

Part 5 Theory and History

31 'A predisposition to cowardice?': cultural influences on aviation   203
    psychology
    Allan D. English

32 Behavioural theory and behavioural technology in the design of   209
    safe systems
    Julian C. Leslie

33 Opening up ATC work: behavioural, cognitive and sociological   216
    perspectives
    Liam Bannon and Dan Shapiro

34 Cooperative work and technological support in Air Traffic Control   223
    D. Randall and R. Harper

35 The organisational context of an interface: the case of ATC   229
    R. Harper and D. Randall

Part 6 Perspectives on Crew Resource Management

36 Extending Crew Resource Management: an overview   237
    Brent Hayward

37 Assessment of non-technical skills: is it possible?   243
    Patricia A.M. Antersijn and Marieke C. Verhoef

38 An operational model for the evaluation of Crew Resource   251
    Management (CRM) skills in Line Operations Simulation (LOS)
    Thomas W. Houle

39	Work group multitasking in aviation *Mary J. Waller*	256
40	Women's learning and leadership styles: impact on CRM *Mary Ann Turney*	262
41	Transfer of the CRM concept into operative medicine *H.G. Schaefer*	269
42	Crossing the cultural boundary *J.M. Davis*	271

Part 7 Automation

43	Automation and accountability *Kathleen L. Mosier and Linda J. Skitka*	275
44	Studying automation in the lab – can you? should you? *Clint A. Bowers and Eduardo Salas*	281
45	Automation and the corporate aviation environment *John A. Wise, David W. Abbott, Donald S. Tilden, Patrick C. Guide and Jennifer L. Dyck*	287

Part 8 Individual Factors

Section A Alcohol

46	Early intervention of alcohol problems among pilots *Dr Fanny Duckert*	297
47	A program to treat alcoholic airline pilots and return them to work *Richard B. Stone*	302

Section B Personality

48	Personality on the flight deck *Greg Stead*	309
49	A comparison of personality characteristics for freshmen entering a university professional pilot program with third-year students and airline pilots *Joseph H. Dunlap and Maureen A. Pettitt*	315

Section C Psychopathology

50 Flying, depression and social disruption 323
    Oscar Quintero

Introduction

Nick McDonald, Neil Johnston and Ray Fuller
Aerospace Psychology Research Group, Trinity College Dublin

Psychology has become both more comprehensive and more diverse in its contribution to aviation. On the one hand there is an increasing emphasis on the more "global" organisational and systems variables in safety, together with a concern for policy formulation and interest in theoretical and cross-cultural issues. On the other hand, the role of psychology has intensified in particular strands of activity such as accident investigation, crisis management, automation and CRM. This book brings these diverse strands together in a "whole system" approach to psychology in aviation.

It is the first in a series of three volumes, numbers II and III being entitled *Aviation Psychology: Training and Selection* and *Human Factors in Aviation Operations*. Taken together these three volumes represent the state of the art of aviation psychology, particularly within Europe, and all three complement the previously published *Aviation Psychology in Practice*.

Collectively these three volumes contain the proceedings of the twenty-first conference of the European Association for Aviation Psychology (EAAP). In recognition of the extensive political and structural changes currently taking place within Europe, WEAAP - the former Western European Association for Aviation Psychology - was renamed EAAP at the conclusion of this conference.

This volume is structured under the following broad headings:

- Policy for Human Factors in Aviation
- Systems and Organisation
- Accident Investigation
- Voluntary Incident Reporting
- Accidents in Ground Handling
- Crisis Management

- Cross-Cultural Factors
- Theory and History
- Perspectives on Crew Resource Management
- Automation
- Individual Factors (Alcohol, Personality and Psychopathology)

The starting point is policy of national and international aviation authorities for the development of human factors research and its application in the industry, addressing the emergent technological and structural changes within the industry. This is followed by a focus on the organisational context, on the relationship of safety to the culture of organisations, and on the practical issues of how to manage change and development in organisations in a way that facilitates the promotion of safety.

The developing role of psychology in the response to accidents, incidents and their aftermath links the following sections. Better understanding and new techniques of investigation are transforming the ways in which accidents are investigated. The use of voluntary confidential incident reports has both enhanced the preventive capability of the aviation system and increased our understanding of the nature of human factors in safety. The collection and analysis of accident data has extended to areas like the ground handling of aircraft. Response to accidents in aviation has also been transformed by a systematic approach to crisis management and the management of post-traumatic stress.

New challenges for aviation psychology are also represented here: the intensifying internationalisation of the industry has brought cross cultural issues into sharp focus; core issues like automation continue to raise both practical and theoretical challenges; and new theoretical approaches, behavioural, cognitive and sociological, are challenging the established methods and models of the sub-discipline. Aviation psychology is beginning to become aware of its own history.

The chapters in this volume also address new developments in the application and evaluation of CRM, and more effective ways of dealing with the the use and abuse of aclohol, and the role of personality factors.

The contents of this book, together with its sister volumes, are as diverse as is the contribution of psychology to the the aviation system. This volume will be of particular interest to those who are involved in policy and management (whether in areas of safety, operations or human resources) in any type of aviation organisation; to those whose responsibility relates to accidents, their investigation, management and prevention; and to researchers, trainers and educators in human factors in aviation.

Nick McDonald, Neil Johnston and Ray Fuller

June 1994

Opening speech to the 1994 WEAAP conference

Brian Cowen, TD, Minister for Transport, Energy and Communications

Mr. Chairman, Guest Speakers, ladies and gentlemen, I would first like to welcome you all to this 21st Conference of the Western European Association for Aviation Psychology. To those of you who have arrived from abroad, I would also like to extend a cead mile failte - a hundred thousand welcomes - to Ireland.

I must congratulate the Psychology Department of Trinity College, and, in particular their Aerospace Psychology Research Group, for the tremendous work they have done in bringing this Conference to Ireland. I would also like to acknowledge the support given to the Conference by such bodies as Aer Rianta, Ryanair, Aer Lingus, the Trinity Trust and Board Failte.

The subject of the Conference - aviation safety - is one which vitally concerns everybody involved in the aviation industry. It is, of course, a subject of more than passing interest to the public who are the users of these aviation services. We, however, who bear responsibility for the provision and regulation of aviation services must have the greater regard for aviation safety and all that those important words imply.

In the early years of aviation development, safety efforts were, in the main, directed towards improving technology, with the main focus being on the operational and engineering methods for combating hazards to aviation safety. A huge amount of endeavour and ingenuity was, for instance, expended in the development of more reliable engines, fail-safe airframes, accurate flight instruments and navigation aids, to name but a few. However, it soon became apparent that human error was capable of frustrating even the most advanced safety devices.

I am pleased, therefore, that this Conference highlights the human factor element of aviation. I note that one of the keynote themes of the Conference is "Developing Theory and Extending Practice", and that many of the issues proposed to be addressed revolve around the application of "Human Factors" knowledge and practice in the aviation context. There has been considerable development and refinement of Human Factors theory in aviation in the past fifty years or so. Unfortunately, and until relatively recently, there seems to have been a lack of practical application of Human Factors knowledge in everyday aviation operations.

When considering the scope and meaning of the term "Human Factors" as applied to aviation, one could easily be forgiven for being slightly overwhelmed by the extremely broad territory which is covered. It is said that "Human Factors" is about people in their living and working environments. It is about their relationship with machines and equipment - the so-called man-machine interface. It is about procedures, standards, attitudes and behavioural patterns. It is about interaction with other personnel, both within the individual's own aviation organisation and also within the so-called sociotechnical system which constitutes the entire aviation transportation system. To help us grasp the scope of Human Factors, the experts have provided us with the conceptual model known as SHEL, which describes the interface between - Software, Hardware, Environment and Liveware.

Statistical analysis of aircraft accidents, while often differing in methodology, invariably appear to return the dismal finding that the Human Factor was responsible in some 75% of occurrences. With the benefit of hindsight, it appears that the resolution of technical problems in the aviation safety equation may have been the easier part of the task. The human error percentage of aviation accidents now seems set to be the most obstinate hurdle to be overcome. Nevertheless, the difficult task ahead <u>must</u> be engaged with vigour.

As one of the I.C.A.O. Human Factors Digests reminds us, the aviation transportation system has many human levels of defence against the occurrence of the aircraft accident. The list is endless - it includes flight crews, maintenance engineers, ground handlers, aircraft re-fuellers, flight dispatchers, cabin crew, airport authorities, fire fighters, air traffic controllers, search and rescue personnel, aircraft manufacturers, airline managers, regulatory authorities and, even, accident investigators. All of the aforementioned are human "elements" in the aviation transportation system. All are subject to and/or concerned with the inescapable fact that human error is an inevitable and normal facet of human behaviour. Human Factors knowledge, training and practice for <u>all</u> of these people is an essential ingredient in the struggle to eliminate the causes of human error in aviation. The complete elimination of all human error is obviously an unattainable objective. However, even at this seemingly insurmountable barrier, the practical application of Human Factors knowledge can help to design aviation systems which are "tolerant" of human error, that is to say that safety factors and safety nets can be in-built which prevent a human error from resulting in a catastrophic accident.

The I.C.A.O. Human Factors Digests place great emphasis on the role of the manager in promoting, within his or her organisation, a corporate culture of safety consciousness and Human Factors awareness. If the management of a particular aviation organisation does not embrace the Human Factor philosophy wholeheartedly, it is unlikely that the stimulus for actions will emanate from below. I am very much aware that the twin pressures of increasing competition and increasing de-regulation in the aviation industry can result in concentration of management's attention to the achievement of production-oriented objectives. Safety-oriented objectives must not become regarded as a sideshow (or worse still, as an obstacle) to the main production effort. The establishment of a safety culture within an aviation organisation must be seen as an integral part of the whole production process which serves to minimise the exposure of both management, employees, customers and the general public to the hazards of aviation accidents. The role which Human Factors has to play in the overall safety strategy must not be underestimated.

At this point I should like to say a few words about the implementation of Human Factors training in Ireland.

Some of our air companies have either their own in-house Crew Resource Management courses or else have acquired the necessary training externally. Some have also used the opportunity of new aircraft type conversion courses to avail of some Multi-Crew Co-ordination training. The newly established State body - the Irish Aviation Authority - which comes under the aegis of my Department, and which replaced the former Air Navigation Services Office of the Department, will continue to play a supportive and proactive role in promoting the air companies' efforts in the Human Factors areas.

I would also like to compliment the Trinity College Aerospace Psychology Research Group in their initiation of the SCARF Programme, or to give it its full title "Safety Courses for Airport Ramp Functions". I understand that Aer Rianta, Aer Lingus and Ryanair are also co-operating in this Programme. On the ab initio training side, the Air Navigation Services Office of my Department, which is now the IAA, issued two Aeronautical Information Circulars in February, 1993, which made the subject of "Human Performance and Limitations" a mandatory examination subject for both Private Pilots and Professional Flight Crew written exams from mid-1993 onwards. A pass at the appropriate level in this subject has become a requirement for the grant of any new licence or rating from 1st January, 1994. In addition, all existing Flight Instructors, who are legally required to be able to instruct in the Human Performance and Limitations subject, must acquire a pass at the Professional level for any renewal of their Instructor Rating after 1st January, 1995. The foregoing arrangements were designed to meet the new I.C.A.O. Annex 1 requirements for Personnel Licensing.

Before concluding, I would like to mention the Government's recently published Irish Aviation Policy document. Safety is an integral part of Government aviation policy. Government policy is committed to ensuring that the highest internationally agreed safety standards are applied to the operation of Irish controlled airspace and Irish airports, and in the regulation of Irish registered and other aircraft operated by Irish airlines, and aircraft crew and maintenance organisations. The past five years the Government has undertaken a major investment programme completely re-furbishing all Irish radar communications and navigational systems in Europe with adequate safety standards and the capacity to meet projected traffic levels. It is the Government's intention, through a continuing investment programme, to maintain and develop the capacity of the Irish systems.

Finally, Mr. Chairman, Guest Speakers, Ladies and Gentlemen, I would like to wish you well in your endeavours here over the next few days. I have no doubt that the proceedings due to take place at this Conference will bring a positive and beneficial influence to bear on safe aviation operation and accident prevention. It gives me great pleasure to now formally declare this Conference open.

Part 1
POLICY FOR HUMAN FACTORS IN AVIATION

1 The future of Human Factors and psychology in aviation from ICAO's perspective

Capt. Daniel Maurino
Programme Manager, Flight Safety and Human Factors
International Civil Aviation Organization

Safety is a major force behind ICAO's activities. It was with the aim of improving safety in civil aviation that ICAO initiated its Flight Safety and Human Factors programme in 1988. The mandate was to make the international civil aviation community more aware of the importance of aviation Human Factors in aviation safety and effectiveness. Given ICAO's international nature, we had to start travelling around the world to spread the gospel. We learned important lessons in our interaction with widely ranging and radically different sectors of the international civil aviation community. I would like to share with you a couple of these lessons which I believe could be of interest to you as well as relevant to the European context.

The most important lesson we learned is that Human Factors endeavours, safety endeavours, training endeavours and any kind of human endeavour have strong cultural components. We humans cannot dissociate ourselves from our heritage. I am not going to dwell into this fascinating topic which others will discuss during the course of this week. I will only point out what I believe to be the most important practical consequence of these cross-cultural issues: there are not solutions valid "across the board". Different contexts might present problems which seem similar on the surface. They are not. The problems might *seem* to be similar, but they encode important cultural biases. Therefore, they require distinct, culturally calibrated solutions. It is naive to assume that simply importing a solution which worked in one context will bring the same benefits to another. Indeed, such attempt might only set a collision course between the biases of the cultures involved, making the problem worst.

Another important lesson we learned is that there is a tendency to deal with cultural issues from a "good guys" versus "bad guys" position. Conventional knowledge suggests that *we* are the good guys and *the others* are the bad guys. Our methods, beliefs and solutions are "good" and must be adapted for other people, whose methods, beliefs and solutions are "bad", inappropriate, outdated and so forth. As we have learned from cross-cultural research, there are no good or bad cultures; there are simply *different* cultures, each one with its own important strengths and weaknesses. The implications for cross-border endeavours are serious. If consideration of cultural variables is only cosmetic, the exported solution will initially *appear* to work because people, following the human tendency to accommodate and avoid being perceived as different, will try to adapt. This will probably cause the symptoms of the problem to disappear. But the roots of the problem will remain hidden under this surface of apparent improvement, ready to backlash. I think I do not need to further elaborate on the safety implications of such a scenario.

We also learned that to get rid of mosquitoes, there is more to be gained by draining the swamp which nurtures them than by devising gadgets or procedures to eliminate mosquitoes one by one. One way to drain the swamp of human error in aviation is through the establishment and continuous support of a safety culture. This is an organizational development which starts high up in corporate management and provides a framework within which safe and effective operational behaviours and practices are fostered and rewarded, and unsafe and undesirable operational behaviours and practices are discouraged. Within such cultures, the allocation of organizational resources to production and safety activities is sensibly balanced. Available evidence suggests the notion that few mosquitoes survive within those organizations which have developed a safety culture.

From the perspective of a neutral outsider flying under the United Nations flag, which are the cultural preferences which make Human Factors endeavours in Europe "different" from those undertaken elsewhere? What are the consequences of these cultural preferences in the outcome - in terms of enhancing effectiveness and safety - of such endeavours? Lastly, how do these preferences hinder the potential integration of European Human Factors know-how with ICAO's Human Factors efforts?

I believe that it is a fair statement that Europe - or Western Europe at least - has yet to break away the equations *Human Factors* = *Medicine* and *Human*

Factors practitioners = medical doctors. It would seem that the region is still dragging beliefs originated in World War Two and perhaps even earlier which portrayed the flight surgeon as the only reliable source of knowledge on human problems. If in managing the ICAO Flight Safety and Human Factors programme I were to restrict my contacts to the formally appointed representatives of European civil aviation administrations, I would deal almost exclusively with medical doctors. Human Factors, as perceived by ICAO, has in reality little to gain from medicine. What we ought to know about health and sickness, their impact on human performance and their relationship to licensing of operational personnel we already know; and it is clearly spelled out under the medical standards included in Annex 1.

ICAO regards Human Factors as a technology concerned with making aviation safer while at the same time allowing aviation organizations to make money, so they can continue to operate *safely*. While there is a contribution of medicine to these objectives, it is certainly not a central one. In fact, my parting thought on this Western European cultural preference is that any attempts to try to improve safety through, for example, more stringent medical standards or perhaps psychological evaluation will unavoidably result in aberrant solutions with regrettable consequences.

As a result of this cultural bias towards medicine, ICAO has had to lean mostly on non-Europeans when looking for support for its Human Factors programme. There is no doubt in my mind that there are European Human Factors practitioners with impeccable credentials. There is no doubt in my mind either that they are very well hidden and exceedingly difficult to find. Although ICAO has been fortunate to spot a few, we continue to rely heavily on expertise the United States, Canada, Australia and New Zealand, with their bureaucratic yet open systems and their more flexible understanding of Human Factors. As a postscript to this topic, I have considerable difficulties in answering the regular enquires I receive about university-level courses on aviation psychology in Europe. I have yet to find one university in Europe which includes a course on aviation psychology in its curriculum. I hear rumours, however, that this may change soon. I will stay tuned.

The very European perception of encyclopedic knowledge as an end in itself rather than as a tool to achieve practical ends seems to maintain a pervasive hold in today's European Human Factors efforts. On the other side of the Atlantic - and the Pacific - there is a growing concern regarding the transfer, integration and most effective application of existing Human Factors knowledge in operational settings. This concern is, by the way, unconditionally shared by ICAO. However, on this side of the Atlantic, the focus seems to remain on the knowledge itself. It would seem that Human Factors knowledge is treasured within some sort of medieval fortress and passed to the operational community during brief openings of the fortress drawbridge. Furthermore, this transfer usually takes place *after* the fact and with the benefit of hindsight. I would suggest to you that if Human Factors has been re-discovered as major contributor to aviation safety and effectiveness, it is largely because of the teaming of practitioners with operational personnel, so that available knowledge can find its way into the realities of everyday aviation operations.

Psychology is another field where cultural preferences make European endeavours quite distinct from other contexts, except - not surprisingly - South America. Like father, like son. The equation in this case would be *psychology applied to aviation = personnel selection (exclusively)*. There is of course no denying the importance of selection in screening out those individuals who later in their careers become a source of constant headaches to flight and training managers and safety officers alike. There is also the very important aspect of eliminating those individuals who lack the basic traits for the profession, thereby saving unnecessary training expenditures in the future. Yet from ICAO's perspective of ICAO, there are significantly larger contributions from psychology to aviation than personnel selection. In fact, I would suggest that in the larger scheme of things, in terms of the aviation system safety and effectiveness, selection is only one contributor. This focus on selection appears rather inconsistent when one realizes that Europe has "revealed" over the last few years a handful of psychologists whose work on sociotechnical systems safety has led to serious reconsideration of long-established aviation prevention practices.

As an afterthought on the subject of psychology, it is also unique to Europe - and again to South America and other pockets of former European influence - that when trying to contact more than one aviation psychologist involved in civil aviation matters, one must go through switchboards of military organizations. This preference contrasts with other sectors of the international community, where military psychologists seldom extend their endeavours beyond the military environment. While there must certainly be strengths in this European preference, one weakness is that knowledge applicable to military environments may not always readily transfer to civilian environments. This further denies a greater support from European aviation psychology for ICAO's Human Factors programme.

In any event, I am a strong believer that psychology and Human Factors will play a central role in aviation safety and effectiveness in years to come. But before discussing the future, I would suggest a quick look into the past. Generally speaking, one could distinguish three "ages" in psychology applied to aviation. The first age ran the early forties to the mid-seventies, and Human Factors was strictly synonymous of medicine, knobs and dials and was the exclusive domain of flight surgeons and engineers. Over this period, clinical, behavioural and cognitive psychologists also made significant contributions to aviation safety by fostering understanding of human capabilities and limitations. All the knowledge, however, was directed towards the tip of the arrow: pilots, mechanics, dispatchers, controllers and so forth. The context within which operational personnel discharged their responsibilities - the system which provided the framework and by force bound them - remained largely untouched and unimproved.

During the seventies Human Factors came into its second age, expanding beyond medicine and design. The late seventies and early eighties also witnessed the blossoming of social psychology in aviation. Crew Resource Management became a world-class citizen, a training technology adopted throughout the world, credited with further improving aviation safety. A fundamental proposal of social psychology, however, went unheeded in most quarters. Social psychologists behind CRM made clear that human behaviour never takes place in a social vacuum, and they emphasized the importance of organizational commitment to CRM. The message of safety as one means to achieve organizational development rather than as an end in itself became loud and clear for those who chose to listen. They were not many.

As the 80's came to an end, and in spite of the success of social psychology, the vision of Human Factors as the last frontier of the aviation system began to crumble under the cold numbers of accident statistics. Rather than questioning the wisdom of the piecemeal approaches pursued, however, the industry redoubled efforts along the same avenues. A general state of isolation prevailed, and more often than not the right hand did not know what the left hand was doing.

Then, on Friday, March 10, 1989, Air Ontario flight 1363, a Fokker F-28, crashed while attempting takeoff from a small provincial airport at Dryden, Ontario, Canada. It was not a major disaster but it deeply shook the Canadian aviation community. A Commission of Inquiry was appointed which after twenty months of work produced a benchmark report, a turning point in established approaches to accident investigation. The philosophy of the Inquiry can be summarized as follows:

> "...The pilot-in-command made a flawed decision, but that decision was not made in isolation. It was made in the context of an integrated air transportation system that, if it had been functioning properly, should have prevented the decision to take off...there were significant failures, most of them beyond the captain's control, that had an operational impact on the events in

> *Dryden...the regulatory, organizational, physical and crew components must be examined to determine how each may have influenced the captain's decision."* (emphasis added)

The Final Report of the Commission of Inquiry into the Air Ontario Crash at Dryden marks the beginning of the third age, through a much needed development: the advent of organizational psychology in aviation. Accident investigations within Australia, the United States, Canada, Finland, Sweeden and France have increasingly followed the path of organizational psychology. By pursuing avenues of action based on organizational psychology the piecemeal approaches of the past will hopefully become memories. The organizational perspective also provides a framework for safety, allowing it to be viewed in realistic terms within the goals of aviation organizations.

There are implications for the entire aviation community in this transition to applied organizational psychology as a safety tool. The challenge for the academic community, beyond the implications in terms of research, has been defined by Robert Helmreich (personal communication) as follows

> *"I agree that no one discipline will be dominant. The problem is to bring together the various disciplines to work on common problems with the breadth that entails. I see one of the greatest challenges as being the production of a new generation of researchers who have the breadth to cross traditional academic boundaries - and I hope we are taking tiny steps in that direction."*

As one who heavily draws from applied research I wholeheartedly endorse the need for this new generation of researchers.

The training and operational communities have also a clear contribution to make. The adoption of organizational approaches to aviation safety involves considerable change. Change, if it is to be implemented through the commitment of those involved, must rest on education. The responsibility to foster such education lies squarely upon the shoulders of managers and trainers.

The regulatory community can support this educational process by including Human Factors-related criteria in the certification requirements for personnel, procedures and equipment. From an international perspective, this responsibility lies with ICAO, but it is up to individual administrations to take over and turn international regulations into national legislation.

For the safety community, the challenge remains to understand the importance of the marriage of theory and practice, the teaming of research and academia with practitioners who can act as a bridge and apply scientific knowledge to operational settings. Significant milestones in flight deck safety have been achieved through the integrated work of researchers and pilots. It is now up to the accident investigation community to close ranks with academia just as pilots did.

Is organizational psychology the new last frontier in aviation safety? I think not. Furthermore, I think that such a mythical frontier does not exist. The passage of time will bring unforeseen challenges which will demand new solutions. The real issue is that we should never sit back, assuming that once and forever we have found the solution for aviation safety. The notion of such a magical solution was implicit in presenting Human Factors as the last frontier of aviation safety, and it was preached in a thousand-and-one opportunities during the past fifty years. The message I am trying to convey - and which I offer to you as my parting thought - is that the battle for safety is an endless quest against a relentless enemy with infinite resources who will never give up.

References

Helmreich, R.L. (1993), *Personal communication*.
International Civil Aviation Organization (1988), *Annex 1, Personnel Licensing*.
International Civil Aviation Organization (1993), *Human Factors Digest No. 7: Investigation of Human Factors in Accidents and Incidents, Circular 240-AN/144*. Montreal, Canada: Author.
International Civil Aviation Organization (1994), *Human Factors Digest No. 10: Human Factors,Management and Organization, Circular 247-AN/148*, Montreal, Canada, Author.
Marx, D., Graeber, C. (1994), *Human Error in Aircraft Maintenance. In Aviation Psychology in Practice*, Johnston, N., McDonald, N., Fuller, R., Eds.
Maurino, D.E. (1992), *Shall We Add One More Defense?* Keynote speech at the Third Seminar in Transportation Ergonomics. 7 October 1992. Transport Canada Development Centre, Montreal, Canada.
Maurino, D.E. (1993), *Management, Safety and Change*, IATA 22nd Technical Conference; Human Factors in Aviation, 4-8 October 1993. Montreal, Canada.
Moshansky, The Hon. Virgil. P. (1992). *Commission of Inquiry into the Air Ontario Crash at Dryden, Ontario*. Final Report, Vol. III. Ottawa, Canada: Author.
Pidgeon, N., O'Leary, M. (1994), *Organizational Safety Culture: Implications for Aviation Practice. In Aviation Psychology in Practice*, Johnston, N., McDonald, N., Fuller, R., Eds.

2 Human Factors, the next technological advance? Issues and needs: a view from the CEC

P.C. Cacciabue and C.J. North
Commission of the European Communities

Ladies and Gentlemen,

I would like to thank you on behalf of the European Commission for the invitation to give one of the keynote addresses at this 21st Aviation Psychology Conference.

The Commission, as you are aware, is basically a "political" body and is primarily involved in setting policy at a European level and developing regulations or standards. I myself am from the Directorate General for Transport (DG VII) and am involved in aviation safety policy and regulation as well as aviation research. The Commission also has the Joint Research Centre, which is based at Ispra in Italy, where they carry out research to support Community policy and initiatives.

I am giving this address mainly from the point of view of DG VII, but also on behalf of the Joint Research Centre.

Since the advent of the jet age, air transport safety has improved dramatically with fatal accidents falling from about 20 per million flights in 1960 to about 1.4 today. This phenomenal improvement in safety has been brought about largely through the introduction of technology (the jet engine, avionics, etc.)

to improve the reliability of the aircraft as a whole and its individual systems, as well as through new design concepts such as 'fail-safe' or 'damage tolerance' for example the duplication of safety critical systems and components. As the modern jet airliner has matured experience, mainly in the form of accidents, has shown us where weaknesses in the design of the aircraft, or in the design requirements, exist. Typically the solution of the design engineer or of the certification authority, has been to design a technological solution to the problem, such as Ground Proximity Warning Systems (GPWS), Stall Warning Stick pushers/shakers, etc.. The result has been that the cockpit is full of buzzers, bells, horns, hooters and flashing lights.

Although, in my opinion, the improvement in safety has been largely technology driven, it should also be recognised that the selection, initial training and recurrent training of airline pilots and the operational procedures for airlines have also changed significantly during this period and that this has had a significant effect on overall safety as well.

However, it is clear that the application of technological solutions alone is not sufficient. The world's most technologically advanced airliner (the Airbus Industrie A320) which contains most, if not all of technological thinking today, and maybe some more besides, has a fatal accident rate that is more than two times higher than the worldwide average and about 4 times higher than the "class leader". This is not because the aircraft and its systems are any less reliable than its competitors, but it is interesting to note that in the four fatal accidents to date on this aircraft, human factors has been a major, if not the, reason for the accident.

The statistics show us, and I know there is some debate on the absolute figures, that over the last 10 years some 70 to 75% of hull loss accidents have had flight crew as the primary accident factor, whereas only 11% can be ascribed to the aircraft and 2% to maintenance deficiencies. Air transport has been growing strongly for many years, and will continue to grow steadily for the foreseeable future. Traffic is likely to double every 8 to 10 years. During this period we have to halve the fatal accident rate if the overall number of accidents per year is to be maintained at current levels.

This is no small task and if we wish to achieve it our efforts must be focused in the areas offering the best safety returns. In my opinion the improvements offered by technology are bottoming out. The statistics clearly show us, without any doubt, that the area offering the best possibility for significantly improving safety is human factors.

Traditionally, the human factors element in an accident has been treated as 'pilot error'. This simplistic approach is not enough. We need to look behind the initial cause and find out what led the pilot to do what he did and how can repetition in the future be avoided. What is needed is an integrated approach which properly addresses human factors in design, manufacture and operation of aircraft and systems, in the selection criteria for pilots and in initial and recurrent training. It must particularly emphasize the man/machine interface - the pilot to the aircraft, the controller to the ATC system and the man/man interface - between pilots, the pilot and the ATC controller and between controllers.

Such an integrated approach can only be achieved with adequate information to enable the designer to treat human factors as a proper design requirement and not as an after thought. Information to enable the regulatory authorities to define meaningful and effective requirements for system and aircraft design, the selection and training of personnel, to enable airlines to define effective operational procedures and for training organisations to define training syllabi and procedures to ensure the necessary communication and interface skills. And finally, information to support a system which gives a warning to everyone when something is going wrong - hopefully before the occurrence of an accident.

The European Commission, through its regulatory and research functions, is in a good position to help provide this necessary information.

Some eight EC Member States have regulations requiring Mandatory Occurrence Reporting (MOR) Systems which deal, primarily, with technical deficiencies or major operational errors, however only a few (4) have computerised systems and none of them are compatible. If you want to use a MOR system as a preventative tool the comprehensiveness and size of the database are very important.

DG VII with the Joint Research Centre, the Member States and the JAA are currently working together to provide a centralized database which will enable the four existing computerised MOR systems to contribute to and have access to the data. In addition we are designing a 'common' MOR system which will enable those Member States without a system (or without a computerised system) to establish one. This initiative, known as ECC-AIRS - European Coordination Centre for the mandatory Accident and Incident Reporting Systems, started back in 1992 following some initial studies in 1990, by the end of 1993 user requirements, software requirements and architectural design were completed. Implementation of the pilot system will take place during 1994 with testing starting in November and project completion in February 1995. At that stage the decision will be made whether to 'commercialise' the system.

Whilst a European MOR system is useful particularly from an aircraft design/maintenance or operational practices point of view, I don't believe that it is enough to support a meaningful human factors approach to air transport safety. What is needed is a European Human Factors Reporting System.

The study that was carried out in 1990 for the Commission into the MOR System also looked at usefulness of a Confidential Reporting System. This study and the subsequent debate led to the Commission funding a feasibility study for a European system by the Technical University of Berlin, which was at that time looking at the possibility of establishing such a system for Germany.

Analysis of existing systems (ASRS, Chirp, etc.) showed that each one had a number of structural disadvantages that led us to believe it would be better to design a European system from a clean sheet of paper. The system would not, however, be designed in isolation and would take account of the existing systems, be compatible with a revised ICAO ADREP format; allow coordination with the MOR system and with accident investigation data.

The key to the success, or failure, of such a system is confidentiality. Without it, there would be no credibility and therefore no confidence from the Aviation Community. All pertinent information should be stored but it should be protected by legal right - the equivalent of professional secrecy. Of course such a system could be open to abuse, for example in the event of industrial dispute or where an employee has a grudge against his employer, and consequently care has to be taken to try to identify and control this problem.

To test such a system the Commission has jointly funded with the German Aviation Authorities the creation of a German confidential reporting system based at the Technical University of Berlin for a 24 month trial period. This system, known as EUCARE, became operational in July 1993 and will continue until mid '95. At the end of this trial period an evaluation will be made with aviation safety experts from the European Community before making a decision on its extension to the European Community as a whole.

Reporting to such a system would have to be as easy as possible - by post or telephone, forms should be as simple as possible - a small number of precise questions should be asked and plenty of space left for descriptive narrative. There would be a two level analysis, with a primary level to react immediately to each report to ensure that all the relevant information is available and the report understood. After codification and data storage, a second level of analysis would take place to look at the incident in a more general context, determine the underlying causes and compare the data with those already in the system to look for similarities and detect trends.

Such a system would be expected to have a satellite architecture, with a small satellite office in each Member State to enable the reporter to make his report more easily and in his native language. The primary analysis would be made at this level as well as any communication between the system and the individual. The satellite office would also process the data and be responsible for local dissemination of safety information. Translation of the narrative part into English would also take place at this level if necessary.

The head office would be located in one Member State, hold the database, and be responsible for the secondary analysis, statistical analysis, trend detection and prepare reports and documentation. The head office would also be responsible for training satellite office staff and analysers to ensure consistency of data and coding.

The output of such a system would be to disseminate information of potential hazards, incident mechanisms and ways to prevent accidents and incidents to all the relevant parties of the aviation community.

Whereas analysis is only as good as the data that supports it, any improvement in safety is only as good as the analysis that takes place.

Consequently, if we are to get the maximum, or even any benefit out of the MOR and Confidential Reporting Systems, we have to be sure that the right staff with the right expertise and training is available for the analysis. This must include not only regulatory authorities and accident investigators, but also airline pilots, operations managers, aircraft designers, air traffic controllers, human factors specialists, etc. Above all, these people must have a good knowledge of aviation and air transport operations and be dedicated to improving safety.

From a regulatory point of view the Commission has established common technical requirements and administrative procedures in the field of civil aviation. These technical requirements have effectively taken the existing JAR codes, primarily for certification purposes, and made them mandatory for the Member States through a Council Regulation. This same regulation also obliges the Member States to become members of the JAA and apply JAA procedures.

These technical requirements are by no means complete and considerable effort is being made by the JAA particularly in the fields of flight crew licensing and flight operations. When these codes are eventually approved by the JAA they will be sent to the Commission to consider their suitability for incorporation into Community legislation.

From a research point of view the Commission is also very active, with human factors related work being carried out in the Joint Research Centre, DG XII and DG VII.
In the JRC, studies have been carried out into Human Factors in Aviation Safety these have focused on the collection and analysis of data from real working environments, the modelling of human-machine interaction for design and safety study purposes, and on the study of real accidents using human factors methods for the analysis of dynamic event sequences.

DG XII has, through the Brite-Euram programme and in particular the FANSTIC project, been looking at the effective integration of future ATM concepts into civil aircraft flight decks as well as the integration of new aircraft systems such as landing and taxiing aids and the associated Man Machine Interfaces.

Within DG VII we have through the EURET programme, been looking at future ATM scenarios (AEGIS contract) and particularly advanced automation and the associated human factors and with the SWIFT contract specifically at the human factors issues related to the future controller working position.

For the future, it is hoped that the 4th Framework Research and Development Programme (with a value of some 13,000 MECU) will be starting at the end of this year and continuing to 1998. Within this framework air transport related research will figure in several specific programmes - Industrial and Materials Technologies (IMT), Telematics and Transport. Human Factors for pilots will probably be treated in both the IMT and Transport programmes, and human factors for air traffic controllers will be treated in both the Transport and Telematics programmes.

As you can appreciate there will be a lot of human factors related activity being carried out in the Commission over the next 4 years. It is also clear from this conference that a lot of work is being carried out by many individuals and organisations in this field but I'm worried that much vital effort and scarce resources are being wasted through a lack of co-ordination and collaboration. What is needed is a focus to try to bring the various threads together to try to ensure that progress in the human factors field is made efficiently, effectively and above all quickly.

As I said before, the reduction in accident rates per flight is bottoming out, growth will result in a doubling of traffic every 8 to 10 years. Unless positive action is taken to halve the accident rate/flight not only for the next 8 to 10 year period but every period thereafter, the number of accidents and fatalities is bound to increase. Aircraft accidents tend to be major events with a large media coverage and high public awareness - it is dramatic "news headlines". Politically we cannot accept to have more aircraft accidents, particularly where the number of fatalities involved in any one could be several hundred.

Air transport safety needs to be improved and improved significantly. Technological development will no longer be enough. The next major improvement in safety can only come from the proper control of the human factors problem.

3 Changes in European civil aviation: challenges to safety and perspectives

Jean Pariès
Inspection Générale de l'Aviation Civile, France

Introduction

The european applied human factors scenery in civil aviation is a rather contrasted one. The major european manufacturer, Airbus Industrie has progressively conquered one third of the world sales, certainly by the means of manufacturing excellent aircraft, but also by setting most of the main cockpit innovations of the last twenty years, finally integrating all of them into the A320-A330-A340 cockpit, with fly-by-wire side sticks, non automotive autothrottles and the removal of practically all conventional indicators.

One would expect that nations which design and manufacture such aircraft are in the best position to operate them properly. As you all know, things did not turn out to be so simple. The leading design country for the A320 is also the country where the strongest opposition has been organised by the pilot unions against this aircraft. Please refrain from the conclusion that this is only a french specific social syndrome. I have worse news: when you look at the statistics, there is some questioning for european people as a whole. Untill today, there has been no accident concerning US operated glass cockpit generation aircraft. In the same time european operators have suffered at least six accidents : Habsheim (A320), East Midland (B737-400), Lauda Air in Thailand (B767), Mont Sainte Odile (A320), Papeete (B747-400), and Varsow (A320). So it is not simply a question of aircraft design or local social atmosphere. And it is not even a question of individual proficiency. When you look at the different european licences and compare them to what is done elsewhere in the world, when you take individual european pilots and check their proficiency, the conclusion is not a shame for Europe. Europe has been a leader for ab initio pilot training programs for years and years. Some of the european airlines have set up human factors training programs which became references in the world: I will only mention the host airline, Aer Lingus, but of course there are other ones.

Unfortunately, we have seen that the safety performance of the european industry is not as satisfactory as one could wish or expect. It therefore seems to be worth taking a look at the big picture, to try and identify the next challenges, as well as the potential contibution of people like you in this assembly.

A rapidly changing economical scenery

First of all, I think we must acknowledge the importance of economical aspects.

The european deregulation

As you know, the air transportation deregulation process which was initiated in the United States in 1978 has been imported into Europe rather recently under a soften form, through the extension of the Rome Treaty and its free competition law to aviation.This treaty had not been applied to the aviation community since 1957. This changed in 1986 when the European Court decided that it should be applicable to aviation as well. Things have then gone through impressive modification. European Community airlines started to live under the reign of the so called "Packages". The measures under the third package which was the last step to the single market have been applicable since the first of january 1993. They are aiming at a free access of EC operators to intra-EC lines, a free fare system, and an harmonized regulation for operator certificate (technical requirements) and licence (economical requirements) delivery.

The changes

Beyond the surface turbulences, deep changes have been consequently induced into the air transportation system, and they will affect all its components. A fundamental evolution is on process: a shift away from the "national flag" concept, which has formed the basis for about 90% of the aviation activity untill now. It will only be slowly and partially replaced by a "european flag" concept. The consequences will be: less protection from governments and public funding, more competition within europe and with the rest of the world, higher productivity requirements and economical constraints, more uncertainty, more diversity in the human components, more sensitivity to regulation discrepancy, especially in the pilot training and licencing area.

Furthermore, european airlines are already facing the consequences of a large discrepancy between the "european" single market and the nation-based airways network, air traffic control system, and airport network. Lack of adequate infrastructure in the air and on the ground leads to extra costs because of longer milage, increased fuel burn, waste of time and the like. According to the Association of European Airlines, airport and ATC related causes accounted for 70% of all delays in 1992. This also leads to higher stress on crew members and ATC personnel, and consequently impacts on safety. Time pressure is a background component to understand the Dash 8 accident at Roissy-Charles de Gaulle airport last year.

The result is hard time for european airlines, which not only have to face the worldwide competition, but have to cope with specific european handicaps in this new game, and above all, have to change their way of living. Most of them are facing very bad economical situations. AEA members as a whole have accumulated historical losses since 1991.

On top of that, it must be said that all these current or anticipated modifications in the european scenery simply add further to a large worldwide mutation in the aviation system, reflected by the extension of the glass cockpit generation and the emergence of a giant integrated data exchange network for navigation, air traffic management, and so on.

It is easy to understand the challenges to safety associated with such a situation. Some of them are related to the economical situation itself: lack of money is an incentive for cutting in the corners. But my feeling is that the basic challenge is the change itself. Air transportation is a highly complex, tightly coupled, underspecified system. Such systems empirically adapt themselves to their environment, using low frequency feed-back regulation. Consequently, they are conservative, they hate changes, especially as far as safety is concern. This does not mean that any structural change will inevitably lead to accidents. The statistics from the NTSB show that commercial aviation in the US was markedly safer during the seven years after the deregulation (79-85) than during the seven years before the deregulation (72-78).

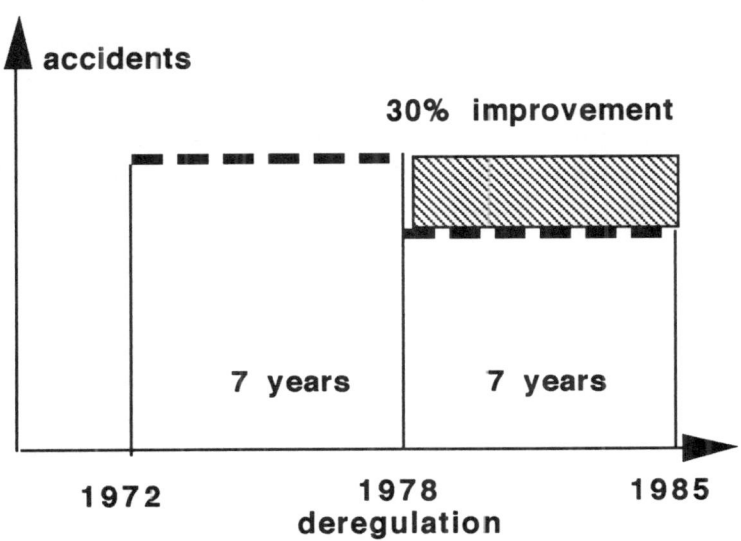

Figure 1 US deregulation experience impact on safety

However this reflects the action of all the components of the system, including the safety regulations enforcement. It is worth noticing in this case that the FAA had anticipated that safety problems could be associated with the economic deregulation, and had implemented a strengthened version of FAR 135 in 1979.

At this point we are naturally invited to look at the european regulations situation.

3- The regulation aspects

Towards a european regulation system

As far as technical and safety regulations in Europe are concerned, the major event is obviously a progressive transfer from the national level to a cooperative european level. This transfer has first concerned the development and the evolutions of the regulations. The actual autonomy of the national bodies in this area has been drastically reduced. All the typical components of a safety regulation system (pilot licencing, aircraft certification, maintenance, operations) are now covered by a european development process within the JAA structure. Furthermore, the responsability of implementing the regulations has also started to shift from a purely national basis towards a european cooperative basis. The certification of the Airbus A340 an A330 was conducted by one single european JAA team. The agreements of maintenance companies will be delivered through a similar process from now, and pilot training and licensing will follow on.

The multiplicity of european aviation organisations

Unfortunately, things are not as simple as suggested above. Indeed there are several "aviation Europes", and things will certainly not getting more simple with the present evolutions on the political field. Aviation Europe is becoming a more and more complex concept. I will not expand on this, I will only picture the situation using the following (well known) diagram of the main european regulatory bodies:

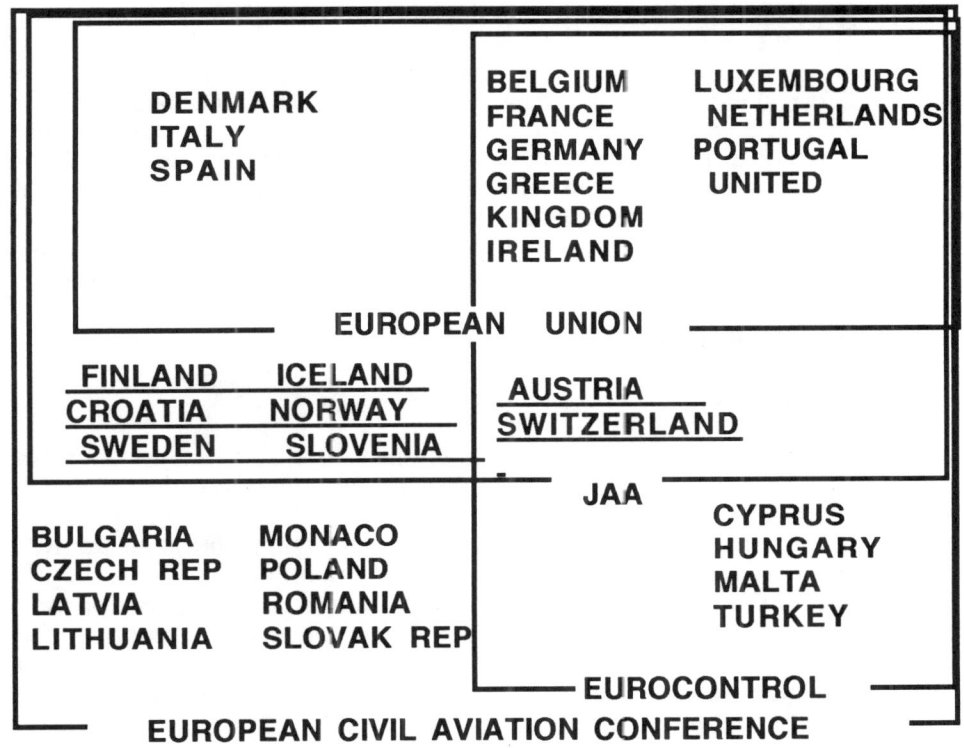

Figure 2 Main european aviation regulation bodies

These organisations not only have different boundaries: they have different objectives, different dynamics, different status and roles vis-a-vis the national bodies.

The challenges of the construction phase

I think a transition like this is a critical moment. We are experiencing a federation process of different national regulations, and such a process tends to be a phase of weakness and conservative behaviour. National regulatory bodies tend to postpone their own national regulation improvements while waiting for the adoption of a common code. Furthermore, the common code itself tends to be rather conservative. Althought one could think that developing a common regulation should be the occasion for modernisation, this is by far not always the case. People have hard time in reaching agreements, and they mainly try to minimize the gap between their present national situations and the future consensus. They have very little energy left to invest into revolutions. Pilot licences is a good illustration of this : an impressive amount of energy has been spent and will continue to be spent on harmonisation aspects, compared to the amount of discussions about pilot training for a better crew performance, for example in glass cockpit aircraft.

And finally, even when a consensus has been reached, the resulting regulation is still nothing else that a single written textbook. We all know the difference between a formal message an it's actual implementation. It will be very difficult to implement a common regulation into similar european practices if the industry has not a minimum common culture, a common background for understanding the needs and the solutions for selection, training, operational procedures, man-machine interface design, and the like.

You in this assembly can deeply contibute to set such a common culture, and therefore it is relevant to take a look at the european human factors tradition.

The european Human Factors tradition

The lack of a european voice

Most of you are researchers or human factors specialists, and I am certainly not in a position to, neither willing to, teach you anything about the european human factors tradition. I would only like to share with you my personal understanding, from the outside, of the european contribution to pratical applications of human factors to flight safety. My point of view is "naive". It means that I will not use sugar coated wordings, although my perception may well be totally wrong. And I will start with a somewhat deceptive report.

There were two major events related to aviation safety and human factors last year in the world. The first one was the second global ICAO seminar hold in Washington DC in april, and the second one was the 22nd IATA Technical Conference hold in Montreal in october. When I remember these seminars, I do not have the feeling that something like a strong "european voice" has been expressed. I do acknowledge that big individual voices from Europe have conveyed some of the most impressive messages, but we all know that the juxtaposition of proficient individuals does not make a proficient team. So the question are: "why?" and "can this be changed?"

A review of the european tradition position

I suggest that a touch of history might help to understand the situation. Let us review the three main trends, or domains, of aviation human factors.

The physiological trend The first trend is physiology and aeronautical medecine. In this field, the european tradition ranks quite honorably on the world market. It is still undoubdetly the dominant one within Europe. To be clear, aeronautical medecine is the only component of human factors accepted by the european aviation systems as a scientifically noble and operationally usefull one. Unfortunately, however, it is commonly accepted outside Europe that this aspect of human factors has lost its leadership and innovative role as far as flight safety is concerned.

The Human Factors trend The second trend is covered by the original american dedicated meaning of the words "Human Factors", and its european counterpart "ergonomics". It deals with the man-machine interface and chiefly refers to laboratory experiments. My feeling is that this domain has been dominated by the US, for theoretical developments as well as for practical applications. As far as Europe is concerned, I can see a big difference between Northern and Southern Europe. It seems that the former was able to follow behind the US leadership. This was not the case for the later. You may find it somewhat caricatured, but I feel that WEAAP is a reflection of this dualistic inheritance.

However, an important evolution originated from Europe in the 70's: the importance of field experiments was acknowledged towards a broader understanding of the man-machine interface, then considered as a coupled system, and the models started to incorporate a model of the human operator himself, as a real component of the system. I know there is one name that can exemplify what I am speaking about without risk of displeasing hundreds of people: Jens Rasmussen. And this name is symbolic of one major fact: that is, this new trend in Europe took place <u>outside</u> the aircraft manufacturing community! While it was flourishing in the nuclear and chemical industry, and even in the air traffic control (ATC) domain, it faced considerable difficulties to penetrate cockpit and instrument design. There has been a strong resistance to the employment of human factors specialists in this area. I think it is worth raising the question "why?", but I don't have the answer.

The clinical and socio-psychological trend The third trend is covered by clinical psychology (adressing selection) and socio-psychology (adressing collective performance). Europe has a strong tradition in this area, even if some ground may have been lost. A good reason for that may be that Europe is bound to ab initio training, due to the lack of military pilots and commuter pilots to feed major airlines needs. But the great superiority of the USA in this field to my opinion is that they were able to <u>apply</u> the academic knowledge to practical pilot training. The Teneriffe accident may be a symbolic illustration: Both a US and a european operated aircraft were involved. On both side of the Atlantic, a lot of thinking was invested towards a training answer to the tragedy. But CRM was born in the US, the big names are american, and all around the world, airlines are using CRM training concepts "made in USA".

However, I can see two major changes in the last ten years.

The emergence of cognitive psychology

The first one is the emergence of cognitive psychology, offering a unified understanding of both individual and coupled performance, with a unified understanding of man-man and man-(automated)machines.systems This approach, which is a rather Europe centered one, has started to lead to practical applications.

I have been involved in the developpement of an academic training course for pilots, and also in the development of a new type of CRM for Air France. Both are widely taking from cognitive psychology. It is very interesting to note that pilots having taken this CRM training have significantly changed their understanding of what is happening in their cockpits, and have taken over the CRM concepts and vocabulary to report incidents. This means that not only individual behaviors, but the collective feed-back of the system can be affected, hopefully to the benefit of safety.

The emergence of the systemic approach

This leads me to tackle a second fundamental change. I think a decisive evolution has occured in human factors approaches during the last few years: the emergence of a macro systemic approach of aviation safety. Some major contributions are coming from the outside, USA, Canada, Australia, but Europe definitely seems to have gained a leading position in this area. Just one examples: the two relevant ICAO Human Factors digests: digest N°7 (Human Factors Investigation in Accidents and Incidents), and N°10 (Human Factors, Management and Organisation) are borrowing from James Reason's model, which is becoming a reference in aviation safety and accident investigation.

Perspectives

This european recovery is good news. But we should be careful not to be over-optimistic. Europe has researchers, theoreticians, and many of the big names now are european. But behind the shop signs and windows, what is exactly standing on the store shelves?

My feeling is that we don't have an integrated system. If we compare the european situation with the US one, we don't have anything equivalent to NASA, neither have we any structure able to centralise and to coordinate the research efforts and link them with the needs and expectations of the industry. We have very few, if any, thematic "aviation" universities offering the whole range of aviation jobs training, including human factors. In most of the cases, european human factors programs are belonging to social science universities, which are living on an alien planet with respect to aviation. This means that they have no real relationship with the aviation world, with the exception of a rather small number of individuals, who may have big names but tend to be lost sheep within their community, and therefore are not necessarilly followed by many students.

In other words my feeling is that european human factors research does exist, but has a tendency to live apart from the aviation world and industry. Furthermore, in spite of several european joined projects, the european research is still firmly anchored to national territories. However, to be fair, I have to add that all this is not true for the ATC domain, neither in France nor at the european level. Other speakers have or will expand on the numerous joined projects in this area, which are dealing with new work place design, air-ground integration and automation programs, socio-psychological aspects of ATC automation, and so on.

Conclusion : a call for joined efforts

There is nothing like a single common market in Europe for Human Factors, and we are still waiting for the First Package of measures towards unification and synergy in this field! The european intellectual tradition is different from the US one, and this is true for human factors sciences as well. As far as aviation practical applications are concerned, and particularly in the cockpit design and pilot training domains, the impact of the european research tradition has not been a major one, and the US leadership must be acknowledged. But although a lot of benefits can be drawn from the US experience, the european aviation industry is facing specific european problems in the context of the complex process of political and economical construction of Europe. A coordinated effort towards a common european approach of human factors in aviation, associating researchers, universities, airlines, training schools, manufacturers and civil aviation authorities therefore seems to be urgently needed, particularly for the benefit of safety.

References

Association of European Airlines (AEA) Yearbook 1992 & 1993, Avenue Luise 350, Bte 4, B 1050 Brussels
The International Air Transport Association (IATA), Proceedings of the 22nd Technical Conference, Montreal, 4-8 october 1993
Boeing Commercial Airplane Group, Summary of Commercial Jet Aircraft Accidents
International Civil Aviation Organisation (ICAO), Proceedings of the second ICAO Flight Safety and Human Factors Global Symposium, Washington DC, April 1993.
International Civil Aviation Organisation (ICAO), Human Factors Digets N° 7 & N° 10

4 The national plan for aviation Human Factors: Federal Aviation Administration implementation

Mark A. Hofmann, Federal Aviation Administration, Washington DC

The human factor has been widely recognized by many, to include the United States Congress, as critical to aviation safety and effectiveness. Numerous studies have indicated that the human factor is absolutely critical for sustaining or improving safety. In like manner, the useability, acceptance, and life cycle costs of systems and products are related to the human factor. These realities call for consistent, long-term support for research, development, analysis, and the application of information related to the human throughout the aviation system.

In recognition of this need, a United States National Plan for Aviation Human Factors was developed and published in 1990. This plan resulted from a series of events which included: an Air Transport Association Human Factors Task Force report concerned with human factors and safety; a Congressional Office of Technology Assessment report dealing with safety; and finally the "Aviation Safety Research Act of 1988". This plan has two overarching objectives: (a) establish a national research agenda which is responsive to the human performance information requirements of the aviation community, and (b) provide guidance to enhance the transfer of this information to the many segments of the aviation community.

The National Plan, now in the implementation phase, is currently undergoing minor revisions as a result of various reviews and experiences with implementation. Volume I, the strategic portion of the plan, which is expected to be reviewed and reissued this year, calls for emphasizing research which leads to enhancements in: (a) "human centered design" of controls, displays and advanced systems, (b) selection and training, (c) information transfer, (d) personal safety and survival, and (e) the measurement of performance and an understanding of variables that affect it. Volume II of the plan which contains the research agenda will be prioritized in the year ahead. In addition, most of the aviation human factors research now being accomplished by the Department of Defense, the National Aeronautics and Space Administration, and the Federal Aviation Administration will soon be accessible through an on-line data base operated by the Department of Defense. This data base is expected to be operational this year.

With regard to plan implementation, the FAA and the others involved with creating the plan have been active. Significant amounts of energy have been devoted to ensuring that research is relevant, documented, and well coordinated. With respect to the FAA, there has been a concerted effort to ensure human factors is an integral part of the research, development and acquisition process as well as regulatory and certification functions. Other endeavors have focused on enhancing the transfer of information through publications, symposia, and professional group meetings. Thus, there is much activity across all elements of the aviation human factors community, to meet the considerable challenges we face.

The remaining part of this paper will describe each of the research thrust areas in more detail and examples of associated projects and products will be illustrated.

Control and display & advanced technology

This objective encourages the identification and application of knowledge concerning the relative strengths and limitations of humans and computer-based technology to the design, evaluation and certification of controls, displays, and advanced systems. A major concern is the development of principles of "human-centered" automation which will enhance overall system performance (Wiener, 1989; Billings, 1991). Typical issues are: (a) degradation of basic skills with the associated performance implications should the automation fail, (b) hesitancy of human operators to take over from an automated system even when there is compelling evidence of a problem, and (c) keeping the operator in the loop and situationally aware of system performance.

Research and products in this thrust include: (a) guidelines for the human factors design, evaluation, and certification of advanced technology flightdeck displays and control systems, (b) human factors requirements guidelines for designing, integrating and evaluating ATC systems for human operators, (c) prototype information system that includes job aid, intelligent tutoring, and electronic documentation for airways facilities maintenance technicians, (d) human factors guidelines for developing, testing, and certifying interface designs of various data link applications, and (e) intelligent tutoring systems and job aids for industry aircraft maintenance personnel and FAA Aviation Safety Inspectors.

Selection and training

The focus of this thrust is the development of enhanced methods of training and selection for aviation system personnel, the support of these methods with training devices and aids, and the establishment of criteria for assessing training needs. Areas of interest include: (a) training for and measurement of effective team performance, (b) education, training, and evaluation of fatigue countermeasures, and (c) the impact of automation on job characteristics and requirements, and the associated consequences for selection and training.

Some of the research and products for this objective are: (a) development of an automated performance measurement system for evaluating flight crew training program effectiveness, (b) tools and reference information for improved performance-based ATC controller selection, training, certification, and retention, (c) training and performance requirements for AF technicians in a satellite-based environment, (d) visual and nondestructive inspection guidelines for aircraft maintenance, and (e) Crew Resource Management (CRM) evaluation guidelines for pilots, air traffic controllers, and aircraft maintenance technicians.

Information transfer & management

The third objective is the determination of the most effective means of information transfer among components of the National Airspace System. Approximately 70% of all Aviation Safety Reporting System (ASRS) reports involve some sort of information transfer problem, suggesting it may be the most common and persistent problem facing the aviation system. Areas of concern include: (a) identifying the most efficient and reliable ways to exchange information between people, between people and systems, and between automated systems, (b) determining what, when, and how information can best be displayed to system components, and (c) designing the system to reduce the frequency of information transfer errors and misinterpretations, and minimizing their impact when they do occur.

Example research projects in this area are: (a) design and evaluation of instrument approach charts, both paper and electronic, (b) ATC/pilot communication errors, (c) human factors guidelines to set policies for data link architectures and procedures, and (d) human factors guidelines for industry/govern- ment communication, data exchange, and support infrastructure.

Personal safety and survival

The fourth thrust deals with areas historically covered by the aviation medical community, with focus exclusively on the aircraft cabin environment. In this context the cabin includes both the cockpit and passenger compartments. There are three major sub objectives concerning health and safety: (a) survivability of crew and passengers following an accident or incident, (b) factors affecting health of crew and passengers, and c) health and medical factors affecting human performance.

Projects in support of this objective include research on: (a) rescue and firefighting performance, (b) the effects of drug and alcohol impairment on passenger evacuation capability, (c) commuter seat crashworthiness, (d) water survival gear for small children, and (e) passenger and crew protective breathing equipment.

Human performance

The fifth objective is improvement in the understanding of the factors that significantly affect human performance in aviation. There are three subthrusts in this area: (a) basic scientific knowledge that will facilitate understanding of baseline human performance, (b) better understanding of the impact of environment (external and internal) on human performance, and (c) improved and standardized methods for measurement of human performance.

Effective applied research is inevitably linked to results from previous basic research efforts. Solutions to workforce performance problems in the future require research in a number of areas: (a) shiftwork and work rest schedules, (b) the influence of organizational and management culture on human performance, and (c) the effective use of microprocessor technology and high fidelity, real-time simulation in aviation studies.

Conclusion

In the rapidly changing environment of the National Airspace System, it is imperative that human factors be treated as a core technology and play a central role in all aviation systems acquisition and development. Automation can potentially bring increased reliability, but only when the capabilities, limitations, and roles of the human operator are clearly understood and utilized in systems design. The National Plan for Aviation Human Factors provides a framework for coordinating human factors research and applying results in order to eliminate accidents and incidents caused by human error. Important research results have influenced system designs, certification and regulation decisions, operations directives, and training procedures. As a community, we have much to be proud of, while recognizing the future presents many formidable challenges and exciting opportunities. The end goal is a safe, efficient, and economically viable National Airspace System.

References

Air Transport Association of America. (1989), *National Plan to Enhance Aviation Safety Through Human Factors Improvements*, Washington, DC, Human Factors Task Force of the Air Transport Association of America.

Billings, C. (1991), *Human-centered Aircraft Automation: A Concept and Guidelines* (TM-103885), Moffett Field, CA, NASA-Ames Research Center.

Federal Aviation Administration. (1990), *The National Plan for Aviation Human Factors* (NTIS PB91-100321), Washington, DC, Federal Aviation Administration.

U.S. Congress, Office of Technology Assessment. (1988), *Safe Skies for Tomorrow: Aviation Safety in a Competitive Environment* (OAT-SET-381), Washington, DC, U.S. Government Printing Office.

Wiener, E. (1988), 'Cockpit Automation,' in Weiner, E. and Nagel, D. (eds.), *Human Factors in Aviation*, San Diego, Academic Press.

5 'How science really works': cultural influences on aviation psychology

Allan D. English
Royal Military College of Canada and Queen's University,
Kingston, Canada

As Europe prepares to move forward into a new era of cooperation, it may be useful to look backwards to see if there are any lessons from the past which could be used as landmarks on this journey into uncharted regions. By so doing, it may be possible to avoid being among those who, having forgotten their history, are doomed to repeat the mistakes of the past.

This paper addresses one of the major themes of this conference, "extending practice," from a historical perspective emphasizing the cultural influences which help to determine "how science really works" in aviation psychology. Research is not conducted in a cultural vacuum. Cultural factors affect assumptions about reality which in turn determine what constitutes scientific activity and the kind of data that are accepted as valid within different societies and organizations (English and Rodgers, 1992).

It has been shown that science is more than "a strictly logical process," and that it is in fact influenced by such other nonrational human behaviours as "rhetoric, propaganda, and personal prejudice," (Broad and Wade, 1982, pp 7,9) not to mention cultural considerations. If one accepts that fierce competition for scarce resources is another characteristic of science, then, those who have the best understanding of "how science really works," could have a crucial advantage in this struggle.

In this paper the following definitions of culture have been used. A national culture is a system of concepts that is perpetuated in a society and serves as a guide for the development of knowledge and attitudes toward life. Similarly, an organization's culture reflects important assumptions, values, activities, and aims (Louis, 1980) that generate common and organizationally acceptable behaviours.

Cultural diversity first became apparent in the field of aviation psychology in World War I, when each nation developed unique aviator selection systems. Each program evolved in a different way depending to a great extent on the professional background of those directing the research. The "equilibrium controversy" was one of many debates among scientists studying ways to cull prospective aviators from the general population of the nations involved in the first great war of this century.

Some of the earliest writings on the subject of aviation medicine had promoted the hypothesis that the semicircular canals of the ear were the primary means by which aviators sensed their orientation in three dimensions. This hypothesis was based on the fact that many birds had a well-developed vestibular apparatus, and from this fact it was deduced that the human vestibular apparatus must be important to the pilot (Alder, 1914). Research published, in 1907, by Robert Barany, a Nobel Prize-winning otologist (a specialist in the ear and its diseases), working in Vienna, inspired the development of techniques to measure the sensitivity of the vestibular apparatus, and some Americans took the lead in modifying these procedures for aviation purposes (Bachman, 1918). Barany's original tests were designed to investigate the condition of patients with diseases of the ear; however, certain researchers used arbitrary and hypothetical criteria to develop tests for fliers (Birley, 1920).

Dr. Isaac Jones, an American otologist selected to establish and ensure standardized aviator testing at US Army recruiting centres, was one of these scientists. As a co-author of the US Army's "Air Service Medical" examination (which almost totally excluded psychological factors), Jones was responsible for the introduction of these complex tests of equilibrium into the selection battery, and candidates who failed them were rejected for pilot training (Jones, 1937).

However, by 1925 it was determined that these tests were "meaningless and misleading," and that, as we know today, "vision...is the most important factor in the maintenance of equilibrium" (Armstrong, 1939, pp 50-1).

But, the approach taken by Jones and his colleagues was not unusual. For, as J.L. Birley, a leading British expert in aviation medicine recalled in 1920, we were "thrown into the rush of war, to be deluged by surprises, confronted with undreamt of situations, and expected at a moment's notice to pronounce expert opinions on subjects concerning which we would sometimes have preferred to confess a profound ignorance" (Birley, 1920, p 1147). In spite of their ignorance, some scientists presented untested solutions to urgent problems when pressed to do so.

Of course the nature of the national culture in question also influenced the outcome. In an era when, in North America, the value of any scientific discipline was measured by its perceived utility to society, appearances were important. Disciplines which produced numerical data from tests which required sophisticated apparatus tended by highly trained specialists were deemed to be more useful than those that did not. The popularity of the equilibrium tests was based both on Jones' advocacy of them, and the belief, fostered by an abundance of empirical data, that they were measuring something useful. However, the use of these tests eliminated many potentially useful candidates despite a desperate shortage at the front.

The "equilibrium controversy" is one example of how science sometimes really works. A prominent specialist in a particular field is asked to solve a problem, and solutions from the discipline he has been working in all his life are those which are adopted. The specialties of those directing a research program do influence its structure, and, therefore the answers that are found. This should come as no surprise. Experts can become isolated in their fields, and, when consulted, often focus on hypotheses and possible solutions that are familiar to them. The "equilibrium controversy" also demonstrates how medical doctors, from their entrenched positions of power in society, came to dominate one sphere of aviation psychology.

The next part of this paper will briefly describe how Canadian psychologists turned the tables and displaced medical doctors as the leading authorities on aviator selection in that country.

Despite its small size relative to the major powers, Canada was a leading member of the Allies in World War II. Perhaps its most significant contribution to the war effort was a massive aircrew training program, the British Commonwealth Air Training Plan (BCATP), which produced over 130,000 aircrew and transformed Canada into what Franklin D. Roosevelt called the "aerodrome of democracy" (Hatch, 1983). Canadian psychologists were an important component in this achievement; however, in 1939, there was some doubt that they were capable of meeting this challenge.

Before the Second World War, psychology in Canada was an immature discipline. Still taught as philosophy at some universities, psychology was in the early stages of development in that country. However, the impending conflict was seen by the Canadian Psychological Association (CPA) as a golden opportunity to advance the cause of the profession by offering its solutions to some of the nation's wartime dilemmas (Wright and Myers, 1982).

In 1938, the CPA began to lobby the leaders of the Canadian National Research Council to be included in the war effort. The Association carefully chose a limited number of programs which it believed would have the greatest appeal to the decision-makers. The CPA had some success in this effort, and a number of experimental psychologists were recruited from Canadian universities to oversee the BCATP aircrew selection program (CPA, 1939).

The involvement of Canadian civilian psychologists and their partiality to actuarial methods for identifying valid and objective measures of aviator potential resulted in a distinctive Canadian aircrew selection process that was indispensable to the success of a program the size of the BCATP. However, the system's most unique characteristic was the use of one of the first flight simulators, the Link Trainer, to help select aircrew on a large scale.

The Link Trainer was developed in the US during the 1930s as a device to train pilots in instrument flying, and, for its time, it was a very sophisticated simulator. After a series of experiments to measure its potential, the Canadian air force adopted a modified Visual Link Trainer (VLT) as an important part of its aircrew selection system. British and American researchers studied the Canadian VLT trials carefully, but they decided not to employ the device for selection purposes on a large scale. Consequently, Canada finished the war as the only Allied nation to employ the VLT comprehensively in pilot selection (DHist, nd).

To avoid giving the impression that the evolution of the Canadian aircrew selection system was the result of some inevitable process of scientific progress, it should be recalled that there were a number of competing selection strategies at the start of the war, and there was no way of knowing which one would prevail. Certain senior military officers were "offended deeply" by the suggestion that human behaviour could be subjected to an experimental trial, and preferred to exercise their own judgement in selecting pilots (Myers, 1972). Medical doctors claimed to be able to assess the "temperamental suitability" of candidates for aircrew duties in the course of a physical examination. And British and American researchers refused to use the VLT for large-scale selection on scientific grounds. However, much like the American otologists of the First World War, Canadian academic psychologists in the Second succeeded in gaining control of aircrew selection in Canada by portraying their discipline as a numerically based, "hard" science. The addition of the VLT added the same level of sophistication to the Canadian aircrew selection process as the spinning chairs of the otologists in the First World War. This combination of empirical data and technological sophistication served to impress decision-makers in a culture where these attributes were admired in a science.

The decision, by those who governed and funded aviation medical research, to put aircrew selection investigations in the hands of psychologists marked a radical departure from previous approaches to this problem in Canada. This action, stimulated by intense lobbying on the part of the CPA, precipitated changes in the selection process which led to the incorporation of methodologies entirely different from those previously employed. But the success of the Association's efforts was due largely to the fact that its leaders agreed to restrict the number of proposals it put forward to those which they felt would be most attractive to national authorities at that time (English, 1992).

This brief description of two milestones in the history of aviation psychology has illustrated how science sometimes really works. National cultures played an important part in determining the profession of those who were placed in charge of the aviator selection programs in question, and organizational cultures dictated the types of solutions that were adopted. The "equilibrium controversy" depicted how, despite its claim to be "the ultimate arbiter of truth" in Western society, science is fallible. Proceeding by deductive reasoning, rather than experimental method, some early researchers in aviator selection established tests to measure a quality that was irrelevant to success in pilot training. And despite the test's flaws, a scientist in an influential position was able to introduce it into a national selection program.

The experience of Canadian psychologists in World War II has demonstrated how many factors impacted on the judgments authorities made in determining which discipline would control the resources allocated to aircrew selection research. While experimental data may seem to be a critical component of any evaluation, it is virtually impossible for bureaucratic decision-makers to have detailed scientific knowledge in all of the contending disciplines. Administrators must often accept at face value the conclusions of competing scientific models. Presented with conflicting evidence, government authorities may resort to such considerations as expediency, availability of resources, anecdotal evidence or subjective impressions to make their choices. The professional community that understands this will be better prepared to influence the process.

Finally, it is worth emphasizing that I am not proposing that science in

Western cultures is an exclusively nonrational activity. Reason plays its part; but it is only one among many human behaviours that influence how science really works.

Acknowledgement

Presentation of this paper was supported in part by the Dean of Arts, Royal Military College of Canada and the School of Graduate Studies and Research and the Department of History, Queen's University, Kingston, Canada.

References

Alder, J.E. (1914), 'Notes on the medical aspect of aviation', in Hamel, G. and Turner. C.C. *Flying*, Longmans, London.
Armstrong, H.G. (1939), *Principles and Practice of Aviation Medicine*, Williams and Wilkins, Baltimore.
Bachman, R.A. (1918), 'The examination of aviators', *U.S. Naval Medical Bulletin*, **12**, 30-41.
Birley, J.L. (1920), 'The principles of medical science as applied to military aviation, Lectures I,II,III', *Lancet*, **1920**, 1147-51, 1205-1211, 1251-57.
Broad, W. and Wade, N. (1982), *Betrayers of the Truth*, Simon and Schuster, New York.
Canadian Psychological Association [CPA], 'Constitution, Correspondence, Minutes and Reports 1938-42, 1971', National Archives of Canada [NAC], MG 28 I 161, Vol.17.
Directorate of History [DHist], Department of National Defence, Canada, (no date), 'Flying training' (Report 74/19), unpublished narrative.
English, A.D. (1992), 'Canadian Psychologists and the Aerodrome of Democracy', *Canadian Psychology*, **33**, (4), 663-72.
English, A.D. and Rodgers, M. (1992), 'Déja Vu? Cultural Influences on Aviator Selection', *Military Psychology* **4**, (1), 35-47.
Hatch, F.J. (1983), *The Aerodrome of Democracy*, Department of National Defence (Canada), Ottawa.
Jones, I. (1937), *Flying Vistas*, Lipincott, Philadelphia.
Louis, M.R. (1980), 'Surprise and sense making', *Administrative Science Quarterly*, **25**, 226-251.
Myers, C.R. (1972), Transcript from the Oral History of Psychology in Canada, NAC, MG 28 I 161, Vol. 26.
Wright, M.J. and Myers, C.R. (eds) (1982), *History of Academic Psychology in Canada*, C.J. Hogrefe, Toronto.

Part 2
SYSTEMS AND ORGANISATION

6 Organisational safety culture and aviation practice

Nick Pidgeon, Birkbeck College, University of London
Mike O'Leary, British Airways and Birkbeck College

Much recent work on the preconditions of accidents and disasters in a wide range of high-technology hazardous systems indicates that human and organizational causes are predominant. This is perhaps not surprising given that individuals, their organizations and groups, and ultimately their cultures are all implicated in the design, construction, operation and monitoring of a technology. Reflecting this, within the civilian aviation community several authors have recently argued that there is now a need to complement analyses of individual human error by an understanding of the role played by broader system factors in aviation accidents (see e.g. Johnston, 1991; Enders, 1992; ICAO, 1993). The paper discusses this issue in three sections. In the first a contemporary case-study illustrating the role of system and organizational factors in aviation accidents, is presented. Second, the theoretical concept of an organizational safety culture is introduced and briefly discussed. In the third section we outline a number of the generic dilemmas associated with institutional design, and which will need to be resolved if attempts to change safety cultures in aviation are to be made.

System failure and aviation: a case-study

The first comprehensive theoretical analysis of the social and organizational preconditions to disaster in large-scale technological systems was by Turner (1978). He concluded that prior to any disaster it is typical to find that a number of undesirable events (particularly involving information and communication difficulties) accumulate, unnoticed or not fully understood, often over a considerable number of years. Turner defined this gradual development of preconditions as the *disaster incubation period*. The incubation period is brought to a conclusion either by the taking of preventative action to remove one or more of the dangerous conditions where these are noticed, or by a *trigger event*, which might be a final critical error, or a slightly abnormal operating condition. This distinction has since been taken up by Reason (1990) in his discussion of *latent* and *active* errors. Reason argues that line-operators (e.g. air crew) often inherit faulty systems directly as a result of management decisions made elsewhere in an organization. In addition, and after the event, the immediate trigger should not be confused with the more systemic background causes.

A graphic illustration of a hazardous situation incubating unnoticed is provided by a recent case-study of the sudden in-flight structural break-up and crash, with the loss of all fourteen lives aboard, of a twin-engined Continental Express Embraer 120 on the 11th. of September 1991 near Eagle Lake Texas. The catastrophic structural failure of the aircraft occurred without warning, during a descent in good weather through approximately 12,000 feet, *en route* to landing at Houston Intercontinental Airport. Neither pilot actions or weather contributed to the accident. Rather, the sudden loss of control and subsequent structural break-up was triggered by the separation of the leading edge assembly from the left side of the horizontal stabilizer on the top of the aircraft's T-type tail.

The US National Transportation Safety Board report (NTSB, 1992) into the accident documents how the failure was not purely a "mechanical" circumstance, but the result of deficiencies rooted in the maintenance, management and regulatory systems surrounding the operation of the aircraft. The probable structural cause of the break-up was the absence of a set of 49 screws in the upper leading edge assembly of the aircraft's T-type tail. However, the precise reasons for this omission were found to reside in the events of the evening prior to the crash, when the Embraer 120 had undergone scheduled maintenance operations to replace the deicing assemblies, known as deice "boots", installed on both the left and right leading edges of the horizontal stabilizer. The operations to change the deice boots required separation of the leading edge assemblies from the aircraft by removal of both the top and bottom rows of screws respectively.

During the course of two shifts over the evening and night, maintenance personnel successfully replaced and re-secured the right-hand leading edge assembly and boot. However, work on the left-hand assembly was started but not completed. A number of factors contributed to this state of affairs including poor supervision and inspection of the work coupled with a complex pattern of errors of communication between the mechanics, supervisors and inspectors of the two respective overnight maintenance shift teams that had worked on the aircraft. These in combination conspired to conceal the incomplete the work on the left-hand assembly.

The NTSB report also points to the operation of more general systemic factors, arguing that "the lax attitude in the hanger suggests that management *did not establish an effective safety orientation* for its employees" (1992, p44, emphasis added), and that this was in all probability a contributory cause of the accident. A related factor concerned the failure of management to properly classify the deice boot change as a safety critical (Required Inspection Item) procedure. Over and above all of this, the final line of monitoring, by the US Federal Aviation Administration in its role as supervisor of correct hanger practice, is criticised in the accident report as having been insufficient to enable detection of probable on-going violations of approved maintenance procedures at the company.

Safety culture

The discussion now turns to the concept of safety culture. This notion is important since it addresses some of the wider organizational causes of accidents, such as the poor "safety orientation" identified in the Embraer 120 case, and in a way that is a significant departure from the traditional human factors approach to safety in aviation. The term first arose in a number of analyses of the implications of the Chernobyl disaster for the Western nuclear industry. Here, the serious human errors and violations of procedures at the plant were interpreted as evidence of a *poor safety culture* (see Pidgeon, 1991). Within Europe the development of an "appropriate" safety culture for nuclear operators is now seen as one important goal of reactor operator training (ACSNI, 1993). And a more general interest in the topic has ensued in attempts to both define and explore the concept (for a review see Horbury, In Press).

Work on safety culture suggests ways in which reliability and safety questions might be linked to more general social science concepts and findings (to the literature on corporate culture, for example), and thereby to established means of empirical investigation. In the social sciences, as well as in common parlance, culture refers primarily to *shared* characteristics of a social group, organization or society. With this in mind Turner et al. (1989) have noted that the discussions of safety culture following Chernobyl are often reduced, on the one hand, to sets of administrative procedures for training, emergency plans and so on, and on the other to individual attitudes to safety. What these discussions fail to address is the crucial shared property that is the defining characteristic of culture.

In our own approach to this issue we view culture as principally involving the *exploration of meaning* and the *systems of meaning* through which a given social group understands the world. Accordingly, we have broadly defined safety culture as the set of beliefs, norms, attitudes, roles, and social and technical practices within an organization which are concerned with minimising the exposure of individuals, both within and outside an organization, to conditions considered to be dangerous (Turner et al., 1989). Such a system specifies what is important to individuals and groups, and explains their relationship to matters of life and death, work and danger. A safety culture is created and recreated as members of it repeatedly behave in ways which seem to them to be "natural", obvious and unquestionable, and as such will serve to construct a particular version of risk, danger and safety. A safety culture also provides a set of assumptions and practices which permit new beliefs about danger to be constructed.

Any discussion of safety culture initially raises two interrelated questions for practitioners. First, are there are "good" or "poor" safety cultures, which vary across organizations and which influence safety performance and reliability? The definition of culture advanced above implies, of course, that in order to improve reliability in complex socio-technical systems we require more than exhortations to air crew and maintenance personnel to "change attitudes towards safety", or indeed to "fly or work more safely". There would seem to be four principal facets of a "good" safety culture: actual (rather then merely symbolic) location of responsibility for safety at *strategic management* level; *shared attitudes of care and concern* throughout an aviation organization; appropriate *norms and rules* for handling hazards; and on-going *reflection* (as provided, for example, by incident reporting and reaction procedures) upon safety practice (see also Lautman and Gallimore, 1987; Pidgeon and O'Leary, 1994). These represent, of course, closely interrelated facets, which in part depend upon and reinforce each other, and which we have argued go together to generate the somewhat elusive quality of a safe climate or culture.

Dilemmas of institutional design

One obvious question is whether the concept of a safety culture can be of utility as part of a proactive process of institutional design for safety? However, it is important to stress that it will be no simple matter to translate the many theoretical treatments of the safety culture concept into practical action. This is because a number of generic dilemmas are associated with any attempt at institutional design (see Hood *et al.*, 1992).

A basic problem stems from the fact that there is evidence within the management science literature to indicate that organizational cultures are notoriously resistant to change. Attempts to change safety cultures solely by management edict or by imposition of external regulation may meet with only limited success. Rather, permanent change may be best addressed through long-term "organizational-learning" (see Toft and Reynolds, 1994). One way in which this arises is through an organization having to respond to its own involvement in an accident or series of incidents.

A second generic dilemma flows from the fact that even if corporate culture can be shown to have changed at the same time as safety performance has improved, it will not necessarily be easy to demonstrate unambiguously that the two are directly linked. Williams (1991) argues that it might be easier to gauge the impact of culture change on an organization through a wider range of measures, including those of quality, reliability, and competitiveness. He concludes, from his review of available studies, that a "good" safety culture may have an influence on safety performance only indirectly, through its relationship with raised quality standards within an organization more generally. This supports what at first may seem a surprising claim: that safety and production goals such as quality or operational reliability may not necessarily need to be traded-off, but may sometimes go hand-in-hand.

A third institutional design question is raised when we consider the fact that large aviation organizations comprise many different, sometimes overlapping, social sub-groupings (e.g. pilots and cabin crew, air crew across different fleets, maintenance and ground handling personnel, different tiers of management etc.), perhaps with their own distinctive sub-cultures. On a much wider cross-cultural level one can also ask whether the concept of a corporate culture, which is derived from Western contexts, will prove useful if applied to airlines from non-Western national cultures. It is doubtful therefore whether a set of unified guide-lines for culture change can be designed to accommodate cultural and resource variations both within and between organizations. On the other hand, all efforts at aviation risk management through institutional design will have to be conducted against the backdrop of pre-existing safety culture(s). One important conclusion that we draw here is that at least some understanding of existing cultures must be gained *before* risk management efforts such as new training, reporting systems, procedural frameworks, and resource management programmes are designed and initiated. This is critical both because existing cultures may generate unintended consequences that subvert the intended outcomes of an otherwise well designed programme, and because the introduction of a new programme always has the potential to change the existing culture. Safe cultures can be harmed as well as encouraged (Horbury, In Press)!

The final dilemma concerns the role of blame in the risk management process, and it is one which is particularly difficult to resolve (see Hood *et al.*, 1992; Johnston, In Press). Blame sets a dilemma because the call for society to place strong sanctions upon individuals and organizations who act unsafely must be balanced against the need to learn from past events. In one sense processes of blaming may be inherent to most social settings, and will always surround the topics of safety, danger and risk (Douglas, 1992). However, as Johnston (In Press) argues, the social functions of blaming should be recognised for what they are, and be clearly separated from the exercise of risk management in aviation. In an ideal world the view of accidents as socio-technical phenomena would be accompanied by an investigative emphasis which seeks for *what* is wrong rather than *who* made the mistake. Thus blame and punishment should be avoided because the knowledge that a "culprit" has to be found whenever an error has occurred will invariably prevent the full and candid reporting of incidents and unsafe events to the detriment of opportunities for learning about the system. At a *corporate* level, however, legal sanction may always be necessary to ensure that organizations set up and maintain effective safety systems. The balance to be struck between the issues of blame and sanction at the individual and corporate level cannot be ignored when questions of safety and institutional design are considered.

Conclusion

Aviation practice must incorporate an understanding of unsafe technical events and individual actions within their social and organizational contexts. In our view a significant part of this social and organizational context is captured by the notion of a safety culture, which is an influential background factor intertwined with ultimate safety performance. The question of whether we can design safe organizations is perhaps the most important issue in risk management today, both for operators of aviation and other high-risk systems. The discussion here should both caution practitioners against approaching this difficult problem with an overly optimistic view, while at the same time indicating some of the ways in which our knowledge about this question can move forward.

References

ACSNI (1993), *Advisory Committee on the Safety of Nuclear Installations: Study Group on Human Factors. Organising for Safety*, HMSO (Health and Safety Commission), London.

Douglas, M. (1992), *Risk and Blame: Essays in Cultural Theory*, Routledge, London.

Enders, J.H. (1992), 'Management inattention greatest accident cause, not pilots', *Flight Safety Foundation Newsletter*, Feb/March/April 1992, **33**(2), p1.

Hood, C., Jones, D.K., Pidgeon, N.F., Turner, B.A. and Gibson, R. (1992), 'Risk management', in *Risk: Analysis, Perception and Management*, The Royal Society, London.

Horbury, C. (In Press), 'Safety culture: future dimensions in the light of new knowledge', *Journal of Health and Safety*, In Press.

ICAO (1993), *Human Factors Digest No. 9: Human Factors in Management and Organization*, International Civil Aviation Organization, Montreal.

Johnston, A.N. (1991), 'Organizational factors in human factors accident investigation', in *Proceedings of the 6th Symposium on Aviation Psychology*, May 1991, Ohio.

Johnston, A.N. (In Press), 'Blame, punishment and risk management', in Jones, D.K., Hood, C., Pidgeon, N.F. and Turner B.A. (eds.), *Accident and Design: Contemporary Debates in Risk Management*, University College Press, London.

Lautman, L.G. and Gallimore, P.L. (1987), 'Control of the crew caused accident', *Airliner*, April-June, 1-6.

NTSB (1992), *Aircraft Accident Report: Continental Express Flight 2574 In-flight Structural Breakup, EMB-120RT, N33701, Eagle Lake, Texas (NTSB/AAR-92/04)*, National Transportation Safety Board, Washington DC.

Pidgeon, N.F. (1991), 'Safety culture and risk management in organizations', *Journal of Cross-Cultural Psychology*, **22**(1), 129-140.

Pidgeon, N.F. and O'Leary (1994), 'Organizational safety culture: implicatation for aviation practice', in N. Johnston, N. McDonald and R. Fuller (eds), *Aviation Psychology in Practice*, Avebury Technical, Aldershot.

Reason, J.T. (1990), *Human Error*, Cambridge University Press.

Toft, B. and Reynolds, S. (1994), *Learning from Disasters*, Butterworth-Heinemann, London.

Turner, B.A. (1978), *Man-made Disasters*, Wykeham, London.

Turner, B.A., Pidgeon, N.F., Blockley, D.I. and Toft, B. (1989), 'Safety culture: its importance in future risk management', position paper for *Second World Bank Workshop on Safety Control and Risk Management*, 6-9 November 1989, Karlstad, Sweden.

Williams, J.C. (1991), 'Safety cultures: their impact on quality, reliability, competitiveness and profitability', in R.H. Matthews (ed.), *Reliability '91*, Elsevier Applied Science, London.

7 Transport Canada's System Analysis and Functional Evaluation (SAFE) Program

James P. Stewart, Director General System Safety Transport Canada

I want to thank Mr. Bob Merrick, Mr. Walter Peters and Mr. Aly Sherif for their contribution in preparing this paper. I particularly want to recognize the efforts of Mr. Walter Peters who, as Director Aviation Safety Analysis and Research, System Safety, led the effort to make the computerized version of SAFE operational.

Background

Two major functions of the System Safety Directorate are to identify system deficiencies in the Canadian National Civil Air Transportation System (NCATS) and to provide advice on where resources can best be used to rectify those deficiencies.[1]

We were concerned that occurrence reports could detail **what** happened but could miss **why** an accident happened. Our concern was compounded since the Transportation Safety Board of Canada could not apportion blame or liability and could not comment on regulatory aspects with a view to enforcement. As part of the Regulatory Authority, we had no such restriction and, indeed, had a responsibility to identify basic failures which resulted in the occurrence even if we imputed blame or liability. We knew that only a clear indication of systemic cause(s), ("the why") of occurrences would lead to effective prevention.[2] We developed a program to analyze occurrence reports, determine systemic causes and categorize those causes in a way which would allow for macro or micro analysis.

Major Premises of the Program

The SAFE program is based on the following premises:

1) any aircraft occurrence represents a failure of one or more aviation systems;
2) any form of occurrence investigation represents a source of system deficiency information;
3) any system deficiency which has the potential to cause an occurrence or aggravate the effects of an occurrence is worthy of study; and,
4) the reason for the system deficiency (the why) must be identified with the greatest accuracy possible even if this ascribes blame or liability.[3]

Safe Categories

As we were interested in the whole National Civil Air Transportation System we developed five main systems for analysis.

1) Personnel - the human element.
2) Equipment - the aircraft, support equipment etc.
3) Environment - the medium in which the aircraft and its crew operates.
4) Regulatory Body - Transport Canada responsibility within the NCATS.
5) Management - management decisions of organizations which control, operate or manufacture aircraft.[4]

Each main system is supported by a sub-system and then by components which serve to narrow the categories and provide a clearer description of the systemic cause. As well, we add a short descriptive phrase to further define the problem.

The Initial Test

We tested the new program using 17 major accident reports and supported this with an analysis of about 60 occurrence reports. We were encouraged, and a little surprised, at the results.

Although the frequency of personnel failures had generally been accepted to be around 80-85% in 1983, we came up with a number closer to 70%. We also identified a high incidence of **Management** factors with the majority of them being in the area of **Supervision**.

The **Management** finding surprised us for two reasons. In 1985, few investigations cited management as causal. There was little emphasis on management factors in occurrence reports. Because the reports we reviewed described major accidents, they were more thorough than those we had for smaller occurrences. It would be seven years before **Management** would be regularly reported upon in occurrence reports without raising eyebrows.

Since the information identifying **Management** as a major factor was deduced from reading the accident report, and not from reading the investigation findings, we gained further confidence in the SAFE methodology. Even with limited information and the crudest of analytical methods, **Management** ranked fourth in a list of why occurrences happened.

Human Performance Limitations

We found the greatest failure was in human performance with the number one factor being **Personnel-Pilot-Judgement**.[5] This substantiated our earlier decision to further emphasize our Pilot Decision Making program. It also spurred us to focus on broader Human Factor Education and to develop management training initiatives. Unfortunately, it also led to severe criticism that we were skewing the data to support our programs to the detriment of other regulatory efforts, such as Airworthiness and Enforcement.

The second most serious factor was Personnel-Pilot-Technique.[6]

Following the introduction of Pilot Decision Making courses, Crew Resource Management training, increased emphasis on human performance concerns and increased awareness of the effect of human performance limitations on causing accidents, there has been a reversal in the precedence of Personnel factors. In the last eight years, Technique has superseded **Judgment** as the leading cause.

The Management Category

Our analysis of the **Management** category revealed that the number one factor was non-compliance with regulations, specifically with regard to direction required by our Air Navigation Orders. We determined that air carriers were not exercising the degree of operational control required; that some companies had no defined chain of command for operational control. This lack of managerial direction manifested itself in reduced supervision, increased non-compliance, reduced training standards and a reduction in the flow of information that managers must pass to their line personnel.

Safe Goes International

In 1987 we presented the SAFE Program to the International Data Exchange Aviation Safety (IDEAS) Committee in Monterey, California. At present, it is in use in one form or another in four countries by Government or private agencies. The SAFE program also bears a striking resemblance to the latest edition of the ICAO ADREP system [7] and the Transportation Safety Board of Canada's TSIS system.[8]

The SAFE system was converted to a computer application with many side benefits and enhancements. We now have a Random Search capability which allows us to search any combination of fields and then allows the analyst to format the report to meet a specified need. This is what I intend to show you today.

Notes

1   Our definition of **system deficiency** is: "The circumstances which permit hazards of a like nature to exist within a system (regional or national)".

2   Regulatory authorities and aviation companies around the world have spent considerable time, effort and resources in responding to superficial causes while, in some cases, ignoring the more serious causes which remain to catch a future unsuspecting victim.

3   The SAFE Program was adapted from a computerized analysis system then used by the Canadian Armed Forces. The Canadian Forces cause factor program has run successfully since the late sixties and is instrumental in reducing military losses.

4   The Canadian Armed Forces used three main components, Man, Machine, Environment. They also had an Operational factor which represented a command decision to accept unlimited risk, a Foreign Object Damage factor and Unknown.

5   At that time, **Personnel-Pilot-Judgement** showed up in 21% of all factors.

6   At that time, **Personnel-Pilot-Technique** was identified in 18% of the factors. Combined with the 21% for **Judgement,** we were faced with a finding that 39% of the factors identified a failure of pilots to deal effectively with their environment. As stated, since that time **Judgement and Technique** have reversed their position.

7   The ICAO ADREP (Accident Data Reporting) system, now known as the Accident/Ient Reporting system, is the current international standard for categorizing cause factors following an occurrence.

8   The TSIS (Transportation Safety Information System) was introduced by the Transportation Safety Board of Canada in 1993. It is used to categorize factors which the Board identifies as a result of their investigations.

8 Safety and learning: safety services in British Airways

Heather Höpfl, Bolton Business School
Callum MacGregor, British Airways

Since 1990 British Airways has brought about significant changes in the style of its Safety Services operations. In part, this has been the result of a decade of change in corporate culture and specifically, a commitment to a radical and philosophical change in the conceptualisation of safety information and to organisational learning.

In 1983 British Airways was in a ruinous financial state and experiencing a number of external pressures to change. The airline had made significant reductions in costs but was finding it increasingly difficult to compete on the basis of cost alone. Many costs, such as aviation fuel and airport charges were outside the company's control. Using Scandinavian Airlines as an exemplar (Carlzon, 1987) attention was directed towards achieving competition advantage via service delivery. Customer service was seen as critical (Bruce, 1987). Colin Marshall, then Chief Executive of British Airways, saw the organisation as demoralised and lacking commercial awareness. From 1983 onwards, Marshall initiated a series of corporate programmes designed to demonstrate a visible commitment to change from top management and to transformation of the corporate culture.

Over a decade of change, BA has acquired considerable experience of promoting transformational change via customer service. One of the primary objectives of the change was to promote business awareness at all levels of the organisation and to help staff to appreciate functional interdependencies. Multidisciplinary teams were set up to encourage collaborative styles of management, and a commitment to management development through higher education was promoted via links with universities. The company was directed towards a conscious opening up to the outside world. The changes in BA stimulated debate in the organisation and, irrespective of how such programmes might be evaluated, the freeing of the former structures offered opportunities for fundamental changes in the style of operations. The concern here is with how the Safety Services unit was able to harness the change in order to adopt new approaches to safety.

In Safety Services, the change in the culture of the airline away from "a military approach to management" (Bruce, 1987, 25) provided the opportunity to introduce changes which were to have a significant impact on the approach to safety in the airline and, latterly, within a broader context. The safety function in BA had evolved since WWII. Its primary task was accident investigation but as the number of accidents declined it took on responsibility for the investigation and analysis of incidents. Historically, safety personnel were drawn from an engineering background and had a technical perspective on the activities of the department. Pilot management teams approved of this technical focus and dealt with operational issues themselves. There was a simple database to record and monitor air safety reports.

In 1989, David Hyde, was appointed as British Airway's Director of Safety, Security and Environment. He appointed Captain Colin Seaman as Head of Safety with a brief to review safety across the airline and to create a structure that was "Fit for the 1990s". The changes led by Seaman rested on a number of factors - the personnel involved; the commitment to and development of an underlying philosophy for safety management; the broad brief of the group and widened areas of influence; the determination to create a sensitive and receptive environment in which safety data could be collected and interpreted; changes in the airline as whole.

Major changes were required. It was decided that the historical data should be destroyed in a symbolic "clean sweep" and a new system introduced. The mainframe database was scrapped and all the categorisations previously used abandoned. The team was geared to setting targets which emphasised the magnitude and the new philosophy. The targets were impressive. The number of open reports was to be reduced from 1058 to 50 and the length of time for an investigation reduced from two years to 28 days. The new tool was a modified PC database which two members of the team, Wright and

MacGregor, had tried and tested on the 1-11 fleet. Data entry to the new system began in August, 1990 with a declared target of having the system live throughout the airline by January, 1991. The development of the system, BASIS - British Airways Safety Information System, is documented elsewhere (Seaman, 1991; Holtom, 1991; MacGregor 1993) but needs to be seen in the context of other critical developments in safety.

MacGregor and Wright were well aware that there were incidents and practices which were not coming to light through the reporting system: "the real story" emerging later. Rich accounts of human factor incidents, interpersonal problems, ambiguities, information difficulties and perceptual matters was generally not available. Given this, Safety Services was resistant to describing quantitative data as safety statistics, preferring to locate this type of data within a wider interpretative context. Some information gaps can be dealt with by appropriate systems but some are much more intricately enmeshed and resistant to exposure. This implies the need to develop a responsiveness within the system to the complex, irrational, embedded, conflictual aspects of information which may be permitted to emerge by a commitment to organizational learning, the acquisition of a dynamic memory, and a resistance to naive quantification. It is the pursuit of the complex and irrational which has kept Safety Services from some of the adverse aspects of corporate culture change which have a specific relevance for safety.

In organisations which regard culture as capable of manipulation, commitment to the organisation is assumed to involve consensus over values. This produces a standardised pattern of behaviours which characterise the company. As organisations become increasingly concerned with routinised patterns of behaviour which support a notion of "service" and "quality", corporate culture becomes increasingly problematic. The strength of the corporate culture is matched by the strength of resistance to it and by patterns of deviance. There are direct implications for safety management. Bureaucratic approaches to safety may produce high standards of performance in terms of that which is presented and measurable or observable. Day to day practice may differ radically, that is, attention may be paid to mere appearances.

Clearly, an understanding of the wider implications of culture change requires a critical awareness of corporate culture as a privileged standpoint and an appreciation what is concealed by its construction. Here, the concern is to examine the extent to which the manipulation of corporate culture reduces safety issues to a declared rhetoric supported by artifacts which may, in turn, reduce a concern for safety to a cosmetic exercise. In such circumstances, safety becomes a matter of methods, manuals and messages. Safety becomes critical to the extent that what is unsafe is concealed by the pursuit of rhetoric, standardised behaviour and quantification.

A number of theorists have wrestled with these aspects of safety. Reason, among others, points to the significance of the "latent failures" (1990: 28) which only become evident when they occur with a "precipitating event" (Turner, 1978) which causes the system to fail. Reason contends that "attempts to discover and remedy these latent failures will achieve greater safety benefits than will localized efforts to minimize active failures" (Reason, 1990: 476-7). Consequently, safety specialists need to direct their attention to the neutralization of latent failures, rather than attempting to prevent "active" failures. Yet, it is generally to the identifiable that most attention is paid. In the face of major accidents and disasters, many organisations are concerned to demonstrate a visible commitment to safety. Unfortunately, this may lead to a well intentioned commitment to the visible aspects of safety at the cost of what is not immediate and apparent.

In his now classic study of disasters, Turner (1978) argued that large-scale accidents have an "incubation period" in which there are a series of unnoticed events which are likely to run counter to established beliefs about the way that the system operates or that risks are defined. Turner encouraged safety researchers to concern themselves with "the cultural disruption(s).... which occur in ways unanticipated by those pursuing orderly goals" (Turner, 1978: 193,201). The pursuit of orderly goals and regulated behaviour is a significant objective of corporate culture. At the same time, the culture of the workplace produces its own taken-for-granted assumptions about the world. The dangers are well documented. However, organisational culture change provides a further level of complexity. Corporate culture with its emphasis on shared beliefs, values, norms and style seeks to construct common meanings for experience. The mechanisms of corporate culture change reinforce a common rhetoric by ensuring the coherence of systems, structures, skills and rewards as a basis for regulating and standardising patterns of behaviour. This coherent and orderly world comes increasingly to a belief in its own constructions (Janis, 1972). The problem is that this orderly world may come to believe its own messages regarding the efficacy of its safety structures and procedures.

This period of order ends when some event draws attention to the discrepancy between the environment as it is believed to be and the environment as it actually is. This forces into the open the "hidden, ambiguous or anomalous events which have accumulated during the incubation period" (Turner, 1978: 201) producing a sudden shift in information levels. The pursuit of coherence imposes the appearance of order on a wide range of behaviours and experiences including the discrepant and irrational. Thus, multiple meanings are likely to be glossed by a privileged interpretation of events. The apparently purposive nature of organisations supports the validity of this interpretation and consensus. Contradictions are concealed.

A second problem concerns apparently consensual values. This conceals dissonant behaviour and experience in organisational members who may demonstrate their resistance to the organisation in a range of unpredictable ways. Airline cabin crew, who in recent years have undergone intensive "customer service" training programmes, acquire a range of strategies to resist the roles that have been laid on them. What needs to be challenged is the "naive preoccupation with shared values" (Linstead and Grafton Small, 1992: 332). The importance of this point lies in other attributes of corporate culture change which via the pursuit of shared values and behavioural regularities have produced apparent consensus and standardised behaviours which may be in conflict with local practice. Some empirical examples of this are apparent in safety management (Guest et al, 1994). A misplaced confidence in artefacts and a paradoxical vulnerability.

Recent work by Turner (1992) has focused on ways in which organisational learning can be used in safety management. In this respect, he argues that new organisational learning requires an appreciation of the processes and multiple perceptions of which organisations are made up; that organisations are like mysteries which have to be unravelled; that the learning cycle is complicated by ambiguities, corruptions of meaning, multiple meanings, symbols and so on; that the assumption of rationality needs to be bracketed: that records and computerized systems need to be regarded as problematic; that assumptions of completeness need to be challenged; that interpretative methods need to be used to get behind taken for granted assumptions. Such an approach may meet resistance. In part, this is because it represents a philosophical commitment to a style of safety management which cannot be quantified nor directly applied at an operational level. The issues which it seeks to keep in play do not yield to analysis or lend themselves to data capture. Safety is viewed as something which cannot be reduced to simple formulations or quantifications. The need to present safety management as an entirely rational activity precludes an appreciation of the irrational aspects of safety. Safety Services in BA has attempted to wrestle with these difficulties.

The culture change in BA provided the opportunity to develop a new approach to safety management. The radical change which followed was the result of a clear endorsement from top management, David Hyde, effective leadership and teamwork, a philosophical base for action, a commitment to a broad conception of learning and a willingness to challenge taken-for-granted assumptions. This translated into an awareness of the complexity of safety data and a resistance to taxonomic and quantitative delusion in the development of the safety information system.

References

Bruce, M. (1987), "Managing People First - Bringing the Service Concept into British Airways", *Industrial and Commercial Training*, March/April.

Carlzon, J. (1987), *Moments of Truth*, Cambridge, Mass: Ballinger.

Guest, D., Thomas, A. and Peccei, R. (1994), Safety Culture and Safety Performance, British Rail in the Aftermath of the Clapham Junction Disaster, *BPS Occupational Psychology Conference*, Birmingham 1994.

Holtom, M. (1991), The Basis for Safety Management, *Focus* Nov 1991, The Flight Safety Committee.

Janis, I.L. (1982), *Groupthink*, Boston: Houghton Mifflin.

Linstead, S.L. and Grafton Small, R. (1992), On Reading Organizational Culture, *Organisation Studies*, 13, 3, 331-355.

MacGregor, C. and Hopfl, H. (1993), A Commitment to Safety, *Disaster Prevention and Management*, Vol 2 No 2 6-13.

Reason, J. (1990), The contribution of latent human failures to the breakdown of complex systems, 27-36 in Broadbent, D.E. Reason, J. and Baddeley, A. (eds), *Human Factors in Hazardous Situations*, Oxford: Clarendon Press.

Seaman, C. (1991), The British Airways Safety Information System, *44th International Air Safety Seminar*, Singapore, Nov 1991.

Turner, B.A. (1978), *Man-Made Disasters*, London: Wykeham.

Turner, B.A. (1989), How can we design a safe organization? *Second International Conference on Industrial and Organizational Crisis Management*, New York, November 1989.

9 Organisational change: the human factor

Brent Hayward, Qantas Airways Ltd, Melbourne, Australia

Introduction

The majority of work carried out in the field of aviation human factors is directed towards improving the safety and efficiency of our operations. This is true whether we approach our jobs from the standpoint of aviation psychologists, pilots, cabin attendants, air traffic controllers, maintenance engineers, ergonomists, educationists, or applied researchers.

However, we are currently witnessing the emergence of an additional explicit goal of our efforts - that of improved bottom line or commercial performance. As human factors practitioners we are beginning to recognize that if we are to gain and to maintain the full support of management for our training programmes, then we must expand our course terminal objectives to include specific "organizational outcomes" in addition to the more traditionally accepted goals of enhanced operational performance and safety (see Beaumont, in press; Hayward, in press).

We have also begun to consider the importance of organizational and national culture in training design and implementation. Several authors (see Johnston, 1993; Merritt, 1993) have extrapolated the seminal cultural studies of Geert Hofstede (1980, 1991) to the aviation environment, achieving amongst other things some appreciation of the difficulties involved in simply transplanting training programmes from one culture to another. We have learnt that ignoring significant differences in organizational or national culture can doom a training programme to failure. However, as observed by Maurino (in press), we should avoid the tendency to think in terms of appropriate or inappropriate cultures, but should think instead in terms of cultural differences, of cultural strengths and weaknesses.

On another cultural dimension, the human factors lessons learnt from working with flight crew are now being applied to a range of specific occupational contexts. For example, Davies and Eagle (1993) have drawn detailed analogies between the human factors of our world of aviation and those of the surgical operating room (SOR). Further, performance measures developed for the evaluation of flight crew have been adapted for use in the SOR environment (Helmreich and Schaefer, in press). Indeed, significant cultural differences have been observed between various occupational categories of the medical profession, including surgeons, anaesthetists, and different branches of the nursing fraternity (Schaefer, in press). We have also heard mention at this conference of the importance of culture in the sphere of Air Traffic Control. At the 1992 Australian Aviation Psychology Symposium, a controller from New Zealand provided his audience with the secret to ensuring a *culture-free* control tower: " fill it with Australians..." (Hamilton, 1993).

Organizational Change in Aviation

Given this recent focus on the importance of culture, it seems odd that we as human factors professionals are either silent, or are all but ignored when our organizations embark upon a process of significant structural and/or culture change. The aerospace industry has more human factors practitioners per capita than any other technologically complex endeavour. We have a wide range of occupational groups working on the development of initiatives to improve all aspects of our operations. At this very conference we have experts from all major domains of our industry, whether their work involves the design of *software* or *hardware,* the structure of our work *environments,* or the selection, training, and maintenance of our valuable *liveware.* We have all been confronted with massive change - within our own organizations as well as within our industry - in recent years. Yet, how many of us can say that our human factors expertise has been adequately utilized in contributing to the planning, implementation and/or management of this change?

We know that employees subjected to significant organisational change can experience high levels of anxiety and stress as they attempt to adapt to new organizational structures, strategies, areas of responsibility and work roles. While in terms of a historical perspective aviation organizations have enjoyed the luxury of operating within an industry of relative stability, all components of our industry have been subjected to unprecedented levels of change during the past 15 years. Indeed, it seems that the single constant factor in our work environments today is the prospect and process of change.

Commercial aviation has been deregulated in many of our markets. Most often this has led to a proliferation of new carriers. The upheaval that follows for established carriers can include increased competition, a shrinking share of an expanding market, lower yield, lower profit margins, increased scrutiny of the bottom line, efficiency reviews, mergers, acquisitions, "down-sizing", the onset of labour disputes, increasing losses, bankruptcy (or protection from it), and in some cases liquidation, together with the massive job losses which usually accompany these events. Aviation has also endured the harsh global economic climate of recent years.

Additional burdens have included the financial pressures generated by the Gulf War, the generally soft air transport market, and the sacrifice of yield in the frantic race for market share which has preoccupied so many airline managements. These factors have precipitated the unprecedented and massive operating losses which have afflicted the global airline community. Indeed, several of the former doyens of aviation are no longer with us. Who could have foreseen that an aviation icon like Pan Am would disappear from our skies with such indecent haste? The pressure created by these events has prompted the emergence of strategic alliances and development of so-called global mega-carriers. However, the "synergies" created by these alliances can themselves lead to significant change and large scale redundancies.

Little and her colleagues (Little, Gaffney, Rosen & Bender, 1990), and Girodo (1988) have detailed the harmful stress effects which have resulted from such turmoil within the aviation community. Unfortunately, as in many other industries, most aviation organisations have given little thought to the effects of such radical change on employees. For example, how will employees react to organisational change? Can we as an industry develop and promote healthy and positive responses to change? What can an organisation do to assist individual adaptation and therefore enhance prospects for the success of the new entity?

The Management of Change

According to Schein (1990), most change begins with the individual. Unfortunately, all too often we have seen that the responsibility for coping with change also stops with the individual. As observed by Callan (1993), very few organizations seem aware of the need to equip their staff with the skills, strategies and resources required to successfully adjust to, and to act as a driving agent for, change. The great irony of this is that if managed appropriately, the human element of an organization can have an extremely positive influence on the success of any programme of change.

Preferred models of organizational development promote the benefits of *incremental change*. This involves introducing change in small and predictable steps, which allow employees the time and opportunity to adapt (Callan, 1993; Dunphy, 1981). Incremental change involves fewer disruptions and less stress for employees than *radical change*, and is thus likely to encounter less resistance from the workforce. As a result, changes introduced are likely to have less negative impact on worker morale, behaviour and performance.

Unfortunately, organizations which decide on making large scale changes to their structure or basic operating philosophies have often been pressured into change by the need to remain competitive or by the arrival of new management. They are thus often impatient to implement change in order to quickly harvest the projected benefits. In such cases the best practice of change implementation is often discarded in favour of expediency. In particular, the recessionary trends of recent years have led employers to disregard the human factors of change implementation, with the justification that times are tough for everyone and that we must all share the burden. In many cases radical change has been employed in the hope of achieving rapid results. This again ignores the positive results that can be achieved by the consideration of how best to assist individuals to adapt to, and to become agents for, the new systems and practices we seek to implement.

Radical change involves significant alteration to the daily functions, responsibilities, and reporting lines of a majority of employees. The threat of job loss or at least relocation is also common. These changes can be highly stressful for employees, and can produce a myriad of negative effects in the workplace. Unfortunately, organizational mergers usually involve the introduction of radical rather than incremental change.

Studies of the effects of mergers (see Kemp, 1987; Fisher, 1994) show that they challenge both the personal and professional identity of employees. Mergers are commonly characterised by high levels of misinformation, and produce elevated levels of anxiety amongst staff. Some individuals can be seen to develop an almost obsessive concern over their continued survival in the organization. Employees typically feel threatened, anxious, confused about their future, and often feel a loss of control in relation to sweeping changes to company procedures, values and reporting structures. They typically also experience uncertainty about which kinds of behaviours are appropriate or valued by the new organization, and about how their own performance will be evaluated and valued in the future.

The cumulative stress and uncertainty produced by a merger is likely to impact negatively on the motivation, productivity and efficiency of employees. While it is difficult to measure the effects of these factors at an organizational level, it is certain that they do not contribute positively to the success of the change process or to the bottom-line performance of the organization. For airlines, customer-service driven and with thousands of front-line staff, the consequences of a mishandled merger can be disastrous.

Strategies for Adapting to Change

Individual strategies for coping with significant change tend to be either problem-focused or emotion-focused. Problem-focused coping strategies are useful in that they involve the individual in taking positive action to modify or eliminate the source of stress by dealing with the situation. However, radical organizational change can overwhelm individuals and lead to feelings of loss of control and powerlessness. This often provokes the onset of emotion-focused coping, which in the extreme can lead to emotional lability, disputes with management and co-workers, domestic disharmony, substance abuse, loss of motivation and attention to task, and resultant performance decrements.

Primary internal coping resources are related to personality traits, and in particular an individual's self-esteem and "locus of control" (Rotter, 1975). External resources and social supports are also integral to an individual's capacity to cope and can include the worker's spouse, family, friends, co-workers and managers. Individuals most vulnerable to the stress effects associated with failure to cope with change can therefore include those with poor self-esteem and high external locus of control (powerlessness), and those without significant external resources or social support networks.

Organizational Strategies. A key strategy for the management of any organizational change is effective communication. This involves the provision of accurate and timely information to all staff members in relation to the nature and pace of the changes to be implemented. Studies of organizational mergers stress the value of open communication with all employees of the merged entity. Effective communication can be achieved through the introduction of regular briefings from management, supplemented by staff newsletters, and staff briefing videos, which can provide regular updates on vision and structure from senior management.

Open and honest communication can itself act as a valuable internal marketing tool. Honourable rhetoric from management can increase staff commitment to organizational change and influence perceptions of subsequent events. On the other hand, many unsuccessful acquisitions have been characterized by buyers making promises of even-handedness during merger negotiations, but in practice exhibiting a marked preference for their own personnel and systems when it came to decision time (Kemp, 1987).

Disregard for the human factor in mergers and acquisitions can be the fast track to failure of the merger to deliver the benefits sought. Research by management consultants McKinsey & Company over a 10-year period showed that only 23 % of US mergers recovered the costs incurred in putting the deal together (Fisher, 1994). Much of the blame for these failures can be explained by companies not taking the time and effort to manage the personal and personnel side of the merger. To guard against this, management must consider the impact that any change under consideration will have on the morale and performance of affected staff.

Giving clear definition and "people shape" to changes in reporting lines, individual responsibilities, career paths, and networks of interdepartmental relationships are important elements of success in organizational change. Workers need clear sets of rules, easily identifiable authority figures, and strong leadership in order to reduce the uncertainty created by change.

The use of charismatic or transformational leadership can also assist staff to cope with organizational change. By effectively communicating their vision for the organization, transformational leaders can empower staff to take positive action and to attempt to control their own circumstances, frequently also enlisting them as agents for the promotion of change. The problem faced by this strategy is that not all managers have the capacity or interpersonal skills to lead change in this manner.

Retention or improvement of worker incentives and benefits is a clear winner as a strategy for helping staff adapt to change. Kemp (1987) reports that two thirds of successful mergers involved improvements to performance incentives, pension entitlements, career prospects, or the introduction of share options. Conversely, in a similar percentage of unsuccessful acquisitions, there was a perceived loss in one or more of these areas.

Conclusion

While there are many important factors to be considered when responding to a desire or need for change, most of these factors involve and impact on the human variable - the very people who will determine whether the the new systems, practices, and the new organization work effectively. It is critical that staff are motivated to accept and adapt to change. Without their cooperation we may be just rearranging the deckchairs... The human factor in organizational change can be neglected - at management's peril.

References

Beaumont, G. (in press). Organizational attachment through resource management. In *Proceedings of the 21st Conference of the European Association for Aviation Psychology.* Trinity College, Dublin, 28-31 March, 1994. Aldershot, UK: Avebury Aviation.

Callan, V.J. (1993). Individual and organizational strategies for coping with organizational change. *Work & Stress, 7,* 63-75.

Davies, J.M., & Eagle, C.J. (1993). Aviation safety programme development: A new perspective from an analogous system. In B.J. Hayward and A.R. Lowe (Eds.), *Proceedings of the 1992 Australian Aviation Psychology Symposium.* Melbourne: AAvPA.

Dunphy, D.C. (1981). *Organizational change by choice.* Sydney: McGraw-Hill.

Fisher, A.B. (1994, Jan 24). How to make a merger work. *Fortune,* 58-61.

Girodo, M. (1988). The psychological health and stress of pilots in a labour dispute. *Aviation, Space, and Environmental Medicine, 59,* 505-510.

Hamilton, D. (1993). Human factors initiatives in New Zealand air traffic services. In B.J. Hayward and A.R. Lowe (Eds.), *Proceedings of the 1992 Australian Aviation Psychology Symposium.* Melbourne: AAvPA.

Hayward, B.J. (in press). Extending crew resource management: An overview. In *Proceedings of the 21st Conference of the European Association for Aviation Psychology.* Trinity College, Dublin, 28-31 March, 1994. Aldershot, UK: Avebury Aviation.

Helmreich, R.L., and Schaefer, H.-G. (in press). Team performance in the operating room. In M.S. Bogner (Ed.), *Human error in medicine.* Hillsdale, NJ: Lawrence Erlbaum Associates.

Hofstede, G. (1980). *Culture's consequences: International differences in work-related values.* Beverly Hills, CA: Sage.

Hofstede, G. (1991). *Cultures and organizations: Software of the mind.* Maidenhead, UK: McGraw-Hill.

Johnston, A.N. (1993). CRM: Cross-cultural perspectives. In E.W. Wiener, B.G. Kanki, and R.L. Helmreich (Eds.), *Cockpit Resource Management.* San Diego: Academic.

Kemp, C. (1987). Managing the human factor can help an acquisition succeed. *Human Resource Management Australia,* 54-64.

Little, L.F., Gaffney, I.C., Rosen, K.H., & Bender, M.M. (1990). Corporate instability is related to airline pilots' stress symptoms. *Aviation, Space, and Environmental Medicine, 61,* 977-982.

Maurino, D. (in press). The future of human factors and psychology in aviation from the ICAO perspective. In *Proceedings of the 21st Conference of the European Association for Aviation Psychology.* Trinity College, Dublin, 28-31 March, 1994. Aldershot, UK: Avebury Aviation.

Merritt, A. (1993). *The influence of national and organizational culture on human performance.* Paper presented at the Australian Aviation Psychology Association Industry Human Factors Seminar, Sydney, October, 1993.

Rotter, J.B. (1975). Some problems and misconceptions related to the construct of internal versus external control of reinforcement. *Journal of Consulting and Clinical Psychology, 43,* 56-67.

Schaefer, H.-G. (in press). Transfer of the CRM concept into medicine. In *Proceedings of the 21st Conference of the European Association for Aviation Psychology.* Trinity College, Dublin, 28-31 March, 1994. Aldershot, UK: Avebury Aviation.

Schein, E.H. (1990). Organizational culture. *American Psychologist, 45,* 109-119.

10 Achieving organisational attachment through resource management

Capt. Graham Beaumont, Qantas Airways Ltd

The realisation that Crew Resource Management can deliver much more than just the operational benefits on which the industry has focused to date is with us. By extending the concepts beyond the flight deck and indeed beyond the aircraft there is an opportunity for every carrier to be not only more profitable but also a more attractive work place. In order to reach this position of understanding, attachment as a phenomenon needs to be explored before looking at the resource management techniques which may be used to achieve it.

The advertising adage "The Person Who Owns The Store Runs the Store' has been and continues to be used to attract customers in a great variety of merchandising endeavours. The reasons for the success of this line of appeal are well founded in the psychological theory of motivation. Perhaps without realising it, patrons of business using this slogan are giving support to the theory of attachment (Steers and Porter, 1979) for in essence there can be no greater attachment than complete ownership.

The process of attachment

As individuals, the development of attachment to any endeavour in life changes forever the attitudes and subsequent behaviours which we apply to that endeavour. The motivators for such change can be many and varied ranging from self preservation through self esteem to financial rewards. Regardless of the driver, the end result is the same, a more committed, harder working individual who is less likely to be absent from the workplace.

To the self employed, the necessity for maintaining such an attitude becomes blatantly obvious when the competition exhibits a stronger commitment and market share declines. To the employee of a large company, the need for the maintenance of this sense of ownership is less tangible but has very definite benefits in the generation of high self-esteem. To achieve this state of mind it is necessary to focus on the big picture, the overall goals of the company. This can be quite a task if the direct involvement of the employee as far as the final outcome is concerned is obscured by the complexity of process and a management which fails to communicate definition to individual tasks. In other words, the employees must be able to identify with the goals of the company and be able to recognise the effect of their efforts on the outcome.

Fostering and nurturing this sense of attachment has benefits for both the employer and the employee. This is a two-way street where compromise on both sides will be necessary to generate the most productive and satisfying environment for all involved. This realisation of mutual dependency is the highest hurdle of all to overcome and may never be surmounted if an atmosphere of trust and respect does not underwrite all interaction between employer and employee. To be most effective, efficient and competitive, the employer (through management) must show understanding and concern for the problems of the employee and the employee must respond with cooperation and enlightenment as to the realities of the global goals of the company.

The theory of attachment as proposed by Steers and Porter (1979) can be viewed as a two stage process. Put simply, there is the initial decision by the employee to join the company. The motives for making this decision can be diverse. Proximity to domicile, perceived opportunities for personal advancement, status, fringe benefits and identification with company goals can and mostly do play a part in this initial decision making process. This is a process controlled by the prospective employee, not by the organisation, a fact that is often given insufficient consideration by managements in their future dealings with employees, for already the process of attachment has begun and an effective management should quickly build on this foundation.

Usually, candidates decide whether they can meet the advertised criteria which seldom annunciate human factor attributes. One has to ask whether it is more appropriate to hire for skills and accept the attitude or hire for attitude and train the skills. The latter standpoint clearly provides the most potential for organisational attachment. The problem of course is definition and interpretation of attitudinal requirements.

At this first stage then, applicants are seeking to make sure that what is being offered will meet their needs and the prospective employer is matching the offered talents to the organisational needs. To ensure that this matching of needs is best achieved it is necessary to communicate correct and complete information about the position and talents on offer. Failure to faithfully complete this important facet will only detract from potential attachment. It has been shown (Wanous, 1975) that realistic job descriptions do not detract from recruitment success. Similarly falsifying experience or qualification records may lead to low self esteem due to inability to complete task requirements.

The second stage of attachment centres around commitment to the organisation or company. It has been proposed (Steers, 1977) that this commitment is dependent upon on the attributes and needs of the applicant, the job itself and the organisation within which the job exists. Strongest attachment and commitment will be achieved by satisfying requirments in all three areas. It is here that the principles of Resource Management can be effectively applied to enhance commitment and build that sense of ownership which is so necessary to employee job satisfaction and consistency of product delivery.

Achieving attachment

It may well be argued that the process of Crew Resource Management (CRM) training development has gone the full circle when considering what is on offer to effect airline crew commitment and attitudinal change on a global basis. Equally, it can be argued that the practical nature of CRM training represents the applied level of the theory of human interaction and this is an area that still requires considerable development to be of use throughout an organisation. That is the focus of what follows.

Satisfaction of the requirements of the person have been touted as necessary to effect attachment. Among these, ambition and the desire to get ahead rank fairly high. How better to cater for this need than to have a system which revolves around participation in the decision making process. A process of involvement, of being heard, where input is valued and the benefits of continuing education and the sharpness of youth can be seen to have an effect on the outcome. Taken one step further, this involvement is really in the management of the company since that process can often be reduced to a series of decision making scenarios.

True participative decision making brings with it a whole gambit of desirable management techniques and subsequent outcomes. Where these hallmarks are not evident you can be sure that some downgraded version of this process is in play. For example as a manager, if you are allowing real participation, the communications within the organisation will be very much two-way, top to bottom and bottom to top. This is necessary to ensure that the knowledge and skills of all those involved are appropriately applied to the situation. The natural flow on from this process is in practice a flatter management structure where the gradient reduction which true participation brings begins to shape the structure. In essence, this can be seen if the difference between three and two person cockpits is closely examined.

Nowhere is this style of management more evident than in the growing use of delegation and subsequent empowerment. As the personal attributes of participants develop or become known, the manager becomes more comfortable with the process of devolution. This action brings with it accountability and the realities of consequence, both of which are as nectar to the achievement oriented person. (Hard and fast seniority systems often deny organisations access to their best resources and certainly lower self esteem in those with talent). All the while the personal needs of participants are being met and commitment and attachment or ownership is growing.
The role that this pivotal CRM instrument can play in satisfying the person and generating high self-esteem is unquestionable.

By pursuing this tack with participation, position descriptions have been effectively changed. It may no longer be practical to define in detail boundaries of responsibility or exact structural positions for the blending which has been effected may defy such demarcation because of the unlimited involvement of all personnel. An effective two-way communication process ensures this involvement level. The added challenges of placement within the structure are tantalising, As an important additional benefit, the practical lack of structure enhances social interaction on the job and steadily generates a family like atmosphere. As far as ownership is concerned, persons who are part of such an organisation are just that, a real part of it.

Used appropriately by all links of the management chain, the process of upward assessment can be of great benefit in the development of managerial skills, particularly as it highlights any mismatch in perceptions of managerial performance. This process is not a performance appraisal system but rather a means of enhancing two-way communication, not only providing feedback for managers but also providing a vehicle for subordinates to effectively express their needs. To be of most benefit, the process must concentrate on behaviours not personalities, providing opportunities for change in a non threatening environment.

Group behaviour

Given an environment where all input is welcomed, it is difficult to imagine that any of the negative effects of group behaviour could survive. However, one would always need to be on the lookout for their presence. Since the dynamics are so vastly different to the traditional management structure, the negative group behaviours which surface will be different. Specifically, pressures of time and self censorship by participants may still come into play, particularly as this type of structure is being established. Nevertheless, the experience of work itself will provide participants with a positive perception of themselves and their importance to the organisational outcomes. In so doing, most expectations of the job will be met. Of itself, the meeting of expectations is a major contributor to commitment to participate on a long term basis. Absenteeism will be reduced.

One aspect of group behaviour which is normally present in a negative sense can actually appear in the positive sense within this type of organisation. Reference is made here to peer group pressure which, in an organisation fostering true participation, is more likely to demand positive group norms because of the high level of attachment. These group norms are likely to cover attitudes to management, output, each other, absenteeism and individual roles within the organisation. History and the good old days will be just that and the focus will be on the job at hand rather than hankering after some mythical workplace utopia.

Making it work

The adoption of this type of decision making process is not the whole story however, since such a process cannot work effectively without some refined communication skills, an ability by participants to adjust their orientation appropriately between the task and the people involved and an awareness of the amount of assertive behaviour which is required to effect the most desirable outcome. All of these skills come as part of accepted CRM training and consequently one could expect that persons having received such training and been given sufficient practice opportunities will be in a better position to participate effectively and thereby develop commitment and attachment to the organisation.

Within an organisation where participation in the decision making process is encouraged, there will be fewer barriers between groups and individuals since communication and interaction will have fostered mutual respect and understanding of each others roles. Empowerment to make decisions implies vertical trust within organisations but it also promotes lateral trust since responsibility and accountability will be spread more uniformly throughout the organisation and an interdependent atmosphere will prevail. In fact the organisation itself becomes part of the interdependency network rather than standing alone as a separate frame work.

Summary

In summarising the positive effects of properly implemented CRM training one could be forgiven for thinking that there is a chance to establish the perfect management system. Unfortunately, in reality such a perfect system does not exist. However, there can be no argument with the proposal that there is a better chance of establishing a better system using the practical tools of CRM. Certainly, the sense of ownership which employees possess and the resultant quality of product delivery can be positively influenced.

References

Fraken, R.E. (1988), *Human Motivation* (2nd Ed) Brooks/Cole Publishing Company Pacific Grove, California.
Gaines, H. (1993), "How Do You Rate?" *Sky* September 1993, 20-24
Steers, R. "Antecedents and Outcomes Of Organizational Commitment." *Administrative Science Quarterly*, 1977, 22, 46-56
Steers, R.M. , & Porter, L.W. Attachment to Organizations. In R.M. Steers & L.W. Porter (Eds.), *Motivation and Work Behaviour* (2nd Ed.), New York, McGraw-Hill, 1979
Wanous, J.P. "A Job Preview Makes Recruiting More Effective." *Harvard Business Review*, 1975, 53(5), 16; 166-168. (a)
Wanous, J.P. "Organzational Entry. From Naive Expectations to Realistic Beliefs." *Journal of Applied Psychology,* 1976, 61, 22-29
Wanous, J.P. "Organzational Entry. The Individual's viewpoint." In J.R. Hackman, E.E. Lawler III, & L.W. Porter (Eds.), *Perspectives On Behaviour In Organizations.* New York: McGraw-Hill, 1977
Weiner, E.L., Kanki, B.G. Helmreich, R.L. (Eds) 1993, *Cockpit Resource Management*, Academic Press Inc., New York.

11 Organisational dynamics and safety

Professor Ron Westrum, Eastern Michigan University

Introduction

Aviation organizations require information flow much as aircraft require aviation fuel. Their success and survival depend, however, on how this information is treated. In this paper I am going to examine three distinct patterns of coping with information used by aviation organizations: pathological, bureaucratic, and generative. The first pattern is typical of highly conflicted organizations, where information is treated as a political weapon. The second pattern is familiar from the textbook description of red tape, etc. Organizations that are bureaucratic are good at handling routine situations, but are bad at dealing with change and with emergencies. The Generative pattern is typical of 'high reliability' organizations and highly creative ones. In these organizations, personnel assume that they have a license both to think and to communicate.

Information is basic to the conduct of complex human enterprises. Without information flow, the parts of an organization would behave as so many 'monads,' each intent on its own purpose and strategy. If one believes in 'pre-established harmony,' this is wonderful. In real operations, it represents disaster. So communication must tie the various parts of the organization together. But how?

Let me ask you to think for a moment about organizations, and how they are designed. Many organizations are still represented by an organization chart that derives from the army or another nineteenth century bureaucracy. It indicates who reports to whom else. An organization chart of this kind is a bad representation of the complex relations of a real organization. Yet it persists, because the hierarchical organization it represents persists. This has certain consequences for communication. Information is expected to travel up through the ranks and down through the ranks, but in real life information must cross the structure laterally, too. Yet this is not shown by the chart. Unlike the relations specified on the chart, lateral communication is informal. A better chart would concentrate on communication, not just responsibility; it would show a network connected in complex ways, not merely a hierarchy.

What I am establishing is that many of the habits that come with the traditional organization may be wrong for the aviation organizations. Coping with complex technology, complex situations, and constant change requires a different style of organization. We need to rethink the organization, and we need to start with communications.

Three Basic Patterns

Just now I would like to introduce in more detail three basic patterns of information flow used by organizations, three styles if you like. They are pathological, bureaucratic, and generative (Westrum, 1993). The chart will help explain them.

Table One: Basic Communication Styles

PATHOLOGICAL	BUREAUCRATIC	GENERATIVE
Information is personal power	Information is routine	Information seen as key resource
Responsibility is shirked	Responsibility is compartmented	Responsiblity is shared
Messengers are shot	Listened to if they arrive	Messengers are trained
Bridging is discouraged	Bridging is tolerated	Bridging is rewarded
Failure is punished or covered up	Organization is just and fair	Failure leads to inquiry/learning
New ideas are actively crushed	New ideas present problems	New ideas are welcomed

Organizations have characteristic responses to evidence of problems or novel ideas. One can trace these responses through the following spectrum:

Table Two: Responses to Anomaly

```
           Encapsulation              Local Fix         Reflective Inquiry
----------*-------------*-------------*------------*-----------*---------------*---------
  Suppression        Public Relations           Global Fix
```

Pathological organizations typically choose to handle anomalies by using responses from the left hand side. Problems are often suppressed or encapsulated. The person who spots a problem is silenced or driven into a corner. This does not make the problem go away, just the message about it! The pathological style is rare, but dangerous where it operates. More likely in aviation is a bureaucratic style. These organizations tend to choose responses from the middle of the spectrum. They do not suppress problems, but they sometimes make light of them or fix only the presenting symptom. They are rigid. Only in the generative organizations are right-hand side responses common. There is a culture of conscious inquiry that tends to root out and solve problems that are not immediately apparent. In generative organizations, people have a 'license to think,' and they investigate widely, taking responsibility for diagnosis and also disseminating the remedies they find.

The Generative Flight Deck

The advent of 'Cockpit Resource Management' meant that flight organizations tried to change interaction from bureaucratic or even pathological patterns to generative ones. Awareness of a need for CRM training grew slowly and not without resistance (Sams, 1987). As both airlines and governments became aware of the need, procedures and philosophies grew in parallel. CRM meant a change from the passive or reactive cockpit to the pro-active one. Now, instead of problem conditions on the flight deck being suppressed, they would be investigated. Information would be shared, instead of being compartmented. More use would be made of the 'total brainpower' present on the flight deck. This included the effective distribution of consciousness over the problems the crew had to solve in an emergency.

Ironically, the need for CRM style patterns of communication paralleled the discovery by business organizations that they needed to encourage lateral communication if the environment was rapidly changing (Burns and Stalker, 1961). One might further have inferred that the more rapidly the environment changes, the greater the need for the conscious management of information to cope with it. Thus, in high- pressure 'operational' environments, training in the handling of information is most important. Going from the single-brain mental workload to the crew mental workload should have meant a shift from a dominance pattern to a 'co-ordinate leadership' pattern; but usually the situation changes before adequate tools to cope with it are developed.

The Generative Organization

Many aviation organizations are still set up along principles developed for organizations in an earlier era, with simpler technologies. Bureaucratic organizations impose 'system,' and they are good at coping with slowly developing problems, but when these organizations are put under stress, their coping strategies often fail. Their most common response to stress, for instance, is typically to impose additional rules and add more structure. Organizational change and high technology make these organizations a dangerous place to work. Generative organizations, by contrast, typically develop through strenuous organizational learning, including much creative trial-and-error. Their members recognize the need for 'distributed consciousness,' and they pursue a 'culture of conscious inquiry' (Westrum 1993). Organizational design is focussed on developing a manageable crew mental workload. For this reason, generative organizations often simplify and streamline their procedures. In contrast to bureaucracies, whose concern is documentation and accountability, these organizations specialize in effective and safe operation through oral communications.

For reasons not entirely clear, social scientists did not pay much attention to such organizations until the 1980's. When the University of California group began studying such organizations, it became clear that 'high reliability' required special organization patterns, habits of thought, and practices (Roberts, 1993). Many of these bear strong resemblance to CRM on a larger scale. The key to the abilities of such organizations is the skillful use of the talents of the team. Generative organizations empower their members, they encourage them to take responsibility, and they encourage lateral communication. They carefully train team members and they monitor carefully both the skill level and the current situational functioning of team members (Rochlin, 1987). Because the organization has carefully cultivated such process skills, it is able to function swiftly and safely, at a very high trust level.

Southwest Airlines in the United States is attempting to be a generative organization (Bovier, 1993). At Southwest CRM is not limited to the flight deck. Instead, virtually all segments of the organization receive training in communication and crew workload management. It is also interesting to note the earlier study by Patterson (1955) in which he shifted the functioning of an air facility from a pathological style to generative one through a skillful intervention. But the key is to recognize that organizational process is more important than organizational structure. While good structures help, they can never be a substitute for the necessary process skills. Self-organization is essential, since no structural arrangement or rulebook can ever anticipate every situation likely to arise.

A generative organization is a thinking organization, self-aware, constantly alert, and constantly re-working its own processes. The 'maestros' in a generative organization set high standards, and especially concentrate on promoting information flow. They encourage group members to inquire, but also to present their information to others. They are good at listening to ideas and problems, and encourage internal 'champions' to pursue improvements. The 'will to think' about improvements is built by visible successes in getting action from management. Lateral communication in such organizations is usually good, since everyone has a license to think and to respond to problems.

Some Problems

Generative organizations sound good, but they are not without problems. One of the observations of Burns and Stalker (1961) about 'organic management (the industrial equivalent of CRM) is relevant here. If the sphere of responsibility is widened, so are the concern and anxiety that go with such responsibility. Many people like to 'know their duty and do it.' Increasing their sphere of attention may bring additional worries with it. The organization has to know how to deal with such worries, and needs to pay attention to the desired scope of attention of those it hires.

And generative organization must be more than a slogan. These process skills require practice, and above all support from the top. Trust is very fragile. The moment trust is broken, bureaucracy will assert itself with new force. Only bureaucracy can provide protection for the person who expects failure. Thus, it is very important that new practices get the support of the top of the organization, in funds, training, and the behavior of top management itself. A study by Boeing of airline organizations, still continuing, suggested that the safety behavior of the organization is shaped by the organization's top management. Let me briefly quote from this report:

'[Management has] acute awareness of the factors that result in accidents, and management reviews accidents and incidents in their own airline and in other airlines and alters their policies to best guard against recurrence. There is a method for getting information to the flight crews expeditiously and a policy that encourages confidential feedback from pilots to management. This management attitude, while somewhat difficult to describe, is a dynamic force that sets the stage for standardization and discipline in the cockpit brought about and reinforced by a training program oriented to safety issues.' (Lautman and Gallimore, 1987, p. 2)

This sounds like the recipe for a 'reflective practitioner' (Schon 1983). Indeed it is. Management must be willing constantly to monitor and re-shape the operational environment, to display a 'hands-on' attitude, and to act not only when things go wrong, but proactively. This means that management must think about its own mental workload. It must make sure that it does not lose 'situational awareness' about what is really happening.

Conclusion

All organizations at some time are pathological, bureaucratic, and generative. Bureaucratic organizations are easy to design and manage, they just don't perform well in aviation. Pathological organizations come about because of strong personalities, who distort structures and rules for their own purposes. Generative organizations are difficult. They must resist the desire to rely on structure alone. Their leaders have to stay alert and flexible. It takes energy to establish such and organization and it takes energy to keep it functioning safely. Generative organizations have to develop; otherwise they become bureaucratic. To paraphrase a statement about democracy, 'the price of generativity is constant vigilance.'

References

Bovier, C. (1993) 'Teamwork: The Heart of an Airline,' *Training*, June, pp. 53-58.
Burns, T. and Stalker, G. M. (1961), *The Management of Innovation*, Tavistock, London.
Lautman, L.G. and Gallimore, P.L. (1987), 'Control of the Crew-Caused Accident,' *FSF Flight Safety Digest*, June, 1-8.
Patterson, T. T. (1955), *Morale in War and Work*, Max Parrish, London.
Roberts, K. (ed.,1993), *New Challenges to Understanding Organizations,* Macmillan, New York.
Rochlin, G., LaPorte, T., and Roberts, K. (1987), 'The Self-Designing High-Reliability Organization: Aircraft Flight Operations at Sea,' *Naval War College Review*, Autumn, 76-91.
Sams, T.L. (1987), *Cockpit Resource Management: Concepts and Training Strategies*, Ph.D dissertation, East Texas State University.
Schon, D. (1983), *The Reflective Practitioner: How Professionals Think in Action*. Basic Books, New York.
Westrum, R. (1993), 'Cultures with Requisite Imagination,' in Wise, J., Hopkin, D.V., Stager, P., *Verification and Validation of Complex Systems: Human Factors Issues*, Springer-Verlag, Berlin.

12 Organisational culture, job satisfaction and work stress: the case of Irish women pilots

Eunice McCarthy and Angela McGinn
Social and Organisational Psychology Research Centre, University College Dublin, Ireland

Introduction

The past twenty years have witnessed a substantial increase in the participation of women in the workforce: during this period women's work participation rates in Ireland have risen from 27.5% (1971) to 33.2% (1992) (see McCarthy, 1994). Coupled with a quantitative change in the workforce participation of women, has been a qualitative change. Women have moved up the occupational hierarchy, assuming jobs with higher status and greater responsibility. In addition, increasing numbers of women are entering non-traditional jobs, increasing the scope of occupations in which women are occupied.

While the participation of women in management is relatively low in Ireland as elsewhere (see Burke, 1993) nevertheless, change has occurred. McCarthy, (1988) in a longitudinal study encompassing forty eight large scale Irish companies demonstrated an increase from 9% to 11% in women's participation in middle management during the period 1972-1984.

This research has suggested that women's access to higher level management and technological positions has been hampered by a constellation of factors. Core barriers to women in management and in senior, high responsibility jobs, suggests four sets of factors as crucial. These include:

- the overall gender culture of the organisation;
- the attribution of limited personality characteristics to women workers by management, i.e., lack of leadership skills, lack of ambition and assertiveness etc.;

- limited access to training and development particularly to high technology - i.e. computer skills, training both internal and external to the work organisation;
- stress arising from work-home demands and conflict. (see McCarthy, 1994).

High Technology and Women Workers

Recent research in the USA, has highlighted a gender gap in informatics education (Martin, 1992). This problem is defined as a significant decline in young women studying informatics and subsequently pursuing careers in the informatics profession. The hypotheses is made that part of this decline can be attributed to the 'male-oriented paradigm pervasive throughout the study and practice of informatics'. For example, Roberts (1989), found the unique aspect of informatics as a discipline to be the encouragement of highly focused, obsessive behaviour as a road to success. He argues that males have been supported by society to behave in this manner more so than women, who are expected to be more 'balanced'. This view echoes Sherry Turkee's (1994) comments in her book *The Second Self*, where she examined the social and psychological aspect of the computer revolution and suggests that the 'male paradigm for computing is decidedly unappealing to women who are nurtured to value interpersonal relations'. Huff, Flemming and Cooper (1992), describe a research programme that investigated the social psychology of human-computer interaction. They confirmed that males and females approach the task of computing in recognisably different ways and that the design of the software itself carries with it a gender-loaded paradigm that can produce differential stress to users depending upon gender.

In a recent issue of 'Women in Technology and Science' (WITS) it was observed that 'although third level institutions have become increasingly aware of the need to attract more women into science and technology, little attention is being paid to the need to maintain women in the technological workforce' in Ireland (WITS, 1994, p. 1). It is further held that many scientific and technical occupations are not 'women-friendly' e.g. supervisors' assumptions about women's ability to do 'a man's job'; exclusion from informal communication networks - all contribute to a significant proportion of women leaving the science and technology workforce. It is assumed here that societal culture and organisational structure share common beliefs and values, relating to women and work in high technology areas.

Organisational Culture, Stress at Work and Job Satisfaction

For the purposes of this article organisational culture can be viewed as the philosophy that guides an organisation's policy towards members and constituents - it refers to 'the way things are done around here' (see Schein, 1990). As such it includes the dominant values espoused by an organisation and the basic assumptions and beliefs that are shared by members of an organisation and that have grown out of its historical evolution. Each organisation has its own pattern of beliefs, practices, values and myths that have evolved over time. Further, as pointed out by Schein (1990), any definable group with a shared history can have a culture and within an organisation there can therefore be many sub-cultures, for example, women workers. Culture also implies the existence of salient dimensions or characteristics that are closely related and interdependent. Organisational culture also embodies key values and beliefs which permeate the societal context in which organisations are embedded. This research taps into organisational culture as experienced by women pilots. The focus adopted endeavoured to isolate dimensions of culture that were gender bound, and the consequences of such enculturation for women occupying the high level technological job of 'airline pilot'.

The organisational culture scale developed for this research consisted of core dimensions, which tapped women pilots' perceived experience of women workers in their organisation, along the dimensions of organisational rewards attained by women workers; the support and consideration received by women; women's participation in decision-making; expectations and change regarding women workers and standards for women.

Research on women, work and stress in high technology jobs in the nursing field (McCarthy and Tiernan, 1987), suggested that stress was associated with lack of training and with interpersonal dynamics rather than with intrinsic job performance where the given skilled training and development was appropriate. For the purpose of the study stress is viewed as a complex interrelationship among a number of variables, rather than a unitary concept (Cox, 1978; Lazarus and Folkman, 1984). The key stressors identified as salient to the job of female airline pilot included:

- task demands;
- relationships;
- gender and sex-role discrimination;
- home-work interface.

Research on women and work has suggested that high job demands, combined with increasing home demands would induce considerable role conflict for women in senior roles (Baruch, Biener and Barnett, 1987). Further Irish research (McGinn and McCarthy, 1989), highlighted the significance of sex-role stereotypes and a gendered culture for the stress experience of women managers. Building on this earlier work, the present research, was designed to explore what stressors impacted most on women pilots. Further, an analysis of the level of job satisfaction of women pilots was obtained. Previous research has suggested that a perceived comparative profile of women compared with men on both intrinsic and extrinsic job factors was a sensitive index of women managers' satisfaction with their work (McCarthy, 1994). A 'working conditions and opportunities for women compared with men scale' was included to tap a comparative male-female profile. As pointed out by Kanter (1994), workplaces and organisations of the future, powered by high level technology, would need to focus more sharply on designing worker friendly systems in which members can obtain satisfaction as well as enjoyment from their work.

Figure 1 below outlines a framework for the women reported on here.

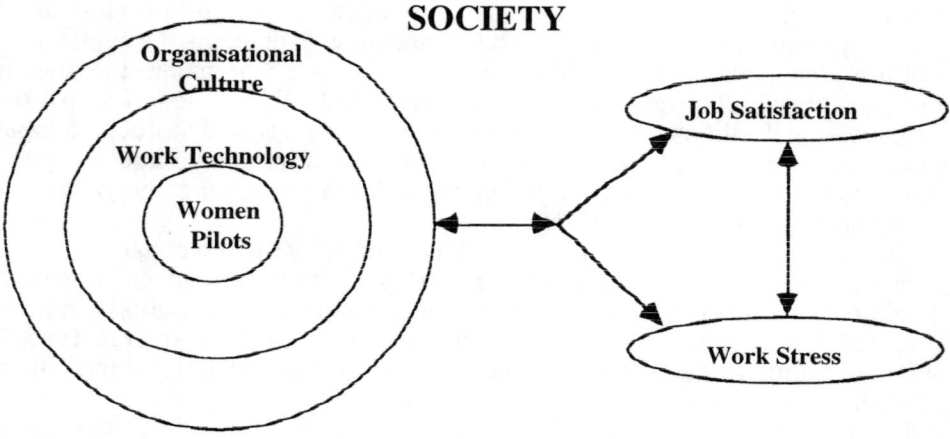

FIGURE 1: A model of the relationship between organisational culture for women, job satisfaction and job stress - women pilots.

In this exploratory study it is proposed that women pilots' experience of job satisfaction, would demonstrate both high intrinsic and extrinsic satisfaction. It is further hypothesised that job stress would be concentrated more on the home-work interface than on the job/tasks demands per se. Further, women pilots perceptions of the organisational culture experienced by women was expected to be relatively positive.

Methodology

This study constituted part of a larger ongoing Irish study on women in management. A sample of women pilots with a national Irish culture were invited to participate in this study which was concerned with tapping the relationship between organisational culture, job satisfaction and job stress. Seven women pilots took part in this study, all were single, four were under 25, three were 25 to 34.

Three measures (adapted from previous research (McCarthy, 1994)) and one measure adapted from Cooper and Davidson (1983) were included are as follows:

- *Organisational Culture for Women Scale (OCFWS) (McCarthy, 1987)*

    Consisted of twenty-three items, designed to tap core organisational culture dimensions e.g. rewards; consideration and support; standards; participation in decision-making and change regarding the potential of women. These items were randomised and presented on a five point ranked scale ranging from positive (+5) to negative (+1).

- *Job Satisfaction Scale (McCarthy, 1987)*

    Consisted of a fourteen item scale, with items reflecting both extrinsic and intrinsic job factors. Each item was presented as a ranked scale ranging from positive (+5) to negative (+1).

- *Working Conditions and Opportunities for Women Compared with that of Men Scale (McCarthy, 1994).*

    This scale included 17 items which reflected both intrinsic and extrinsic job factors, and which compared men and women on a three point scale ranging from 'Better', 'No Difference' to 'Worse' (range +3 to +1).

- *Job Stress Scale (adapted from Cooper and Davidson, 1983)*

    Included a forty-two item scale, designed around four core dimensions: Task; Relationships; Discrimination Related; Home-Work Interface. These dimensions were also suggested by previous research McCarthy and Tiernan (1987), McGinn and McCarthy (1989). Scale item responses ranged from no stress (+1) to considerable stress (+4).

Background data was obtained relating to age, work experience, work training etc. The training and development manager of the airline facilitated the administration of the questionnaire.

Results

Analysis of the Organisational Culture for Women Scale (OCFWS) demonstrated an overall positive response. In the view of women pilots their organisation demonstrated:

- confidence and trust in women (100% agree);
- is progressive in its policies and attitudes towards women (100% agree);
- is a woman friendly place (100% agree);
- action taken to promote women's participation in my organisation (71% agree);
- Women's voice is not heard (72% disagree).

This positive profile clearly indicated that the airline company is perceived as being supportive of women at a macro level. As perceived by women pilots their organisation
- sets high standards for women managers;
- encourages women to seek further training and development;
- allows women to be autonomous.

On the more negative side, participation in decision-making is not perceived as being actively promoted.

It is of interest that these women pilots are on the whole undecided in their perception of the extent to which management 'see women as wanting to learn' to the same extent as they do men. Further, there is agreement that managers may exclude women from informal discussions about work. The traditional perspective, that women have skills and potential that the organisation is 'unaware' of suggests that the organisation in some aspects of work development are tied to some core gender limiting beliefs.

These patterns of response suggest that questions that refer to women's situation only, generate relatively positive responses, while gender comparative questions which compare women's opportunities with their male counterparts, yields a more negative response. Thus, it appears that comparative statements tap into sensitive nodes more so than the macro statements that refer solely to women's position. These findings, support earlier work (see McCarthy, 1994) and provide an additional perspective on those aspects of gendered culture that needs a re-structuring and a remodelling.

Job Satisfaction

The overall mean score of the 14 item job satisfaction scale was positive (4.11) with the women pilots reporting that they were satisfied with their work. The only areas that had a mean score lower than 4 were relationships oriented (with colleagues and superior) and conditions oriented (pay and hours). The job satisfaction variables which yield most satisfaction for women pilots are as follows:

- The chances I get to learn new things (100% satisfied);
- The opportunity for using my own ideas and actions (86% satisfied);
- Opportunity for promotion (86% satisfied);
- Feeling at doing something well (71% satisfied).

Perceptions of working conditions and opportunities - women compared with men.

The results of the 'working conditions and opportunities for women compared with those of men scale' indicate that no areas emerged where women were treated more favourably than men. The dominant profile in which women pilots perceive no difference between the extrinsic job rewards received by women compared with men in their organisation, is as follows:

- Financial award (no difference 100%);
- Working conditions pensions, holidays (no difference 100%);
- Flexible work arrangements (no difference 100%);
- Working conditions hours (no difference 100%);
- Comprehensive work experience (no difference 86%);
- Opportunity for training within/outside the organisation (no difference 86%);
- Job security (no difference 86%);
- Availability of a mentor (no difference 86%);
- Mobility in the job (no difference 71%).

A number of items however highlighted differences in the treatment of men and women. Some 57% of women reported that in their organisation women's opportunities for advancement/promotion and interesting work were worse than that of men. They also indicated that women's involvement in the decision making process was less than that experienced by men (57%). These findings resonated with salient aspects of the organisational culture scale as delineated above.

Job Stress

The 42 item stress scale can be subdivided into four dimensions:

- Task (17 items)
- Relationships (6 items)
- Gender Discrimination (12 items)
- Home Work (7 items)

Women pilots clearly indicated that job factors such as work overload, level of control, degree of power and influence and conflicting job demands were not a source of stress for the majority. Slight/moderate stress was related to issues such as 'making presentations' and time pressures and deadlines. In all the sample presented as exhibiting competent coping with potential job stressors that they may encounter. Their ability to cope effectively, can be understood in terms of the challenge training and development they experience, as well as perhaps matching what Kobasa (1986), describes as the hardy personality, that is, one who has a great sense of control, commitment and challenge in their work setting. The presenting profile of these women pilots, suggests a level of resilience and competence that acts as an important internal resource.

Relations with same sex and opposite co-workers are relatively stress free. The social support received from colleagues is viewed positively by women pilots. Areas where social support can be enhanced includes greater support from superiors and less isolation.

Analysis of the gender and discrimination dimensions, indicated that these concerns are satisfied with the training experience they obtain compared with men. Further, the organisational policies and guidelines under which they work, are attuned to their values and beliefs as women.

Areas where 'slight' stress is experienced refers to traditional attitudes e.g.

- 'being excluded from the old boys network at work';
- 'experiencing prejudicial attitudes from members of the male sex at work';
- 'having to perform better at my job than male colleagues'.

The home-work interface dimension, taped more potential sources of stress than did the other three dimensions. Demands of work on private/social life is a source of slight/moderate stress for some, while the dilemma concerning when to start a family is problematic as well. The dominant pattern emerging from women pilots' response to the job stress scale clearly suggest that work related job demands are competently coped with by women pilots.

It is the arena of home-work interface that commands the greatest concern for these women. Given the complex and demanding nature of the work of women pilots, balancing the tightrope of personal, home and work needs will not be easily resolved. As observed by Auster (1993), given the multiplicative nature of tightropes, women in demanding jobs, will have to use multi-contextual approaches in many spheres to be constantly self-conscious and also to monitor others' reactions and interpretations.

Conclusions and Discussion

An exploratory study with a small sample of women pilots working with a national airline, yielded a profile of these women's perceptions of the organisation culture as experienced by women, gender comparison and working conditions and opportunities, job satisfaction and job stress of women pilots.

The overall emergent profile, delineates women pilots as experiencing high levels of job satisfaction and relatively low levels of job stress. Their perceptions of salient gender and organisation culture dimensions, suggests that they perceive their organisation as a supportive, rewarding context for women, with a proactive policy of equal opportunity. Subtle gender differences surfaced when respondents were asked to contrast women's work experience with that of men. A sense of limited awareness regarding women's potential emerged, added to a view that the informal network can exclude women. Further, these women pilots presented as coping constructively with potential job stressors. The area which presents as challenging the adaptive and coping efforts of these women is in the balancing of family/home and work demands.

The glass ceiling metaphor has been used to describe the subtle barriers to advancement experienced by women. Auster (1993), argues that what is hindering women's career advancement is not a ceiling, but gender bias. Gender bias refers to stereotyping and preconceptions that result in the unequal treatment of women.

Gender bias can be classified as both overt and covert, organisational and interpersonal. In the case of the women pilots included in this study, it appears that they have not only broken a glass ceiling, but more important they have penetrated the hard-core, high technology ceiling, which so frequently inhibits women's advancement and development in the highly skilled cognitively demanding information technology work settings of today. The supportive organisational culture identified by the women pilots, provides a trusting context which enables these women to experience a work setting which embodies ongoing learning and valuing of both sexes.

These findings suggest that a more extensive study of women pilots be conducted across a number of airlines, to isolate both barriers to change and those positive initiatives that are generating new gender equality learning cultures matching structures and processes for women in high skill, high technology work domains. New insights derived from proactive equality oriented work cultures, could generate new cybernetic understandings of the process of change and gender equality required for the organisations of tomorrow.

References

Auster, E. R. (1993). Demystifying the Glass Ceiling. Organisational and Interpersonal Dynamics of Gender Bias. *Business and the Contemporary World,* Vol. V, No. 3 Summer p. 47-68.

Baruch, G. K., Biener, L. and Barnett, R. C. (1987). Women and Gender in Research on Work and Family Stress. *American Psychologist,* Feb. p. 130-136.

Burke, R. J. (1993). Women in Corporate Management: Introduction. *Business and the Contemporary World.* Vol. V. No. 3, p. 3-9.

Cooper, G., Davidson, M. (1983). *Stress and the Women Manager.* oxford: Martin Robertson.

Cox, T. (1978). *Stress* London, Macmillan.

Huff, C. W., Flemming, J. H. and Cooper, J. 91992). 'Gender Differences in Human Computer Interaction'. In Martin, C. D. and Marchie-Bayman, E. (Eds). *In Search of Gender Free Paradigms for Computer Science Education.* The NECC Monograph Series, International Society for Technology in Education (ISTE) 1787 Agate Street, Eugene, OR 97405 USA.

Kanter, R. (1994). 'New Challenges in Strategic Organisational Change'. Paper read at National Conference 1994. Irish Institute of Training and Development, Dublin.

Lazarus, R. and Folkmar, S. (1984). *Stress, Appraisal and Coping* New York: Springer.

Martin, C. D. (1992). 'Addressing the Gender Gap in Informatics Education'. In R. M. Aiken (Ed.) *IFIP Transactions. Education and Society.* Vol II, p. 239-245.

McCarthy, E. (1987). 'Organisational Culture For Women Scale'; 'Working Conditions and Opportunities for Women Compared with Men Scale'; Job Satsifaction Scale'. Social and Organisational Psychology Research Centre, University College Dublin.

McCarthy, E. (1994). 'Changing Contexts and Women and Work in Ireland' Dublin (In Press)

McCarthy, E. and Tiernan, J. (1987). *The Impact of New Technology on workers and patients in the Health Services in Ireland.* European Foundation for the Improvement of Living and Working Conditions. Brussels.

McGinn, A. and McCarthy, E. (1989). *Job Stress and Women Managers.* Dublin. Social and Organisational Psychology Research Centre, University College Dublin.

Roberts, E. (1989). 'Women and Computer Science'. *Tough Questions Student Pugwash Magazine.* Fall Issue, 4-5.

Schein, E. H. (1990). 'Organisational Culture' *American Psychologist* Vol. 1. ps 109-119.

Turkee, S. (1984). *The Second Self: Computers and the human spirit.* New York: Simon & Schuster.

Wits (1994). *Women in Science and Technology.* Dublin.

13 Psychology and Air Traffic Control: who cares?

Bert Ruitenberg, IFATCA Executive Vice-President Professional

Introduction

Although The International Federation of Air Traffic Controllers' Associations (IFATCA) is frequently found in the list of organisations that provide speakers to technical aviation-conferences, our presence at this scientific gathering is a new experience that we feel warrants a style of presentation that is different from our usual approach.

In an attempt to adapt the format to that of more scientific presentations, this paper will build on three propositions that correspond with the themes of this Conference.

For the theme "linking theory to practice", the model developed by Professor J. Reason for the analysis of the breakdown of complex systems will be applied to the introduction of TCAS (Traffic alert and Collision Avoidance System).

For the other theme, "developing and extending the core areas of aviation psychology", we will have a closer look at the Selection and Training of Air Traffic Controllers (ATCOs). But first this:

Proposition #1

"There are many people in this audience who would appreciate a quick introduction to IFATCA."

IFATCA is the independent non-profit, non-political, non-industrial, Professional Association representing over 13,000 Air Traffic Controllers in more than eighty (80) countries world-wide. The Federation actively participates in Working Groups and Panels of the International Civil Aviation Organization (ICAO). IFATCA also maintains a close working relationship with the International Federation of Airline Pilots' Associations (IFALPA), the International Air Transport Association (IATA), the International Labour Office (ILO), the European Civil Aviation Conference (ECAC) and Working Groups on Aviation Matters in the European Parliament.

It is especially relevant to mention that IFATCA is a member of the ICAO Flight Safety and Human Factors Study Group, and actively participates in the ICAO Regional Seminars on Flight Safety and Human Factors. IFATCA also presented a paper at ICAO's 2nd Global Symposium on Flight Safety and Human Factors.

Proposition #2

"Air Traffic Controllers are not primarily employed to control air traffic."

Although the statement from that proposition may come as a shock to some of you, in many countries it is still just to true to be good.

It is a reality that most qualified Air Traffic Controllers are engaged in giving On-the-Job Training (OJT) to student-controllers. In other words: the students control the traffic, the qualified Controllers monitor and coach the students (and intervene in the traffic-situation where necessary). Once a student passes his/her final check, he or she becomes a qualified Controller and after a period of typically two years gets a student assigned to him/her in turn.

Meanwhile, the first-mentioned qualified controller has been busy coaching further students, for there seems to be a perennial shortage of staff in ATC.

And yet it seems so simple: analyse what attributes a qualified Air Traffic Controller uses in his work; define selection-criteria based on those attributes; select and train a person to become an Air Traffic Controller; let that person control air traffic. How can there be a world-wide shortage?

It should be understood that the existing shortage is not a result of lack of training-efforts, but rather of a lack of training-output. The recognised figure for the fail rate of OJT-students in ATC is around 75%, in spite of highly sophisticated selection-procedures including psychological tests.

This of course implies that qualified Controllers spend most of their career sitting behind student controllers, for the shortage is never over. In that way, controlling air traffic is not their primary job but merely a prerequisite in order to be able to train students.

Without pretending that IFATCA has THE answer to this problem (for a problem it is!) we would like to submit that maybe the analysis of the attributes a Controller should possess is incomplete. If an Air Traffic Controller's career involves giving OJT (which is a demanding task, in a complex operational environment) one of the selection-criteria should be the ability and motivation to teach!

Not everybody can teach, nor does everybody have the desire to teach. ATCOs are no exception to this. Yet they all are expected to give OJT, and often without the benefit of any instructor's course too.

IFATCA would like to invite those of you who are involved in determining selection-criteria for ATCOs to give this matter some consideration.

Proposition #3

"TCAS is not improving safety the way it might."

TCAS TCAS was the Reagan-administration's answer to a number of mid-air collisions in the USA in which quite a few lives were lost. Legislation was passed that every aircraft with more than 30 seats operating commercially in the USA should be equipped with a device that gives the pilots advice for evasive action when another aircraft gets too close. (Detection of other aircraft is subject to such aircraft operating a transponder.) A first deadline for fitting all aircraft with TCAS was found too tight and therefore was extended to the end of 1993.

Reason-model Now, let's have a look at the Reason model (with which most of you probably are familiar). What it says is: in complex systems, such as the aviation-industry, an accident is the result of a number of Latent Failures combined with one (or two) Active Failure(s). "Pilot Error" or "ATCO Error" should in fact read "System Error".

What is important to realise is: if there has been an accident, it is wrong to just take disciplinary action against the pilot or the ATCO and think you've solved the problem that caused it. If there is no change in the system, the same mistakes will be made sometime somewhere by another pilot or ATCO, thus causing another and similar accident.

Therefore, to improve the safety of the system after an accident, it is necessary to make changes in the system. Changes in the earliest levels of the Reason-model, i.e. the levels of the Regulators and Decision-makers, are the most effective for system safety.

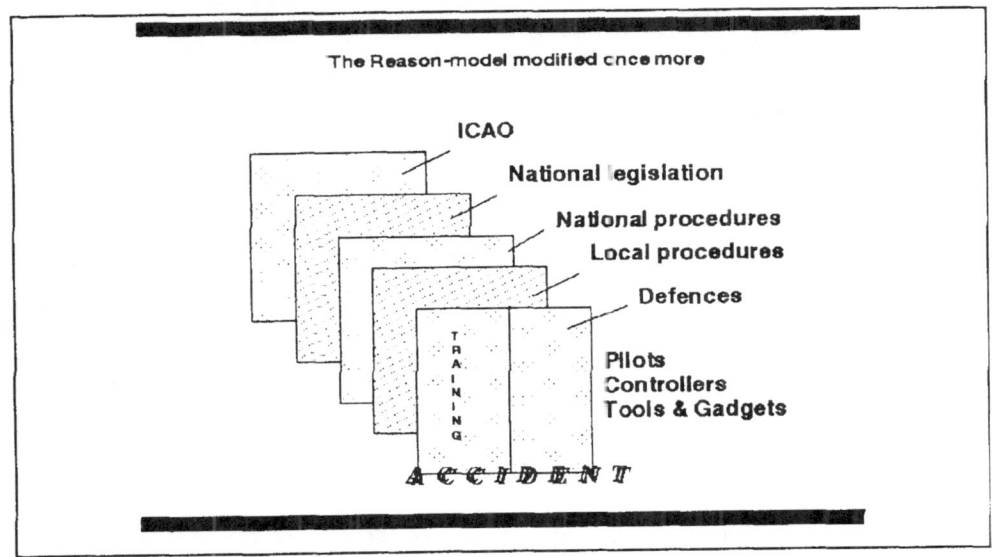

Figure 1: amended Reason-model

Figure 1 again depicts the Reason-model, but this time in a slightly different way. This version shows the various levels of regulation to which international aviation is subjected. It also shows that the last layer of defence between regulation and an accident is that in which we find the pilots and ATCOs. This layer is enhanced by the components Training and Tools & Gadgets. When we apply this model to the introduction of TCAS this can be translated to mean that because the whole of the existing ATS-system with its regulations has failed, a technical tool is given to one of the groups in the last line-of-defence with a view to making the system safer.

At this point it is interesting to note that in the case of TCAS the industry couldn't quite keep up with the pace of the legislators. The manufacturers didn't meet the envisaged technical specifications, the airlines were unable to equip all their aircraft in time, and last but far from least, there was virtually no training given to pilots on how to use the tool - nor to Air Traffic Controllers, for that matter. Yet TCAS is a reality today!

Effects and solutions   But rather than just give a tool to those in the last line-of-defence, it would have been better to change the rules, regulations and/or procedures in order to prevent future accidents. Some mid-airs involved VFR-traffic that strayed into the path of IFR-traffic. If for example the airspace-classification would be changed to "IFR only" or "IFR/CVFR", and the approach-procedures for the airports involved would be amended accordingly, it can be argued this would do more to improve the safety of the system than the present TCAS implementation.

In other words (ref. fig. 1), start working on the regulation-parts of the system before adding extra tools to the last line-of-defence!

Safer or unsafer?   Furthermore IFATCA is concerned that, contrary to its purpose, TCAS has the potential to make the aviation-system less safe than it was.

In a conversation between IFATCA and a senior ICAO official, ICAO said that due to the introduction of TCAS the mathematical chance of a mid-air collision has become much smaller, therefore in the near future the ATC separation-criteria between aircraft could well be reduced.

Allow us now to take you back to the Reason-model. We've seen that, because the system is unsafe, a tool is given to pilots: the last line-of-defence. No other coherent changes are made to the system. So: it remains as potentially unsafe as it was, it is only hoped that the last line-of-defence will better serve to keep accidents from happening. In ICAO's reasoning that new tool in the last line-of defence is now used to justify a reduction in separation-criteria that were considered inadequate to begin with!

Maybe an analogy can help illustrate the situation here, for which we would like to compare TCAS to the airbag-systems that are nowadays built into many family-cars.

Just like TCAS, airbags are meant as a last resort to prevent the ultimate disaster from happening. No car-buyer expects to ever use it, but it feels safe knowing it's there anyway. TCAS is meant to provide a similar feeling to pilots.

But unlike what seems to be the trend in aviation, no legislator that we know of is considering a structural slackening of existing road-traffic safety-rules, such as doing away with speed limits, minimum braking-performance or minimum requirements for tyre-profiles, just because cars are now fitted with airbags! In aviation however, the installing of TCAS in aircraft has immediately triggered many so-called trials to see if existing separation-criteria (i.e. safety-rules) can be lowered. That is not what TCAS was meant for!!

Epilogue TCAS can serve a purpose, but in the way it is being implemented it does add little to the safety of the aviation-system. IFATCA calls for caution to prevent TCAS from becoming detrimental to aviation-safety instead of enhancing it.

Therefore the IFATCA Policy on Airborne Collision Avoidance Systems reads:

> "IFATCA recognises that the development of airborne collision avoidance systems should be encouraged. However it must be accepted that the primary means of collision avoidance within a controlled airspace environment must continue to be the air traffic control system which should be totally independent of airborne emergency devices such as ACAS. Autonomous airborne devices should not be a consideration in the provision of adequate air traffic services."

Conclusion

The answer to the question from the title of our presentation, "Psychology and Air Traffic Control - Who cares?", could be: we all do. But the title can also be a challenge: who cares (enough) to carry out further research on these subjects?

In the interest of international air safety, IFATCA is ready to assist anyone who does.

Part 3
ACCIDENTS/INCIDENTS AND THEIR AFTERMATH

Section A
ACCIDENT INVESTIGATION

14 Investigation of Human Factors: the link to accident prevention

Peter G. Harle, Transportation Safety Board of Canada

History

In accident investigation, traditionally investigators have tended to focus on the proximate cause; specifically, they have identified the unsafe acts committed by the operator. Since the pilot is usually the first one at the scene of the accident, there has been a tendency to focus on "pilot error" often attaching blame for the failure of the pilot to assess the inherent risks in his actions, such as continuing into instrument meteorological conditions under Visual Flight Rules (VFR), descending below published minima, deviating from established procedures, etc. Hence, accident reports typically have depicted **what? when? and who?** with a factual travel log of the occurrence, micro-second by micro-second examining the crash dynamics. Investigators have focused on the personnel failures, often with much finger-pointing, such that the Honourable John Lauber of the National Transportation Safety Board of the U.S. speaks of the **"whodunit?"** approach to accident investigation. On a world-wide basis, accident reports have seldom depicted accurately **why? and how?** the occurrence came about. They have provided little assessment of the events preceding the accident with a full consideration of all the potential contributing factors.

In analyzing accidents, all too often the situation was ripe before the accident; the experts were saying "it is just a matter of time". All too often, normal, healthy, competent, experienced, well equipped personnel were implicated in the accident. They did not have any intention of committing suicide; on the contrary, they often had strong motivation towards mission accomplishment. But, often, they had committed the same potentially unsafe act hundreds of times before - successfully. Daily, we see incidents pointing to latent failures that are present within the aviation system. Designers, planners, and managers often knowingly (but sometimes unwittingly) accept the inherent risks of these failures in the system. Sometimes pilots are not even aware of those risks, such that some observers have called pilots the "unwitting inheritors of all the system's defects".

So, when investigators ask "why do normal, healthy, qualified, experienced, well equipped, personnel commit unsafe acts?" they must strive to better understand the context in which these errors were committed.

A systems approach to investigations

Figure 1 SHEL Model

This suggests a need for an alternative approach to accident investigation, whereby we consider the total latent situation when the unsafe acts were committed. A systematic approach is required. One useful model is the SHEL Model offered by Elwyn Edwards, as modified by Frank Hawkins. (Hawkins, 1987) This model focuses on human beings (Liveware). In addition to understanding the physical, physiological, and psychological factors affecting the pilot's performance, we must examine the interfaces between the crew and other personnel in the aviation system (Liveware), their equipment (Hardware), their operating environment (Environment), and the effectiveness of all of the system support that is put in place for them (Software). By examining all blocks and interfaces of the SHEL Model in Fig. 1, the contributory factors creating the context in which normal people were implicated in accident causation can be evaluated.

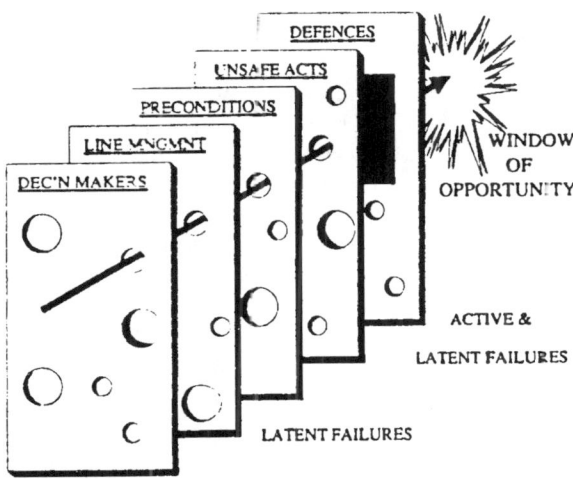

Figure 2. Reason's Model

More recently, Dr. James Reason of the University of Manchester, has offered another systematic approach which considers the whole production system - in our case the entire aviation system (Reason, 1990). Fig 2 depicts this layered approach. One layer depicts the unsafe acts undertaken by flight crews and other personnel. Fortunately, the aviation system has many structural defences built-in to mitigate the circumstances of such unsafe acts. But, Reason goes further than focusing on the immediate circumstances of the accident. He would have us examine all of the pre-conditions at the time of the occurrence, including such things as crew fatigue, stress, accepted operating practices, etc. He defines a fourth layer, to depict the effects of line management in such areas crew scheduling and training, dispatch, standard operating procedures etc.

An finally, Reason includes a layer representing all senior decision-makers; those of the carrier, the manufacturer, the regulator, and the unions. Reason notes that these decision-makers frequently make "fallible" decisions.

Under a particular set of circumstances, a window of opportunity may be created for an occurrence. All the system's defects sit latently waiting for someone to commit an unsafe act thereby triggering a potential accident scenario. If the system's defences work, a benign incident results. If they fail, the result may be a tragic accident.

Given this expanded appreciation of accident causation, a new approach to investigation is required. The new text "Aviation Psychology in Practice", (McDonald, Johnston and Fuller, 1994) includes a chapter which summarizes the systematic approach to accident investigation advocated by ICAO. This approach requires collecting data in the diverse areas suggested by Elwyn Edward's SHEL model and analyzing them to identify the latent safety deficiencies in the system, as evidenced by the higher three layers of Reason's model; i.e. the pre-conditions, line management, and the decision-makers.

Training the investigator

Such an approach to accident investigation requires new knowledge, skills and attitudes on the part of the investigators. The balance of this paper will describe the experience of the Transportation Safety Board of Canada in preparing its investigators to better understand the human behaviour preceding an aviation occurrence, such that appropriate remedial measures can be implemented.

The process began with a review of the operating assumptions of the TSB. For example, it was noted that, while the TSB employs several Human Performance Specialists, there are insufficient resources to permit a Specialist to attend each investigation.

Most occurrences are investigated by investigators who through training and experience have developed the skills necessary to investigate highly technical and complex aspects of occurrences. Where necessary, technical specialists are consulted to provide specific assistance and guidance. But, by and large, the data gathering and analysis are conducted by generalist field investigators. In summarizing his expectations of the Human Performance course in a precourse questionnaire, one of the investigators aptly described this concept: "I do not expect to become a Human Factors expert as I do not expect to become an engineering expert; however, I must be aware of the types of Human Factors elements to look for and where to go for help."

Recognizing that the investigators will frequently have insufficient formal training to address particular issues, the in-house Human Performance specialists are available on a consultancy basis to assist the investigators. Furthermore, when investigating Human Performance at the extremes of any normal distribution of human behaviour, the consultant services of professional experts outside the organization can be obtained.

Course development process

Just as we advocate a systems approach to investigation, we followed a systems approach to course development. A formal assessment of our investigators' and analysts' needs was conducted. The tasks they are required to perform in an investigation were carefully analyzed. Suitable training methods and strategies were selected to best facilitate the course members' acquisition of the knowledge, skills, and attitudes necessary to complete these tasks in the field. The course is modified in the light of end-course evaluations. And ultimately, the effectiveness of the course over time will be validated to facilitate follow-on training.

Learning objectives

Having surveyed and analyzed the investigators' needs, five broad learning objectives emerged. Upon course completion, all investigators and safety analysts should be able to: -

- Discuss the basic concepts of human performance that frequently
- impact on transportation safety;

- Identify human performance deficiencies which may degrade transportation safety;
- Apply a standard methodology for the conduct of the investigation and analysis of human performance issues;
- Draw reasonable inferences from their investigations and analysis for the findings, reflecting the appropriate level of certainty; and,
- Record human performance data for macro analytical purposes

Of note, these objectives are written in performance-oriented terms. The investigators are expected to be able **to do** specific things as a result of this training. To assist with the development of the training program, the services of a consultant who has a good working knowledge of the aviation industry and an extensive experience in designing and delivering adult training programs were retained.

TSB approach

In its simplest terms, the course can be viewed as four blocks: collect data, analyze data, record data, and write accident report. In other words, the actual sequence that an investigator performs his duties is followed. For each of these blocks, various terms, models, and principles are discussed, and the tools and tasks necessary for completing the investigative actions are applied.

The knowledge portion of the course comprises developing an understanding of the SHEL model described by Hawkins (Hawkins, 1987) and the "REASON" model (Reason, 1990). In addition, to better understand the nature of human error, Rasmussen's Skills-, Knowledge- and Rules-based approach is examined. (Rasmussen, 1990). The investigators then develop skill and practice in applying these concepts in real situations, mimicking field behaviour with case studies in group activities.

Of prime importance, they learn that Human Factors investigation is not something that you add-on to a normal investigation. Rather, Human Factors considerations are an integral part of every phase of the investigation.

Focus

The focus of the training efforts is on the question **"What will I do on Monday morning"?** The possession of theoretical knowledge by the investigators will be of little use if they lack the skill and confidence to apply these concepts in their daily work.

Typically, one week courses try to cram a lot of information into intensive lectures. Thus, a key strategic issue in course development was: How much learner involvement could we afford in a one week course? With the volume of material to be covered, intuitively little time could be spent in syndicate work. Yet, the over-riding consideration was how would we best be able to help our people perform back on the job? Since people tend to retain 10% of what they read and 20 % of what they hear (vs. 90% of what they say and do), we opted for high learner/group involvement - even though it meant covering less content. Therefore, much of the course is spent in syndicates, working on practical case studies. To the extent practicable, we have tried to create situations where the course members can mimic the behaviour required in actual investigations. We promote continuous personal involvement in the learning process, and we try to create a climate where the course members enjoy the process, believing that people tend to remember best what they had most fun doing.

Attitudinal change

In putting the course together, it became apparent that in addition to the five formal learning objectives which had been established, a major attitudinal shift would be required if the training was to be effective. For example, we realized that many of our investigators view human factors with some kind of mystique. Therefore, we have tried to demystify the subject of human factors - putting academic concepts into practical and workable terms, understandable to the field investigator.

For a number of reasons, many of our investigators have developed a cynicism towards the practicality of human factors investigations. For those, we must help them develop a respect for the fundamental need for emphasizing this aspect of their work, and to realize that efforts expended on these often non-material issues are worthwhile.

Many of our investigators are not aware of the organizational resources available today to help them in their investigation of human factors. Without academic credentials, many felt they were not competent to address Human Factors issues. Thus, during the training program, we aim to develop their knowledge and willingness to use all the resources available to them; for example, the services of our medical staff for physiological issues, our behaviourial specialists, our engineering laboratory staff for computer-based anthropometric modelling, our library services for literature searches, etc. Furthermore, recognizing the limitations of a one-week course, we must strive to motivate our course members that the course is just the beginning. We are striving to provide them with a framework and the motivation to facilitate continued learning through the balance of their careers for the investigation of Human Performance issues.

Results

To date 96 TSB staff members and 15 non-TSB personnel have participated in the training program. Some of these were very experienced, some very junior, some highly cynical about human performance as a discipline, or the TSB's attitude towards it, and some were very enthusiastic, or at least anxious to find a better, more systems-based approach to their work. The majority of those who have completed the training are now enthusiastic in their desire to try to apply this new approach. While the validation process has only just begun, feedback to date suggests considerable success in meeting the course objectives. But, back on the job many of the graduates are experiencing the natural disappointments of applying new approaches. Considerable reinforcement on the job will be required to hone their newly acquired skills. This follow-up phase is just beginning.

Conclusions

In summary, accident prevention is critically linked to the adequacy of the investigation of Human Performance issues. The aviation system contains a complex of inter-related latent deficiencies at all levels of the system. Almost daily there are benign incidents which demonstrate the existence of these potential system failures. From time to time, healthy, experienced, competent personnel commit unsafe acts which breach all the system's built-in defences, and an accident occurs. Unfortunately, often it is not until there is a judicial inquiry into a major accident that the latent safety deficiencies in the system are identified, validated and communicated to responsible authorities for corrective action.

These latent failures in the system can be identified by competent investigators. The TSB has taken a systems approach to the development of a course specifically designed to meet the needs of its investigators and analysts. The underlying principle is that generalist investigators can develop their skills to collect and analyze the Human Factors information essential to initiating effective accident prevention measures - just as they do for engineering, metallurgical, or aerodynamic issues. Investigators must also learn when to seek appropriate professional assistance.

However, in view of the major attitudinal changes necessary at both the individual investigator and the organizational level, considerable follow-up and reinforcement will be required to ensure the effective and lasting application of the systems approach to occurrence investigations.

References

Hawkins, F.H. (1987), *Human Factors in Flight,* Gower Technical Press, Aldershot, UK.

McDonald, N., Johnston. N. and Fuller, R. (eds) (1994), *Aviation Psychology in Practice,* Avebury Technical, Aldershot.

Reason, J.T. (1990), *Human Error,* Cambridge University Press, New York, USA.

Rasmussen, J. (1987), "The Definition of Human error and a Taxonomy for Technical System Design", *New Technology and Human Error,* (eds Rasmussen, J., Duncan, K. and Leplat, J.) John Wiley & Sons, Toronto, Canada.

15 The contribution of aviation psychology to the investigation of aircraft accidents of German Armed Forces

Burkhart Falckenberg, Diplom-Psychologe, GAF Institute of Aviation Medicine

In principle, the German Armed Forces Director Flight Safety has the task to investigate flight accidents and incidents of all three services of the German Armed Forces. The investigation is conducted by a board consisting of a chairman, an accident investigation officer, a technical officer, a flight surgeon, a representative of the flying unit in which the accident happened as well as other experts if required.

In the past, the German Armed Forces' aviation psychologists have only participated in exceptional cases. These were mainly fatal accidents for which no plausible reasons could be found in the course of the initial investigations. At the office of the Director Flight Safety, German Armed Forces, people were obviously satisfied with the psychologists' work. This experience and the fact that technical factors had become ever less important as possible causes of flight accidents while human factor had become more and more decisive made the German Armed Forces Director Flight Safety work towards a routine participation of psychologists. This planned new regulation met with varied and rather mixed response by the flying units, it ranged from agreement to even objection.

There may have been various reasons for a negative attitude: one important reason was certainly the fact that people simply did not know enough about psychology and the work of the psychologist. Sometimes, the psychologists' special field may even have been associated with that of psychiatry. In contrast to those states where a psychologist is assigned to every flying squadron in addition to the flight surgeon or at least is present in the units as a unit psychologist on a regular basis, the German Armed Forces only employ aviation psychologists at the GAF Institute of Aviation Medicine. This fact may have been another reason which caused some people to be rather sceptical about the aviation psychologists' participation as that institute is the only organisation within the German Armed Forces to conduct medical examinations at regular intervals, thus having a major influence upon flying personnel's careers. Finally, some of the commanders may "subconsciously" have been concerned about the results the investigating psychologist might come up with, i.e. that factors might additionally have played a role in the accident which rather have to do with organizational aspects or similar marginal conditions. In order to counter these concerns from the very start, it was the policy of the Director Flight Safety German Armed Forces, to always consult a psychologist, also in the case of accidents caused by technical failures. Thus, a psychologist appearing at the site of the accident was nothing special or extraordinary anymore.

In my following presentation, I would like to talk about the methods the psychologists apply and about their first experiences in this field which is comparatively new to the German Armed Forces' psychology. Fortunately the flight accident rate is very low, i.e. it is 0.25 (related to 10,000 flying hours), and only a total of 43 accidents have happened since 1989, which is also a relatively small number. In addition, psychologists were not consulted for all, but only for 32 accidents in the initial phase. Consequently, it certainly cannot be expected that I will present remarkable scientific findings or that impressive statistics have been the result. 15 different types of aircraft were involved in the accidents that have been investigated and the missions also varied a lot, which meant that a comparison would hardly have been feasible.

But what is the actual task of the psychologist? The psychologist mainly concentrates on the areas of information processing, on the individual's competence for action under increased stress, on the quality and degree of the individual's flying and general motivation as well as on the type and intensity of crew co-ordination and social interactions. If required, the flight psychologist extends the scope of his investigations to include ergonomic aspects as well as organisational, operational and further circumstances.

The objectives of psychological investigations of accidents are:
- Finding out about the psychological backgrounds of actions leading to an accident (the causes of the causes),
- pointing to possible habits of behaviour of the individual which must be considered hazardous,
- relating concrete behaviour to more general laws of psychology,
- pointing out to dangerous procedures, regulations or group norms,
- referring to aspects of cockpit design or other technical factors which are impractical or even dangerous from an ergonomic point of view and
- suggesting and proposing measures to prevent accidents.

As a consequence, the psychologist's investigation work has to be done step by step, comprising several levels of analysis. Although we do not have an extensive check-list (like the Canadian Air Force, for example), the psychologist however, proceeds according to a relatively fixed scheme. First he must examine the sequence of events which finally caused the accident from a psychological point of view. In this context, it is also particularly important to consider factors relating to the situation which may have had an indirect or direct influence on the accident, such as the situation immediately before starting on the flight (pressure of time in preparing the flight, unexpected change of the flight plan, etc.) Finally, it will be decisive to clear up the possible causes behind the established or supposed reasons for the accident to the extent that they are related to the human factor.

When the psychologist has received the information of the flight accident he will join the respective unit as soon as possible. There he will be briefed by the investigating officer who will inform him on the first findings. The psychologist will know about the flying environment and will also have experience as a passenger in combat aircraft but normally will not be a pilot himself and will even less likely be accustomed to the type of aircraft involved in the accident. Therefore, this briefing will frequently comprise information on the aircraft itself, on its aerodynamic characteristics or other technical details that are of importance in this context. Having a look into all the documents available so far, such as preliminary reports, minutes of interviews, photos or other documents such as the cockpit voice recorder will be an important part during that first briefing.

The question arises whether the psychologist should also visit the site of the accident. This decision must be taken for each individual case. In the case of accidents during final approach, during landing or in the case of helicopter accidents close to the ground, an on-site inspection of this kind may be rather suitable for clarifying psychological factors related to perceptual factors. Furthermore, the investigator may get a clear idea about where and in which chronological order the accident happened. Should the possibility arise, it may be helpful in some rare cases to fly the route the aircraft took all over again, particularly in the case of accidents that happened close to the ground. The next crucial point in the investigation will then be interviewing the persons involved in the accident, provided the accident was not fatal. These interviews should be conducted as soon as possible as people do not reconstruct details of the course of the accident if the period of time between the accident itself and the examination is too long. Another problem is the fact that the person involved in the accident may receive additional new information from other sources, thus perhaps changing his memories of the course of the accident or making false hypotheses himself.

For persons who were injured in the accident, the time of interview, which is frequently only the first of a series, of course mainly depends on their physical state, which is a question that has to be answered by the flight surgeon. In this context, it is of equal importance that the person concerned may still suffer from a shock or at least be in an emotionally labile condition, which would make it irresponsible to conduct an interview.

This point leads us to a very important question of a different nature, i.e. how the role of the investigating psychologist is to be defined - should it be that of an investigator or therapist? In particular cases, it may happen that a person involved in an accident prefers to turn to the psychologist primarily for advice and consequently speaks more openly to him than he would to somebody who is "only" an investigator. In a situation of this kind, the psychologist and the person concerned should agree on what may be included in the investigation report later in order to avoid abusing the patient's confidence. However, the investigating psychologist should basically be aware of the fact that his function is going to be that of an investigator.

Further difficulties may arise with respect to the psychological investigation of the persons concerned: in the case of retrograde amnesia, seriously injured patients will not be capable of reconstructing details of the course of the accident. As things usually happen very fast up to the moment the accident takes place, the persons involved in it sometimes simply cannot remember details or the correct chronological order. On the other hand the psychologist must always be aware of the fact that some of the statements made may serve to protect the person involved, in particular if he seems to have acted negligently or incorrectly, thus trying to avoid criminal prosecution or disciplinary punishment or claims of recourse, a reaction which is quite understandable. As a matter of fact, the prosecution has access to the accident investigation material in contrast to some other states where there are usually two separate files on the accident. This may actually impede the clearing up of all circumstances that led to the accident, considerably. However, it must also be expected that people make false statements for completely different reasons, i.e. in order to protect themselves when they are afraid of losing face (nobody likes to admit having made a mistake).

In addition to reconstructing the course of the accident and clarifying other situational factors, the psychological investigation will also and in particular concentrate on the person's flying career and his general biography.

For this purpose, the investigating psychologist will have a variety of documents at his disposal. As a rule, he will examine the result of the psychological selection prior to flying training as well as data from the flying screening. This information will of course in many cases not be very comprehensive, in particular if a relatively long period of time has passed in the pilot's flying career. However, in particular cases, this data, too, may provide valuable hints, especially if it is confirmed by information gathered at a later point of time, for example during flying training, and if a certain personality trait that might be seen in context with the accident runs like a "red thread" through the entire career.

Additional important information may be gathered from the individual flight record of a person involved in the accident, enabling the psychologist to assess his career as an aviator, his proficiency, special capabilities and also weak points. The impression gained with respect to the person's performance and personality is completed by interviewing his superiors, the flight surgeon, instructor pilots and other persons of reference. In very rare cases in which already exploratory investigations have resulted in clear indications of possible weaknesses in the person's performance, it may become necessary to conduct an examination based on psychological tests.

In general, all of the written documents mentioned before will also be available in the case of fatal flight accidents, of course. In this context, the cockpit voice recorder - if available - may be of particular importance as it enables the psychologist to go beyond the normal scope of evaluation (reconstruction of the sequence of events and the crew members interactions) and analyse the recorded material and perhaps even assess the qualities of the voices recorded, which may provide an indication of the persons' emotional state.

The psychologist who normally is able to gain a personal impression of the person involved in the accident must, in the case of fatal accidents apart from documented evidence, rely on the statements made by the persons of reference he interviewed. In such a situation it turns out to be particularly important to collect as much information as possible and make persons of reference from the victim's personal environment talk about their experiences. In this context it does not come as a surprise that there may be a lot of resistance to interviews of this kind at first and that it may take some time "to break the ice". Furthermore, many a detail may be covered up as a result of a wrong sense of comradeship.

In some very rare cases it could become necessary or at least useful to question relatives of crew members killed in accidents, too, for example if the investigations conducted so far point to a personal conflict situation which might have played a role for the accident. As both the investigator and the person interviewed are exposed to extreme strain during an interview of this kind, this possibility should only be considered in very exceptional cases.

The pieces of information gathered in this way from various sources will finally all be included in the psychologist's investigation report. An essential part of this report is the analysis of the sequence of the accident in the light of psychological findings. However, it must be understood that some questions with respect to details of certain facts or certain interrelations will have to remain unanswered or may only be formulated as hypotheses or probabilities. Just like the preliminary reports by the other members, the psychological investigation report will be submitted to the investigation board, serving as one of the basic documents for the board's work. But now, the psychologist is confronted with another, indeed basic, problem of his work within the framework of flight accident investigation. The psychologist must, just like the flight surgeon, abide by professional discretion as laid down in German law. However, the implementing regulations issued by the German MOD for the work of physicians and psychologists specify that psychologists acting as expert witnesses are bound by professional discretion only to a limited extent. But there are no clear definitions as to the psychologist's obligation to pass on any relevant information, which means that this decision obeys his personal criteria. In practice, the members of the Accident Investigation Board are informed about the detailed contents of the psychological report and may take the findings laid down in this document into consideration. They are strictly bound to secrecy as far as matters are concerned that go beyond the scope of their work on the board. Nevertheless, disclosing his findings more often than not is a tightrope walk for the investigating psychologist, but very strict observation of the protection of data privacy - which basically is to be appreciated - will probably continue to rather impede comprehensive clearing up of the causes of accidents in the future.

16 Report on air traffic accident on 27 December 1991 at Gottröra, AB County

Kristina Pollack, Swedish Armed Forces, Sweden

The Board of Accident Investigation finds that the accident was caused by SAS' instructions and routines being inadequate to ensure that clear ice was removed from the wings of the aircraft prior to take-off. Through this, the aircraft took off with clear ice on the wings. In connection with lift-off clear ice came loose and was ingested by the engines. The ice caused damage to the fan stages of the engines which led to engine surging. The surges destroyed the engines.

Contributory causes were : the pilots were not trained to identify and correct engine surges; ATR - which was unknown within SAS - was activated and increased engine throttles without the pilots' knowledge.

As a result of its investigation the Board of Accident Investigation is submitting 15 recommendations.

References

Pollack, K and Bostrom, S (1993) Human Factor Report, Official Appendix 385 in Report C 1993:57; Air Traffic Accident on 27th December 1991 at Gottrora, AB County, Sweden. Case No.L-124/91.

Section B
VOLUNTARY INCIDENT REPORTING

17 The quantitative analysis of qualitative data: methodological issues in the derivation of trends from incident reports

Don Harris, Department of Applied Psychology, College of Aeronautics, Cranfield University

The relationship between hazards, incidents and accidents is not an easy one to quantify. Heinrich (1959) suggested that for every industrial injury accident there were 30 minor (non-injury) accidents and 300 hazardous incidents. Other studies have confirmed this pyramidal relationship between these categories, however, their ratios are likely to be dependent upon the type of industry and the definitions used. Incident reporting is a vital step in any safety system. Van der Schaaf (1991) suggests that the analysis of near-misses provides the link between highly visible and detectable (but rare) accidents and very frequent, but almost invisible, potentially dangerous behavioural acts. The regular analysis of incident data can eliminate or reduce the risks in a system before they combine in such a way as to culminate in an accident.

Van der Schaaf outlines three basic purposes of a confidential incident reporting scheme:-

Modelling   the detection and analysis of factors leading to an accident.
Monitoring   the analysis of trends of known risk factors to establish the effectiveness of a safety management system.
Motivation   to encourage vigilance and impart a sense of involvement and the ability to make a positive contribution to improve safety.

If an incident reporting system is to be useful, the nature of the data that it collects must be clearly understood, as should the relationship between the data and the sequence of events in an accident. In aviation incident reporting schemes, such as the UK-based Confidential Human Factors Incident

Reporting Programme (CHIRP) and the US Aviation Safety Reporting System (ASRS), most of the reports submitted will be atypical and abstruse, and because of this the derivation of long term trends may be difficult. Analysis of reports at too low a level my lead to what Reason (1990) has described as 'tokenism', and as such their analysis may only provide a minimal improvement in safety (if any). For meaningful analysis to be undertaken, incidents need to be subsumed into larger categories and an emphasis should be placed on identifying the reasons *why* things happened, rather than merely describing *what* happened.

The reasons why incidents occur (or in an incident reporting system, why the reporter thought that they occurred), have been described by Reason (1990) as condition tokens. The actual error(s) themselves are designated as unsafe acts. There is a 'one to many' mapping of condition tokens to unsafe acts. For example, high workload (a condition token), perhaps caused by air traffic control instructions, may contribute to any one of hundreds of potential errors being made (unsafe acts). Because of the nature of this relationship, it is almost impossible to predict which unsafe acts will be committed as a result of a given condition token. Therefore, analysis of incident data must encompass the investigation of both unsafe acts and their psychological precursors. The scope for effective interventions is far greater at the latter level.

Confidential reporting schemes have a central role to play in the enhancement of aviation safety. However, due to the qualitative nature of the data collected in them, (usually in the form of an unstructured narrative), it is difficult to identify and quantify any meaningful longer-term trends. This potentially limits their effectiveness (*qv* Van der Schaaf, 1991), although it is also worth noting the caveat to be found at the beginning of any ASRS search request; the power of incident reports lies in the qualitative nature of the report narrative, which tries to explain what happened and why. Nevertheless, to identify recurrent problems and new problems, some quantitative data concerning the frequency of occurrence needs to be culled from these reports.

Incident reports often provide a valuable insight into what happened, however they may not paint the whole picture about why something transpired. This is especially problematical when the 'why' component involves hypothetical, psychological constructs, such as workload. In-house reporting systems (*eg* the British Airways BASIS programme; O'Leary and Fisher, 1993) are attempting to rectify this, however, some method must to be devised to analyse *post hoc* the influence of psychological factors underlying past incidents in the extensive existing databases, and then quantify these data to produce meaningful trends. This data is too valuable simply to be disregarded.

To elicit trends from the analysis of qualitative data it is necessary to code the narratives into some kind of framework. Utilising the framework of human error within a system context posited by Reason (1990) such a framework should include both the psychological precursors of the incidents and a description of the errors themselves. Failure to include a description of the condition tokens will result in merely a description of what happened, without providing any appreciation of why it happened.

The *post hoc* coding of data, however, has methodological problems associated with it. For reliable categorisation of events to be achieved, it is necessary that there is agreement between two (or more) independent raters about the factors involved, thus going someway to avoiding subjective biases. However, as a precursor to inter-rater reliability, there must also be intra-rater reliability. High levels of inter-rater reliability will never be achieved unless individuals are also consistent in their interpretation of events.

To illustrate these problems and principles, data from the narrative reports of 67 incidents involving high-technology, wide-bodied commercial aircraft, provided by the NASA ASRS database, were subject to *post hoc* coding of events by two different raters. The coding framework was derived from two sources. The first was the proforma utilised by British Airways in its BASIS programme. This questionnaire is sent to crews reporting an in-flight incident in an attempt to elicit the contributory factors that resulted in an event occurring. For the purposes of the analyses contained herein, certain aspects of this proforma were modified to make it compatible with the nature of the data available. These are outlined in table one. In addition to these factors, the problems associated with high-technology aircraft flown under Flight Management System (FMS) guidance, described by Sarter and Woods (1992), formed the corpus of another seven categories of problem. These categories are described in table two. The items derived from the BASIS programme reflect the more abstract, psychological precursors of events. The categories elicited from Sarter and Woods address more specific, concrete questions of the data contained in the narrative reports, (although it should be noted that this distinction between the concrete and abstract is by no means perfect).

The raters were given specific instructions that they should only code the presence of a category if it was ***explicitly*** referred to in the narrative. All ratings were conducted independently. One rater was a pilot, the other a human factors specialist. Several days after the initial categorisation of events, the raters were again asked to code the narratives (without reference to their previous assessments). From these data the initial intra-rater reliabilities were established. The objective was to continue this process until the intra-rater reliabilities were over 95% for each of the categories for each of the raters.

However, after four passes through the report narratives (with two to three days between each categorisation exercise in order to minimise any potentially confounding memory effects), two of the categories derived from the BASIS proforma (workload and cockpit ergonomics) had still failed to attain the desired degree of intra-rater reliability. Thus, the inter-rater reliabilities reported in table three, were calculated at the end of the fourth categorisation exercise.

Table 1. Psychological precursors of incidents, derived from the British Airways BASIS programme.

Errors of omission or commission attributable to:-	*Misunderstandings attributable to:-*
Distraction/interruptions	Misleading manuals/QRH
Time pressure	Misleading displays
Lack of stimulation	Misunderstanding ATC communications
Tiredness	
Ergonomics: flight deck design	Misunderstanding intra-cockpit communications
Contributory factors underlying poor crew performance:-	Misunderstanding ATC procedures
	Misunderstanding cockpit procedures
Equipment failures	
Visual illusions	
High workload	
Insufficient or inadequate training	
Insufficient or inadequate monitoring	
Environmental stressors	
Morale/crew cooperation	
Fatigue	

Table 2. Problems encountered in the control of aircraft when flying under FMS control (adapted from Sarter and Woods, 1992)

Misunderstanding of flight management system logic	Uncommanded mode transitions
Failure to recognise what aspect of the system was in active control of the aircraft (MCP or CDU)	Lack of confidence in flight director commands
	Monitoring active target values
Data entry problems	Data propagation within modes of the FMS
	Lack of familiarity/experience of using the FMS

Table 3. Inter-rater reliabilities for incident classification

Category	Reliability	Category	Reliability
Precursors of events			
Distraction/interruptions	100%	Misunderstanding c/pit procs	98%
Time pressure	86%.	Equipment failures	97%
Lack of Stimulation	92%	Visual illusions	100%
Tiredness	92%	High workload	86%
Ergonomics: flight deck design	89%	Inadequate training	94%
Misleading manuals/QRH	100%	Inadequate monitoring	95%
Misleading displays	91%	Environmental stressors	100%
Misunderstanding ATC comms	91%	Morale/crew cooperation	97%
Misunderstanding c/pit comms	81%	Fatigue	98%
Misunderstanding ATC procs	94%		
FMS associated problems			
FMS logic	98%	Flight director commands	98%
MCP/CDU control confusion	98%	Monitoring active target values	98%
Data entry problem	97%	Data propagation	100%
Uncommanded mode transition	97%	Lack of experience	100%

It will be noted from the inter-rater reliabilities presented in table three, that there was far greater agreement in the classification of the specific problems associated with the FMS than with the more abstract, psychological precursors of events. Subsequent to the exercise, the raters indicated that their greatest problems were with the categories of 'time pressure' and 'high workload'; 'cockpit ergonomics' and 'misleading displays'; and 'tiredness' and 'fatigue'. There was often some difficulty in distinguishing between these categories. It was also suggested that in many cases, it was not for the raters to suggest if some aspects of the conduct of a flight were 'inadequate' on the basis of the information available. Additionally, the category of 'visual illusions' exhibited an artificially high agreement as there were no instances reported of this phenomena in the reports examined.

In the results presented, it must be borne in mind that just because it was not possible to elicit the presence of one of the psychological precursors to an incident, that is not to say that it was not actually at play. It is worth noting a further caveat to be found when requesting an ASRS search; data derived from reports of this kind are open to various sources of bias. However, what can be known, is that these reports reflect at least the lower bounds of the frequency of a certain categories of occurrence.

These results suggest that the *post hoc* coding of psychological precursors from incident data is likely to be unreliable. The validity of the technique may also be questionable as it cannot diagnose the presence of all the precursors. It only provides some estimate of the frequency of occurrence of those states that were most available to the reporter when submitting their account of events. The technique being used in the BASIS programme would seem to be a promising way in which confidential reporting schemes should progress, giving a more comprehensive coverage of precursors of incidents and a description of the incidents themselves. What can be derived from the *post hoc* coding of reports with some degree of reliability are specific events relating to specific items of equipment, although this does err on the side of tokenism, increasing reliability while perhaps decreasing validity.

Acknowledgement

The author would like to thank NASA and the Battelle ASRS office for providing the data used in this analysis.

References

Heinrich, H.W. (1959). *Industrial Accident Prevention (4th edition)*, McGraw-Hill, New York.

O'Leary, M. & Fisher, S. (1993). *British Airways Confidential Human Factors Reporting Programme: 1st Year Report*, British Airways PLC., London.

Reason, J.T. (1990). *Human Error*, Cambridge University Press, Cambridge.

Sarter, N.B. & Woods, D.D. (1992). 'Pilot interaction with automation: operational experiences with the flight management system', *The International Journal of Aviation Psychology, 2* (4), 303-321.

Van der Schaaf, T.W. (1991). 'A Framework for Designing Near Miss Management Systems', in Van der Schaaf, T.W., Lucas, D.A. & Hale, A.R. (eds), *Near Miss Reporting as a Safety Tool*, Butterworth-Heinemann Ltd., Oxford.

18 'Too bad we have to have confidential reporting programmes!': some observations on safety culture

Mike J. O'Leary, British Airways and Birkbeck College, University of London

Introduction

At an ICAO Human Factors (HF) conference last year, ICAO's Steve Corrie remarked: "It's too bad we have to have confidential reporting programs!". As I had been helping to set up and run the British Airways Confidential Human Factors Reporting Programme (CHFRP) for the last two years, the remark took me by surprise. However, he made a good point as confidential reports are difficult to validate objectively and it can be difficult for management to accept information from people who wish to remain anonymous. Management who are not committed to a human factors reporting programme might dismiss information from it as anonymous axe grinding and miss entirely the genuine concerns of professional line crews. Thus an open reporting system in which both sides can freely discuss reported safety problems is a desirable asset for a safety manager's toolbox.

Confidentiality would be necessary in an environment in which the safety culture is not exemplary, e.g., where a reporter of an unsafe or potentially unsafe situations fears, rightly or wrongly, that he or she may be disciplined because of the event. So what about British Airways' CHFRP. Firstly is it at all necessary? Are we getting more, different or better information through it than from other sources. Is it necessary to have a confidential programme or could the information be obtained more efficiently and more usefully without the confidentiality guarantee. If our confidential programme does work then is there a deficiency in BA's safety culture?

British Airways Safety monitoring and reporting programmes

To answer these questions I will describe British Airways' safety culture in the context of its safety reporting and monitoring programmes. Then I will offer some evidence showing why a CHFRP was needed.

British Airways run air and ground safety reporting programme which requires all staff to report safety related events. For flight crew, the events which require the filing of an Air Safety Report (ASR) include all of those required by the Civil Aviation Authority's Mandatory Occurrence Reporting Programme. To encourage the filing of ASRs, British Airways states clearly that information from an ASR will not normally be used to bring disciplinary proceedings against flight crew. This would only occur in cases of wilful negligence or criminal intent and no-one in Safety Services can recall when such proceedings were last instigated. Discussion of the event with one's flight manager or any necessary retraining is not considered a disciplinary procedure.

The ASR programme is highly successful. It was fully reorganised some four years ago and the software, BASIS, developed by our own pilots and engineers is now used by many airlines around the world. All ASRs are stored in the BASIS database and easy reporting and trend analysis with graphical output is built in. The success of British Airways ASR programme is told in two statistics. The ASR filing rate has doubled since the beginning of 1991 and the number of reports assessed as high risk has decreased by two thirds between January 1992 and December 1993. This suggests both that our reporting culture has improved from an already high level and that our risk management strategy has been successful.

SESMA is a Flight Data Recording (FDR) programme which monitors the safety health of our fleets' operations while guaranteeing our crews complete anonymity. The FDR for each flight is scanned for operational 'events' which lie outside what are considered to be safe norms. All events are stored in the BASIS database and the more serious are discussed at a monthly meeting of technical managers, and BALPA representatives. If this group considers the event serious enough the BALPA representative will be charged with discussing the event with the flight's captain.

At this point the BALPA representative is given the name of the captain by Bill, a member of flight operations administration. Bill is the only person who has access to the information which can identify the flight crew. Any information offered to the BALPA representative by the captain is then reported back to the next monthly SESMA meeting and published in an unidentifiable form in the monthly SESMA report to management and in the monthly fleet newsletters. This programme is a highly valuable safety tool and is a rare collaboration between flight crew, union representatives and flight management in a safety programme which satisfies the interests of all groups.

British Airways believes that it has a good safety culture. Nothing however is perfect and of course we do have both line pilots and flight managers whose attitude towards the other is less than exemplary. We have learnt that a change of Flight manager can affect the number of flight crew volunteering for positions as CRM trainers. There are also line pilots who are proud of the fact that they have never nor will ever use a voluntary reporting program and will try to find reasons for not using the mandatory reporting systems.

However, these exceptions are rare as is demonstrated by the co-operative spirit of all involved with the SESMA programme for the last 25 years and the ASR statistics described above.

Do we need another reporting programme?

With a successful operational monitoring programme and a well supported ASR programme, do we need another reporting programme? We decided over two years ago that the answer to this question was Yes, and our CHFRP was born. The programme is run by line pilots and the names of the reporters are known only to those few crew involved in dealing directly with the HF reports. The issues raised in the reports are communicated to line management on a regular basis and great care is taken to maintain the anonymity of the reporters. The workings of the programme and its successes are not reported here but some indication of the benefits it offers can be seen below in the ASR and the HF report describing the same incident.

Air Safety Report: "Under ATC control we were ahead of another aircraft. ATC instructed other aircraft to orbit right and we became concerned about this traffic's position. Another very urgent instruction to orbit was heard and the co-pilot then saw the other aircraft overtaking us on our right hand side. Estimated separation was 200 metres laterally and 100 feet vertically."

Human Factors Report: "This was a very close airmiss which at the time did not provoke much of a shock reaction. However, once safely on the ground adrenaline induced shock affected all crew. This shock seemed to increase as time went on and even more after talking to the ATC controller when we realised how deeply shocked he was.

Some 90 minutes after the airmiss before next sector, we became aware that we were not concentrating properly on the pre-flight checks. I know that I was moving switches around without paying attention to my actions. We all stopped our checks and, instigated by the captain, discussed whether we were fit to operate the following sector. We had to make a great effort to push out of our minds the drama of the previous sector and concentrate on the job."

The Air Safety Reports are not anonymous and are required reading for flight managers. The Human Factor reports are read by only a very small number of line pilots who work for Safety Services which is totally separate from the Flight Operations department. We believe the organisation of the programme allows a freer and more complete level of reporting by flight crew. Moreover, we have recently introduced a 'Callback' procedure whereby we telephone all reporters who give us their name. With this pilot to pilot communication procedure we often receive valuable information from crew who return the form as 'not applicable to human factors'. Therefore we would argue that British Airways does need a CHFRP and gains much by its confidentiality and by it being organised and run by line pilots within an autonomous Safety Services department. So if, as I believe we do have a relatively good safety culture and yet we benefit from a confidential HFRP then is Steve Corrie wrong or is there something missing from my analysis.

Aviation safety culture

Pidgeon & O'Leary (1994) argue that a good safety culture is characterised in four ways: 1) it originates at the level of strategic management; 2) concern for safety is distributed and endorsed throughout the organisation; 3) there is a clear set of flexible and effective norms and rules which govern safety behaviour; and 4) there is ongoing proactive reflection on unsafe events and incidents and about safety in general. From points 1 and 2 it is clear that for a good aviation safety culture, management must establish the norms and other groups such as flight crew must accept and share these norms. However, in any aviation organisation there are many functional sub-groups, each of which might have its own distinctive sub-culture which will directly influence how it responds to the company's established safety objectives. Unless we understand these subcultures, success in spreading an organisation's safety culture to all sub-groups might at the very least be unpredictable. Perhaps there is a clue here to the apparent discrepancy between the apparently good safety culture in British Airways and the need for confidentiality in its safety reporting programs. Maybe the flight crew sub-culture makes it difficult to accept at face value the good will and good intentions of management. It may be that the flight crew sub-culture may lead it to misperceive the positive safety culture elsewhere in the organisation.

Influences on flight crew safety sub-culture

Let us not forget that the pilot is, like any other employee, dependent on the high regard of his superiors for the continuation of his employment. With this in mind, perhaps a look at the influences on and the characteristics of the flight crew subculture will lead us toward the goal of establishing a safety culture which allows open and free reporting of safety events. To highlight possible conflicts between the corporate culture and the pilot subculture I will briefly discuss a few selected factors and influences that might impact negatively on flight crew's acceptance of the organisation's safety culture..

Flight crew personality characteristics. There is a general finding that pilots score highly on self reliance scales and are considerably more Internal on Rotter's Locus of Control scale (Wichman & Ball, 1983) than the average population. Other psychoanalytic research suggests that a strong internal locus of control can be associated with high levels of guilt. Pilots, therefore tend to take responsibility for all mishaps whether or not they were under his or her control and if this leads to guilt then it is possible that the pilot will be less likely to report an untoward event whatever the cause. In the UK. this aspect may well interact with the inherited tradition of post second world war RAF pilots who naturally monopolised the post war commercial flying situations. . That military culture was probably not totally conducive to the practice of telling your superior officer that you had made a silly mistake.

Relationship with flight management. Trust between flight crew and management has to be at a very high level before flight crew freely report safety incidents which reflect badly on themselves. Unfortunately the relationship between flight crew and flight management is often soured by industrial disputes in which pilots representatives and pilots management are on opposite sides and try to discredit each other. If such discrediting is successful then in the industrial dispute the pilot - flight manager relationship and safety reporting might become just collateral damage.

Relationship with strategic management. Senior management have the responsibility of setting the foundations of a good safety culture. However, they also have duties to other groups such as shareholders which may lead them, in cases such as take-overs and industrial disputes, to take decisions which act against the economic interests of flight crew and other employee groups. Often these decisions will seem arbitrary and unreasonable to the employees and it is vital that senior management separate the industrial arguments from the safety goals which it espouses so that safety and safety reporting survive the dispute. I wonder if any management is or ever can be always successful in this task.

Impact of the legal framework. Lord Denning in the case of Alidair vs. Taylor in 1978 ruled that: "There are activities in which the degree of professional skill which must be required is so high, and the potential consequences of the smallest departure of that high standard are so serious, that one failure to perform in accordance with those standards is enough to justify dismissal." When that high standard can be reduced by fatigue, stress, poorly designed equipment or procedures, or the confusion induced by technical failure, this legal judgement does not encourage the free and open safety reporting culture that is our goal.

Relationship with society. - Neil Johnson (1994) argues most cogently that allocating blame and punishing those who contribute to an accident or incident does nothing to improve safety and further the understanding of risk management. Yet society appears to need a focus for its anger or grief in the unhappy aftermath of an accident. Hunting the villain may be appropriate in criminal circumstances but it is totally counterproductive if the goal is the understanding and prevention of accidents.

Conclusions

,,Aviation's primary goal is a safe arrival and a good safety culture is a statement of intent to arrive safely. I believe that a better understanding of the issues introduced here can lead to strategies which will allow us to counter such negative influences and lead to improvements in safety culture, even in good safety cultures such as that in British Airways. With such improvements we will move ever closer to the goal of full, free and open safety incident reporting. In turn this will lead to fewer unsafe arrivals.

References

Johnston, N. (1994), 'Blame, punishment and risk management', in Hood, C,. Jones, D., Pidgeon, N. and Turner, B. (eds), *Accident and Design*, UCP

Pidgeon, N and O'Leary, M.J. (1994), Organisational safety culture: Implications for aviation practice', in Johnston, N., McDonald, N. and Fuller, R. (eds), *Aviation Psychology in Practice*, Avebury Technical, Aldershot.

Wichman, H. and Ball, J. (1983), 'Locus of control, self-serving biases, and attitudes towards safety in general aviation pilots', *Aviation, Space and environmental medicine*, **54** (6) 507-510

19 Self-report means under-report?

R.S. Elwell, Psychavia Ltd

Introduction

In historical terms there has been a downward trend in aircraft accident rates (Diehl, 1989). However, as the accident rate has decreased the proportion of the total attributable to human error has increased. Estimates of the human error component vary. The Lufthansa World Accident Survey (Lufthansa, 1994) found cockpit crew errors accounted for 74% of causal factors in operational jet losses between 1983 and 1992. Reason (1991) quoting a US National Transportation Safety Board source for airline operations gave broad causes as: pilot error 54%, non-aircrew error 46% and weather 42% (Note the NTSB accept multiple causes for an aircraft accident).

For commercial rotorcraft, the NTSB cited the pilot as the cause, or a related factor, in 64% of American commercial helicopter accidents (NTSB, 1981). In the UK Army Air Corps, Vyrnwy-Jones (1984) reports that "pilot error" is the cause of 75% of their helicopter accidents, whilst in the United States Army the figure is 80% (Shanahan, 1984).

Lewis (1975) reviewing USAF accidents declared "..over 50% were caused by human error." Chappelow (1984) identified a human factors contribution (but not described as "error") in all but four of the 66 RAF accidents that occurred in the ten year period he analysed. Lee (1985) reported that 76% of all Australian aircraft accidents over a ten year period were attributed to human factors. There are a variety of other figures quoted for human error involvement in aircraft accidents, but a general range between 50% to 90% is common (Diehl, 1989). The sheer diversity of figures quoted reflects the difficulties of definition and mensuration as well as the questions concerning the accuracy and reliability of the data collected (Adams, 1982).

An inadequate explanation for the change from mechanical and operational causes to questions of human performance is that advances in aircraft design, construction and maintenance have not been accompanied by improvements in the reliability of the human component in the system. However, this disguises the fact that the opportunity for aircrew error most frequently occurs when aircraft systems or external agencies have failed. The pilot is the last last line of defence against an accident.

It is also important to realise that the terms "aircrew error" or "pilot error", although cited as causes of accidents in accident reports, serve only as a description of events. The term "error" does not provide an explanation for the accident (Ruegger, 1990; Nagel, 1988). Moreover, Chais and Simpson (1985) argue that neither flight experience, nor pilot qualifications, provide an adequate means in themselves for eliminating human error as a cause factor in accidents.

Table 1 is from Lufthansa (1994) and shows percentage of jet losses between 1961 and 1990 for different phases of flight. This is further related to their exposure to those flight phases, if one assumes that the flight has a duration of 1.6 hours. It is clear that most time is spent in the cruise, where fewest accidents happen. The approach and landing account for 57% of accidents, but for only 6% of exposure. Take off and climb account for 30% of accidents, in 20% of exposure. Of interest to the analysis presented subsequently, only 2% of accidents occur during the 20% of the time spent on the ground.

Table 1: Operational Jet Losses 1961 - 1990

Flight Phase	Losses	Exposure
Take Off	23%	1%
Climb	7%	19%
Cruise	3%	40%
Descent	8%	14%
Approach	33%	5%
Landing	24%	1%
Ground	2%	20%

In Chais and Simpson's (1985) analysis of a random sample of rotorcraft accidents, flight duration is not given. Percentages of accidents for different phases of operation are shown in Table 2. Again, a majority of accidents occurred during the descent to land, 41%. Note however that 19% of the accidents occur during low level flight, an unusual flight regime for big jets.

Table 2: Helicopter Accident by Phase of Operation

Flight Phase	Losses
Ground/Air Taxi	20%
Take Off/Climb	10%
Cruise	10%
Descent to Land	41%
Low Level Flight	19%

Whilst accidents are fortunately rare events, incidents (which have the potential to become an accident, ie they are near-accidents) are much more common. Incident data therefore tends to be regarded as a good substitute for the limited accident data (Wells, 1991; Van der Schaaf, 1991). At a more trivial level, much of human behaviour consists of correcting error conditions, automatically and continuously, to achieve a desired outcome; see Figure 1. There is a continuum between many instance of error correction, fewer incidents and very few accidents.

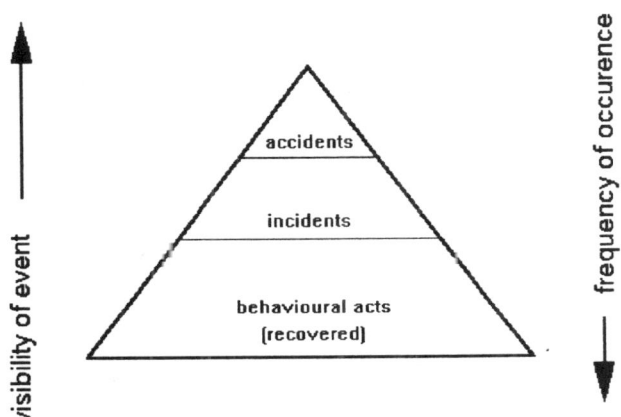

Figure 1: The relationship between accidents, incidents and errors

Incident data will only be of value if it reflects what happens when accidents occur. It is often surmised, but difficult to establish, that this is not the case. Considering whether incident data does accurately reflect accident causation is the purpose of this paper.

It has been suggested that on most occasions when pilots make serious errors these are seldom reported; this reluctance was the rationale underlying the Aviation Safety Reporting System (ASRS) established in the USA (Hardy, 1990; Billings, 1991). Similar, although not identical systems have been established in the UK with CHIRP (Confidential Human factors Incident Reporting Programme) (Green, 1985) and in other countries.

There are formal incentives for pilots to report their mistakes to ASRS; ie an immunity from possible prosecution. In contrast, there has been a reluctance to contribute to CHIRP

Having started the day at 0500 Local for an 0715 hrs T/O to Rig "A" and Rig "B" (5 sectors) we duly returned to Aberdeen by 1015 and were then "stood down" (no facilities for rest on base) until 1300 Local for a 1400 hrs T/O to Rig "C". On the return leg at about 1600 I was awoken from a "cat-nap" by the co-pilot asking me if I was awake. Fortunately the aircraft has both height and heading holds and also, we were both very aware of being very tired and overheated in our survival suits (Bright sun - OAT + 4 deg C). Ever cold air failed to alleviate the tiredness. I finally deselected the holds and flew "manually" to keep myself awake. This was not "fatigue" but the effect of a bad night's rest before an early start with a split shift to a late finish, on a hot day, in survival suits. And it was all quite "legal" for duty hours.

Feedback No 14, page 4

Figure 2: Extract from "Feedback"

for fear that anonymity may be compromised (eg Frow, 1993). Besides describing ergonomic deficiencies and breaches of discipline, pilots have used CHIRP to make complaints against what they see as unsafe or illegal practices by their employers, see Figures 2, 3 and 4. That certain employers do take sanctions, or dismiss, pilots who complain about safety measures is publicly documented (Bennetto, 1994; Creighton-Clarke, personal communication[1]).

The SINTEF 'Helicopter Safety Study' (Ingstad et al, 1990) is a major source of incident data. The study investigated the contribution of a variety of "risk factors" to the safety of North Sea helicopter operations. The investigation considered the operational, engineering and management factors contributing to safe flight in support of oil exploration and exploitation and examined three helicopter companies from the UK, one Dutch operator, and the single (at the time of the study) Norwegian company. Researchers collected interview, questionnaire and accident/incident data from the operators.

In contrast to the previously described reviews of "pilot error", the analysis in the SINTEF study attributed only 20% of incidents to "pilot performance", which they defined as, "The degree to which the pilot(s) can be depended upon to act in a manner required." This meant "pilot error" (Sten, personal communication). The majority of incidents in these companies' databases arose from engineering and maintenance deficiencies, even though most were raised by pilots.

After several weeks of rosters of five consecutive nights I informed ops that I would not be doing the fifth night due to extreme fatigue.

On the 4th night whilst en route I was told to change frequency and although I wrote the frequency down I didn't select it. I found this out at the next reporting point when I asked for a direct routing.

Letting down, me PNF, Wx good. PF calls for both on the ILS. I selected both VORs to the ILS but failed to change the DME. The PF had a lot of problems assessing speed relative to distance to go.

At 500ft on the altimeters things looked wrong and I realised we both had QNH selected.

At this stage full flap was called for. I selected it and the PF said "Sorry, that was a little fast".

Colleagues subsequently went on to complete the 5th night but one of them had been told "There are 10 pilots waiting for your job".

Feedback No 28, page 10

Figure 3: Extract from "Feedback"

HEADS THEY WIN, TAILS YOU LOSE

Some years ago this Freight Company accepted a contract for a weight greater than the structural maximum allowed for the type of aircraft.....

.... The heavier ones are unable to lift the maximum structural load let alone the contracted load. With a combination of poor weather, maximum load, minimum sensible fuel uplift and in the interests of safety some freight has to be left behind.

The client has complained to the Company and in turn the Flight Ops. staff have all received a letter from the management of the Company stating that they are expected to ensure that freight is not offloaded. The thinly veiled threat of redundancy and job losses if the contract is lost is very obvious.

.... I am convinced that if a Captain is involved in an incident through "bending the rules" he would receive no support from the Company at any enquiry. In fact he would be "thrown to the wolves".

Feedback No 31, page 5

Figure 4: Extract from "Feedback"

If the incident data collected during the SINTEF study accurately represented accident data one would expect 50% or more of incidents to be due to deficiencies in pilot performance, ie pilot error. To examine this discrepancy, the incident reports from one of the three offshore helicopter operators, based in the UK, were re-examined.

Method

During the SINTEF study, incident databases from all the helicopter operators had been collected. A primary risk factor was allocated to each incident, based upon an interpretation of the circumstances described in narrative accounts of what had happened. This is referred to as RF1. In addition, a secondary risk factor (RF2) was sometimes allocated. The secondary risk factor was a circumstance or condition which in itself did not precipitate the incident, but by being present allowed the incident to develop.

> **To illustrate:** a progressive crack in the fuselage might be attributed to maintenance/inspection, ie RF1. If the the area of the crack was not normally visible during inspection, RF2 would be design/maintainability. If the crack was not easily seen because inspection of an offshore based aircraft routinely took place on an exposed helideck RF2 would be management/economy.

Results and Discussion

A summary of one operator's incident reports for the period of the study are presented here. However, company personnel were not consistent in the terms they used to describe phase of flight. Therefore, in Table 3, the descriptions they used are shown collapsed into three categories: "Cruise", "Climb & Descent" and "Ground".

> **Note:** that one incident was labelled "On ground and In Flight" and has been discarded from this analysis. It concerned an engine cowling which was discovered unlatched whilst in the cruise.

Table 4 shows the risk factors associated with incidents. For ease of analysis, these factors were collapsed into four categories representing people, procedures, equipment and the environment. This is shown in Table 5. Relatively few incidents attracted an additional RF2 and in consequence, these supplementary factors are not considered further.

Table 3: Phases of Flight

Ground	Climb & Descent	Cruise
Daily Inspection	Hover	Cruise
Start	Take Off	En-route
Post Engagement	After Take Off	
After Landing	En-Route Descent	
On Ground	Approach	
On Deck	Final Approach	
Parked	Finals	
Turnaround	Landing	
Servicing	Winching	
Storage		

> The five factors of human error were collapsed to the category of "People Errors". To this category were added "Maintenance Diagnosis" and "Training". In this latter, solitary incident report, a training captain allowed a tail strike during a one engine inoperative landing.
> "Maintenance Procedures", "Operational Procedure" and "Helideck Obstruction" were collapsed into the category "Procedural Errors".
> "Equipment Failings" encompass "Failure Inducing Design", "Faulty Manufacture" and "Component Reliability".

133

"Environment" contains "Birdstrike", "Ice/Rain" and "Unknown". This latter category consists of those occasions when the fault could not be reproduced on the ground.

Table 4: Risk Factors in Different Phases of Flight

Factor	Cruise RF1	Cruise RF2	Climb & Descent RF1	Climb & Descent RF2	On Ground RF1	On Ground RF2
Human Error - Pilot	1	2	1	3	6	0
Human Error - Maintenance	5	1	3	1	6	2
Human Error - Passenger	0	0	0	0	1	0
Human Error - Helideck	0	1	2	0	3	0
Human Error - Groundcrew	0	0	0	0	1	0
Operational Procedure	0	0	0	0	1	0
Failure Inducing Design	13	4	1	0	12	5
Faulty Manufacture	0	0	5	2	0	0
Component Reliability	19	1	1	0	11	0
Maintenance Diagnosis	2	0	2	0	2	0
Maintenance Procedures	0	2	1	0	3	3
Helideck Obstruction	0	0	2	0	1	0
Birdstrike	0	0	0	0	2	0
Ice/Rain	0	1	1	0	0	0
Unknown	0	0	3	0	1	0
Training	0	0	1	0	0	0

Table 5: Risk Factors by Category

Category	Cruise RF1	Cruise RF2	Climb & Descent RF1	Climb & Descent RF2	On Ground RF1	On Ground RF2
People Errors	8	4	9	4	19	2
Procedural Errors	0	2	3	0	5	3
Equipment Failings	32	5	28	6	23	5
Environment	0	1	4	0	3	0

There were 40 "Cruise" incident reports and 44 "Climb & Descent" reports. From the Lufthansa (1994) and Chais and Simpson (1985) summaries we would have expected significantly fewer incidents in the "Cruise" than in "Climb & Descent". Eight "Cruise" and nine "Climb & Descent" reports were attributed to human error, although as can be seen from Table 7, a very small percentage of these are attributable to pilots. Nineteen attributions of human error occurred from a total of 50 incidents occurring whilst the helicopters were on the ground. The data, as percentages, are presented in Table 6 and shown graphically in Figure 5. Note that the percentage of people errors on the ground (38%) is approximately the same as the percentage of errors whilst in flight (40.5%).

However, if the pilots' contribution to these figures is extracted as a percentage of all reports of error there is a change, see Table 7. Although approximately similar percentages are found for "Cruise" (12.5%) and for "Climb & Descent" (11.1%), a considerably larger number of the errors that are made "On Ground" are attributable to pilots (31.5%).

Making the conservative assumption that half the error reports for each stage of flight should be attributable to the pilot, a one-way chi-square suggests the difference in reporting between flight and on the ground is significant ($p < 0.05$, $\chi^2 = 6.26$, $df = 2$). Increasing the expectation of pilot error to 75% increases the value of χ^2 to 17.85, $p < 0.001$.

Table 6: Percentages of Primary Risk Factors

Category	Cruise	Climb & Descent	On Ground
People Errors	20	20.5	38
Procedural Errors	0	6.8	10
Equipment Failings	80	63.6	46
Environment	0	9.1	6

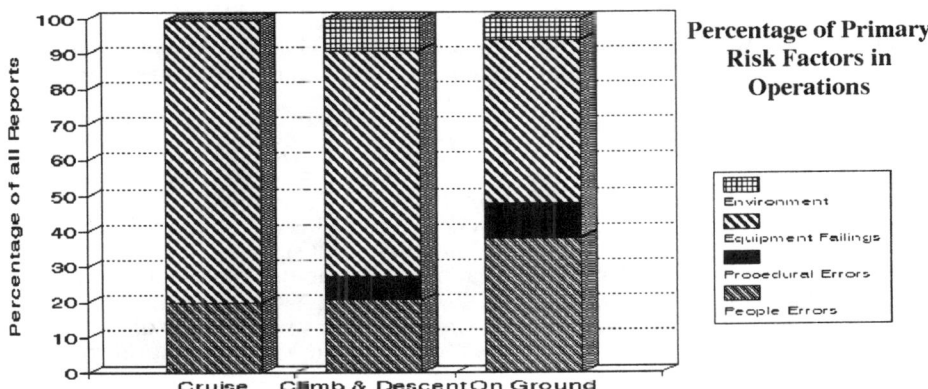

Figure 5: Percentage of Primary Risk Factors in Operations

This analysis is even more conservative than may first appear because many of the "On Ground" incidents are reported by maintenance personnel when a pilot was not near the helicopter, ie during servicing and maintenance. In contrast, all in-flight reports are raised by the pilots.

The most parsimonious explanation is that it is difficult for pilots not to raise reports when they have an incident on the ground. The events, the occasions of incidents and of the pilots' subsequent actions, are likely to be observed by others. Aircrew thus have little choice about making a report. When flying, nobody except the aircrew themselves may know that something untoward has occurred. If the pilots are embarrassed, or expect to be punished if they report the incident, they may be tempted not to do so. Pilots are not responsible for design or maintenance failures. They are, however, considered accountable for their own mistakes.

Table 7: Pilot Error as a Percentage of all Instances of Human Error

Category	Risk Factor 1	Risk Factor 2
Cruise	12.5	50
Climb and Descent	11.1	75
On Ground	31.5	0

Conclusion

The original suggestion that aircraft incident databases accurately reflect accident causation is not supported by the analysis presented here. In particular, it seems probable that occasions of pilot error are significantly underreported when pilots themselves make the reports.

Consequently, this analysis supports the establishment and maintenance of confidential reporting systems such as CHIRP. Despite the acknowledged sampling biases of such schemes they provide evidence of incidents which would otherwise remain unreported.

Notes
1. Captain Creighton-Clarke remonstrated with his employer about breaches of flying regulations. He was dismissed, ostensibly for other reasons, but an industrial tribunal upheld his claim that his dismissal was due to complaining about unsafe and illegal practices.

References
Adams JA (1982) "Issues in Human Reliability" *Human Factors,* 24(1), 1-10
Bennetto J (1994) "Pilot sacked after safety complaints" *The Independent,* 21 March 1994
Billings CE (1991) "The automatic human" *Aerospace,* 18(3), 14-19
Chais RI & Simpson WE (1985) "Investigation of Technology Needs for Avoiding Helicopter Pilot Error Related Accidents" NASA, ORT TR-2384
Chappelow JW (1984) "Human Error in Aircraft Accidents: A Review of Psychologists' Reports on Royal Air Force Accidents 1972-1982" Royal Air Force Institute of Aviation Medicine Report No 633
Diehl AE (1989) "Human performance aspects of aircraft accidents" in RS Jensen (ed) *Aviation Psychology*" Aldershot: Gower Technical
Frow I (1993) "A Sideways Look - No 1: There must be a Better Way" *The Log,* Journal of the British Airline Pilots Association, 54, 6
Green R (1985) "The UK Confidential Human Factors Reporting Programme" Proceedings of the XVI Conference of the Western European Association for Aviation-Psychology, Helsinki, Finland
Hardy R (1990) "*Callback*" Shrewsbury: Airlife Publishing
Ingstad O, Rosness R, Sten T, Ulleberg T, Rausand M & Lydersen S (1990) "Helicopter Safety Study: Main Report" Trondheim: SINTEF Report No STF75 A90008
Lee RB (1985) "Analysis and Evaluation of Human Performance Factors in Aircraft Accident Investigation" Proceedings of the XVI Conference of the Western European Association for Aviation-Psychology, Helsinki, Finland
Lewis ST (1975) "Human Factors in Air Force Aircraft Accidents" *Aviation, Space and Environmental Medicine,* 46(3), 316-318
Lufthansa (1994) "World Aircraft Accident Survey" Frankfurt, Germany, Flight Operations Inspection and Safety
Nagel DC (1988) "Human Error in Aviation Operations" in EL Wiener and DC Nagel (eds) "*Human Factors in Aviation*" London: Academic Press
NTSB (1981) "Special Study: Review of Rotorcraft Accidents, 1977-1979" Washington DC: National Transportation Safety Board Report NTSB-AAS-81-1
Reason JT (1991) "Identifying the latent causes of aircraft accidents before and after the event" Proceedings of the 22nd International Annual Seminar of the International Society of Air Safety Investigators
Ruegger B (1990) "Human Error in the Cockpit" Zurich: Swiss Reinssurance Company
Shanahan DF (1984) "Medical Aspects of Helicopter Safety and Crashworthiness" in "Aeromedical Support in Military Helicopter Operations" AGARD Lecture Series No 134
Sheridan TB (1981) "Understanding human error and aiding human diagnostic behaviour in nuclear power plants" in J Rasmussen and WB Rouse (eds) "*Human Detection and Diagnosis of System Failures*" London: Plenum Press
Van der Schaaf TW (1991) "Introduction" in TW Van der Schaaf, DA Lucas & AR Hale (eds) "*Near Miss Reporting as a Safty Tool*" Oxford: Butterworth-Heinemann
Vyrnwy-Jones P (1984) "A Review of Army Air Corps Helicopter Accidents - 1971-1982" Royal Air Force Institute of Aviation Medicine Report No 632
Wells AT (1991) "*Commercial Aviation Safety*" Blue Ridge Summit, PA: Tab Books

Section C
ACCIDENTS IN GROUND HANDLING

20 Towards an integrated approach for ramp safety management

Hans Oude Egberink, Traffic Research Centre, University of Groningen

This paper was inspired by an analysis of ground handling accidents and incidents data from a number of individual companies that has recently been carried out in the framework of the European SCARF project (Safety Courses for Airport Ramp Functions). It is argued that any company, whether ground handling company, airport authority, or airline, that carries ground handling activities should actively and systematically collect and analyze data on accidents and incidents that occur on the ramp.
The paper concludes with a proposal for a standardized routine in the framework of what might be called a of Ramp Safety Management Tool (RSMT) for the follow-up of accidents on the ramp, including formulating and carrying out countermeasures. A first outline of this routine is presented.

The problem

In contrast to the safety of flight operations, ramp safety is not a major issue in the airline industry. Generally speaking, there exists no such thing as a safety culture on most airport ramps. This is quite surprising because the direct and indirect costs of accidents and incidents on the ramp are enormous, not only in terms of money involved, but sometimes also in terms of human suffering. If a medium sized airline company calculates that the overall annual costs (direct + indirect) of ground handling accidents and incidents only at its home base must be at least some US$ 20,000,000, then the overall industry loss as a result of ramp accidents and incidents alone must be many hundreds of millions of dollars p.a. White (1993) quotes an estimate of an average US$ 20,000 damage caused per rampworker p.a.

Apart from the financial consequences of accidents, especially European companies are by now more or less forced to respond more actively to accidents on the ramp, given the new European legislation regarding occupational safety and health. Actually, this legislation implies no more than that an airport, like any other place where people work, should be a safe place, and that this safety is the company's responsibility. I would also like to refer here to Kerkloh (1992) who presented the view that companies should look after their workforce like they would after their capital resources.

The current situation

An airport platform, especially on larger airports, is a very busy working environment. As a consequence of the design of most airports there is only very limited working space around parked aircraft. In this limited space, many people have to do their job, very often under time pressure, using all kinds of vehicles and equipment that are not always remarkable by the quality of their ergonomic design. Time pressure is a frequent phenomenon in cases of *delay recovery*, i.e. situations in which every effort is made to have an aircraft that has come in late, leave again on time, or at least with a delay that is as small as possible.

Accidents and incidents related to ground handling of aircraft are a very frequent phenomenon. On many airport ramps they literally happen every day. And still it seems as if many companies take the occurrence of ground handling accidents for granted, treat them like acts of God, or accept them after the old saying 'you cannot make an omelette without breaking eggs'. Of course, whenever it is considered necessary, disciplinary actions against the employee(s) involved are taken and existing regulations are adapted or new ones are provided. But very often this is done on an ad hoc basis and there is no well funded policy behind it. E.g. with a number of ramp accidents it may very well be that adequate countermeasures could, at least partly, consist of adapting existing -, or supplying new Standard Operational Procedures for carrying out certain tasks. On the other hand, it is very often the case that adequate SOP's for a certain task do exist, but that in certain situations they are just not adhered to. One of the important reasons for this is that in ground handling of aircraft there is a very important rule which in practice supersedes many safety regulations and which states that, no matter what, the aircraft has to leave on time. As a consequence of this rule, we often see that employees are allowed, or even expected, to break many a (safety) rule as long as the aircraft leaves on time AND as long as they do not cause any damage or injuries to others than themselves. The trouble starts when this last prerequisite is not met.

What should we do

The current situation with regard to safety during ground handling of aircraft must be considered as undesirable. One of the first steps that have to be taken is that, as it is the case in flight operations, management of ramp safety should become an integral part of the overall management of ramp activities. This step implies a sensitization to safety, followed by a commitment to safety, of all levels of ground handling management. In this process, accident data can play an important role.

The importance of collecting accident related data

The most important reason why collection of ground handling accident data should take place is that, if it is done properly, it enables a company to gain insight in the nature and size of the problem with regard to the causation of the accidents as well as the consequences.
Good quality accident data will enable a company to:
- set priorities with regard the safety measures that have to be taken
- formulate adequate countermeasures.
- evaluate countermeasures

We could also quote ICAO Annex 13 here, which states (with regard to flight accidents) that *'The fundamental objective of the investigation of an accident or incident shall be the prevention of accidents and incidents. It is not the purpose of this activity to apportion blame or liability'*.

What types of information should be collected

Roughly speaking, there are two main types of information that should be collected:
1. information on the accident causation process:
    - what happened
    - who was involved
    - how did it happen

- why did it happen and what factors played a role

Many companies already collect some accident information. But very often there exists a parallel with the standard registration of road accident data by the police, which, in many countries, leads to knowledge on WHAT happened and to some extent HOW an accident happened, but not WHY an accident happened. And especially this last information can be considered as crucial in terms of accident prevention. To take the analogy a little further: the primary goal for accident data collection in both systems is often the same: find someone to blame for the accident.

2. information on the outcome of the accident:
- what type of injury was caused to whom
- what caused the injury
- what was the damage to equipment, aircraft, installations (type, location and size)
- what were the consequences (absence, delays, cancellations, etc.)
- what were the costs

A first step towards collecting more information about the causation of accidents, with a little more emphasis on human factors aspects of this process is the experimental IATA/APRG ground accident report form which is currently used by a number of airline companies.

Who should collect the data

In many companies it is currently the case that a ramp worker's (immediate) superior reports on an accident and subsequently collects the necessary data on that accident. There are several reasons why it might be better if the data collection would be done by some other party. Firstly, there is the hierarchical relation that exists between the ramp worker and the reporting person, which might result in biased information. Secondly, it may also very well be that the superior somehow played a role in the accident process. There are many examples of accidents in which ramp workers, e.g. due to time constraints, disregarded safety regulations with the explicit consent of their superior. We wholly agree with White (1993) who pleads for an independent, fulltime and fully qualified ramp accident investigator with competence in the field of human factors.

Ramp safety management using accident data: suggestions for a standard approach

In many companies there is quite a lot of information available on accidents and incidents and their consequences. The problem, however, is the fact that very often this knowledge is fragmentary, i.e. it is scattered over several departments, and there is no one who has an overview. For a typical accident resulting in aircraft damage, equipment damage as well as injuries to an employee, it may very well be that information on the causation of the accident is with the ground handling department, on the injuries sustained with the medical department, on temporary staff that has to be hired because of the injuries with the personnel department, on the resulting flight delays with the operations department, on the damage types and costs with the company's repair shop, on angry passengers who missed their connecting flight, walked away and swore never to come back with customer's department, etc. As a consequence of this situation, the available information is not used optimally. It is our experience that even within a department, sometimes accident data collection is more or less considered as a goal in itself. E.g. data on the causation of an accident are collected but just stored and used for almost no other purposes than to take disciplinary action against the employees involved.

What I would like to propose here is that companies that do ground handling should start to actively monitor and analyze safety on the ramp using *all* available accident data on a regular basis. An integral part of the monitoring process would have to be the feedback of all pertinent information on accidents, including the results of analyses, to the departments that were involved. This feedback should have a routine follow-up that could actually consist of the question: 'what has been done with the information and are any actions that have been taken acceptable?'. This whole process could be significantly enhanced if the company would have a central ramp safety department or group, whose main task would be the collection, analysis and interpretation of all available information regarding ramp accidents. An first important prerequisite for such a department or group would be that the people working in it should be independent, i.e. should not stand in a direct hierarchical relation to the employees working at the ramp, ground handling management, or other suppliers of information.

A second prerequisite would be that these people should be given enough authority in the company, in order to ensure that
- they will be taken seriously
- proposals they make are actually picked up, i.e. at least given serious consideration.

This can only happen if there is a high commitment to safety in ground handling up to high levels in a company's management.

I do not propose here to create a new stream of forms and other paperwork, i.e. literally move a copy of all of this information to a central point, although, in smaller companies, this might be an option. Rather, given the rather high level of automation and the availability of computer networks in many companies, access to this information could be made available via a computer program at one central point in the company. The program should function as an analysis tool that allows the user to crosslink all information from the available sources.

A useful and simple first exercise to identify possibly relevant departments in a company that could have information on the causation or outcome of an accident would be to design a number of plausible accident scenarios and systematically take these through all departments in that company.

Concluding remarks

Based on our own observations, we would argue that today, the farther we move away from actual flight operations, the less safety plays an important role. If, however, ground handling of an aircraft is regarded as an integral part of the flight cycle, and I see no reason why this should not be the case, this situation should change drastically.

I am very well aware of the fact that the points that I have presented here involve investments, or in other words, have financial consequences. I am also certain, however, that compared to the current costs of ramp accidents, these investments will only be very small and that, within a limited time, these investments will start to bring profit, both for the employees involved in ramp accidents as for the companies they work for.

References

ICAO (1988), *International standards and recommended practices on aircraft accident investigation; Annex 13 to the Convention on international civil aviation.* 7th edition. Montreal.
Kerkloh, M. (1992), *The socio-psychological consequences of personal injuries on the ramp - the Frankfurt experience.* Paper presented at the International Air Transport Association seminar 'Creating the safety culture on the ramp', Miami, Florida, 26-27 October 1992.
White, G. (1993), *Safety in ramp operations.* Paper presented at the 22nd technical conference Human Factors in Aviation, Montreal, Canada, 4-8 October 1993

21 The use of international data in the analysis of accidents

George White and Nick McDonald
Department of Psychology, Trinity College Dublin

The ultimate cost of damage to an aircraft while it is on the ground, especially if unreported or unrecognised, is its potential for a major flight disaster. Secondly, an accident on the airport ramp can generate a substantial human cost to both the individual and family affected.by a death, serious disablement and chronic injury There are huge direct and indirect costs to the industry of ground damage to fragile and expensive aircraft, to damaged vehicles, equipment and structure, together with the financial costs of injury and death to personnel. These collectively represent a serious and unnecessary haemorrhage of scarce resources.

The aviation industry, especially in the economic climate of today, has a powerful vested interest in reducing ramp accident generated costs. This vested interest is the engine which should drive the industry and the national and international regulatory agencies, to address, in a cost efficient way, the human failure aspects of ramp accidents.

It is necessary to establish the type of accidents which are occurring and the related causal factors, as a first step. Until recently, in marked contrast to the flight phase, there has been no systematic collection by the international aviation community of data concerning the contributions made by human factors to ramp accidents.

Since 1990 the Aerospace Psychology Research Group, based in Trinity College Dublin, has been collaborating closely with the Ramp Safety Group of the IATA Ground Handling Council in research into the development of a more comprehensive and consistent reporting system, the analysis of the data and practical application of the results to new training initiatives. A new accident report form was developed. It was designed for ease of use and struck a balance between obtaining usable information and the maximum which could be expected from a busy ramp manager. It requested, inter alia, details of the circumstances of the accident, the personnel category involved, (no names) and identification of causal and contributory factors selected from coded protocols. It also requested information on the consequences of the accident - damage, injury and direct/indirect costs together with actions taken and recommendations made.

The accident reporting system has three main objectives:

1. *causes*

   The systematic investigation of human factors aspects of ramp accidents, together with other causal and contributory factors. A complete and reliable picture of the pattern of causation of ramp accidents is essential to developing a programme of preventive measures. Human factors underlie a very large proportion of of accidents on the airport ramp and have received little systematic attention up until now.

2. *norms*

   The establishment of industry norms of accident rates in terms of the frequency of different types of accidents per index of exposure (number of aircraft departures, number of vehicles or pieces of equipment, for example). Such norms provide the basis for the evaluation of trends over extended periods of time, and enable individual enterprises to compare their performance with the norms within the industry.

3. *costs*

   Obtaining information on costs (both direct and indirect) and other consequences of ramp accidents (personnel injuries/fatalities, flight cancellations and delays, damage). Only through the quantification of the consequences of ramp accidents (particularly the financial costs) will it be possible to provide a cogent rationale for significant investments by the industry in measures which will enhance safety on the airport ramp.

The system was designed as a "one-work-process" operation for the reporting agencies; that is, the report form is designed so that each accident report could be filled in by one person at one time. This was to minimise the administrative burden of reporting and maximise the number of reports submitted to the system.

A six month preliminary trial of the reporting scheme was carried out from January to June 1993, which produced 600+ reports. The reporting worldwide participants were the 13 representative members of the IATA

Ground Handling Council Ramp Safety Group. Reporting confidentiality and anonymity were strictly maintained with de-identification of the reporting source. This IATA/ APRG database centered in Trinity College Dublin dealt with reports in which damage occurred to aircraft, vehicles/equipment or facilities.

The reporting system groups contributory factors into five main categories
1. Regulations or procedures not followed.
2. Equipment misused or defective
3. Organisational failures.
4 Behavioural (performance) failures
5 Hazardous physical circumstances.

These main categories of contributory human factors involved in **aircraft** damage are represented in the data base by the following percentages:

Regulations /Procedures: 57%
Equipment 31%
Organisational: 25%
Behavioural: 70%
Physical circumstances: 25%

For **equipment** only damage accidents, the picture is very similar with BEHAVIOUR/PERFORMANCE FAILURE accounting for 76% and REGULATIONS/PROCEDURES NOT FOLLOWED at 55%

If we examine these behavioural and procedural factors in more detail for the combined data for **aircraft and equipment** accidents the following picture emerges:

Failure to see: 27%
Poor judgement: 24%
Spatial misjudgement: 22%
Poor discipline: 17%
Other factors each < 7%

The same exercise for the REGULATIONS/PROCEDURES NOT FOLLOWED group shows the following picture :

SOPs not followed 33%
Safety regs. not followed 26%
Traffic regs. not followed 15%
Other factors each <1%

These figures tend to show that perceptual judgement failures are predominant in the behaviour/performance data . It is also clear that regulations not followed were a salient group of factors. Further analysis of the data determined the degree to which these results were independent of each other. Did the misjudgement accidents happen because of the intrinsic unavoidable difficulty of the task or were those involved in the accidents ignoring SOPs and regulations? The analysis showed that for **aircraft accidents** 65% of the misjudgement problems were associated with a breach of procedures or regulations and for **equipment accidents** the figure was 60% Therefore, while demanding spatial /perceptual problems are present in the various tasks associated with servicing aircraft, there is a clear problem of personnel failing to adhere to SOPs and regulations. In this respect it is very relevant that the factors of poor discipline and inadequate supervision were identified in 25% of all accidents. Incorrect use of equipment and limited space were each reported in ten percent or more of the accidents.

A more detailed analysis of accident reports in relation to selected types of equipment involved in both vehicle/equipment damage and aircraft damage accidents is underway. This analysis focusses upon the causal and contributory factors, phase of operation and the narrative reports pertaining to individual types of equipment. It aims to elucidate in as much detail as the reports allow the issues which need to be addressed in relation to each piece of equipment. This analysis is in progress. Completion of the detailed analyses of individual pieces of equipment will lead to the identification of common trends.

For example, analysis of 52 accidents inolving **container/pallet loaders** which resulted in aircraft damage indicated that:

The positioning of equipment close to the aircraft and the manoeuvering of the equipment around the aircraft were both heavily involved in accident causation.

Overwhelmingly these accidents involved visual and spatial problems made up of failure to see (involved in 27% of accidents), misjudging spatial position (40%) and poor judgement (27%). 42% of accidents involved failure to follow regulations or procedures, 37% involved incorrect use of equipment and 10% defective maintenance.

Detailed analysis of the individual accident reports indicate that a major problem concerns a mismatch between the equipment being used and the aircraft being handled and this implicated particular aircraft types. In addition defects in the ergonomic design of equipment were also highlighted.

Identification of contributory factors should not be seen as a definitive allocation of causes. The main relevance of this procedure is to make it easier to begin to design countermeasures which can help to eliminate or ameliorate a problem. It should always be born in mind that the assignment of contributory factors necessarily involves an element of interpretation and is susceptible to reporter bias, subjectivity and errors of judgement. While major efforts are necessary to clarify ambiguity and ensure understanding of all aspects of the reporting process, problems of reliability, consistency and interpretation in different cultures remain.

Analysis of accident reports is ongoing, but at this stage it is possible to highlight a few general themes which link a large number of ramp accidents. This commentary should be regarded as provisional.

PROCEDURES

Standard operating procedures require a comprehensive review. This review should pose the following questions, amongst others:
- are the procedures adequate to guide action?
- is the task adequately specified for procedures?
- are procedures compatible with other operational goals?
- do operatives know the procedures? How are they promulgated?
- is there adequate monitoring and enforcement of procedures?
- what consequences normally follow failure to follow SOPs (when no accident ensues)?

Visual/Sensing Devices on Equipment and Facilities

Much ramp equipment is clearly defective in terms of making provision for adequate vision and spatial judgement. This is an issue of basic ergonomics which should not pose insurmountable technical or financial problems.

Equipment Positioning

Many accidents occur at the aircraft stand because the positioning of other equipment is not always anticipated. The possibility of improved standardisation of equipment positioning and movements around the aircraft should be explored. This should include a review of unnecessary equipment movements or positioning.

Ramp Resource Management

The provision of adequate personnel resources, adequately trained and motivated, clearly aware of the company's goals and priorities is a basic requirement of a safe operation. A major general implication points to the importance of the development of more effective training for the management of human resources on the ramp at all levels of the enterprise (management, supervisory, trainers and operatives).

Section D
CRISIS MANAGEMENT

22 'It's not over yet': mitigating the effects of disasters and traumatic incidents

Gerard P.S. Jackson, Metropolitan Police, Heathrow Airport

Over 90% of people are likely to suffer some reactions similar to the symptoms of Post Traumatic Stress Disorder after they have been exposed to a traumatic incident which is outside their normal experience, though few develop the full blown syndrome.

A study involving Police Officers who worked at the scene of the Lockerbie disaster found absence due to sickness increased by 58% the year after the disaster compared to the year before. Absence due to accidental injury increased by over 300%.

This has resource implications for all organisations. Even if we do not care about our staff at all, people are likely to be absent from work and even if they are at work they may be accident prone and unable to concentrate. Some people recover naturally after a period of weeks but the majority of people recover more quickly if steps are taken to reduce their levels of stress before the incident, during the incident and afterwards.

The proposal then is to provide a comprehensive system of care for people who are likely to be involved in managing a crisis such as aircraft disaster and also less traumatic incidents such as accidental death or injury during aircraft operations. The proposal consists of 5 phases:
1. To select appropriate staff for particular jobs.
2. To train staff for those jobs and prepare them psychologically
3. To manage staff in the most appropriate way
4. Provide short term support after the incident
5. Provide whatever long term support is required.

Selection

Selection of personnel to be involved in traumatic incidents is obviously seldom possible. However, it is possible to identify, in advance, personnel who it is intended to utilise, in the event of a severe crisis, to do particularly traumatic tasks.

Staff should have a reasonable level of existing life experience. Young people often have greater difficulty in placing the experience of the incident alongside the rest of their experience. They should have a flexible nature with a resilient sense of humour. They should not have had too much previous exposure to trauma, personal or work oriented. People recently bereaved or involved in trauma are likely to have particular difficulties. They should have good personal relationships and support networks. Exposure to traumatic incidents is likely to adversely effect an already unstable relationship. It will help if they are part of a supportive working team.

Training

The training should be of two types:-
a) Training staff to do the actual job envisaged
b) Increasing their awareness of the psychological effect of involvement.
Both types of training will have the effect of minimising the 'surprise' factor. It is much less stressful to do work you are thoroughly trained to do.

Staff management

Staff need to feel cared for and anything which helps that feeling develop should be encouraged. Exposure to the incident may need to be limited but managers should not be over anxious or over controlling. The dividing line between workers becoming over-involved to the extent where they become a liability, and allowing workers to complete a job they have started can be a difficult one to identify, but the stress caused by taking a worker out of a situation before his or her task is finished may be worse then leaving him or her to finish the job.

Workers often express resentment that their efforts were not noticed or appreciated by management so a word of two of acknowledgement and praise every now and then is helpful. 'Gallows' humour is often used to help workers to cope and should not be discounted. The team should be made to feel supported by the management, and inadequate resources or equipment will increase stress levels.

Sufficient breaks should be allowed preferably at a time when the workers themselves feel the need. Additionally workers who leave because of obvious distress should be seen and encouraged to talk about their distress. This is so that, after an opportunity to vent their feelings, they can return to work.

Before the team go off duty it will be helpful if each member has a chance to have a 15 or 20 minutes conversation with a manager or outside individual just to talk through any outstanding concerns he or she may have. An acknowledgement of a good job done under difficult circumstances is appropriate at this time. Staff should be told that a full debriefing will follow within the next few days

Short term support

Within 24 to 72 hours after the incident a team debriefing should be held. The model suggested is called Critical Incident Stress Debriefing (CISD) and can best be described as a psychologically and educationally based group discussion which has been carefully designed to achieve two main goals. First, it is intended to mitigate against the impact of the event in order to limit the damage incurred by personnel. Second, it has been designed to accelerate normal recovery processes in normal people who have normal reactions to abnormal events.

A CISD is not psychotherapy, psychoanalysis or group therapy. Neither should be it be seen as in any way similar to, or combined with, a debriefing on the practical issues arising from an incident. One of the most important issues for a trained CISD team is to clearly recognise that the population is not a psychiatric population but a population which is normal and has simply been exposed to an event which has temporarily overwhelmed their abilities to cope effectively.

The CISD process should not be viewed as a final, absolute "do or die" intervention technique. It is one of the earliest steps in a process of recovery. There is always room for additional therapeutic contract and the debriefing team should recognise that one of the great values of the debriefing is in the window it provides into the group to assess the need for further intervention.

If it was a very large incident several debriefings will be necessary as the number included in any one meeting should be about 15 or 20 maximum. Attendance at the Debriefing should be mandatory. In many organisations, if the system is of the 'opt in' type workers are unlikely to admit that they need any help and will not attend. Members of the group should not have any other duty to perform at that time and it may be necessary to set aside as much as 5 or 6 hours after a large incident to allow sufficient time to accomplish the tasks. The debriefing will occupy a shorter time for a smaller scale incident. It will be helpful if some form of light refreshment is available in the room and toilets should be close by. Participants should be encouraged to use the toilets before the debriefing starts and interruptions from external factors should not be permitted. Critical Incident Stress Debriefing consists of seven phases:-

Introduction Phase

The task here is to motivate the team and set the ground rules. The group is encouraged to participate actively in the discussions which is to follow and at the same time they are told that they do not have to speak. The issue of confidentiality is heavily emphasised. Finally, the group is told how the debriefing will proceed and that if anyone leaves the room in distress one of the debriefers will go with them to offer support. They will be encouraged to return to the the debriefing.

Fact Phase

The participants are asked to say who they are, what their role was in the incident and what happened during the operation. A brief synopsis of the operational activities is usually sufficient. It is helpful if all the participants have a knowledge of the whole of the incident. Before the debriefing starts they may be in possession of only some of the facts and it helps in the mental organisation of the events to have the gaps filled in.

Thought Phase

The task here is to get participants to discuss the first or most prominent thought which entered their mind during the incident. This is frequently the first time that the members of the group have had the opportunity to personalise their experience by expressing their personal thoughts on the situation.

Reactions and Feelings Phase

This is undoubtedly the most emotionally powerful part of the debriefing. People could be asked to answer the question "what was the worst part for you personally?" This phase should try to elicit how people felt and encourage them to talk about their emotional reactions. Emotional Reactions such as anger, fear, frustration, grief, loss, emptiness, guilt, helplessness are very common during debriefings. All the feelings are accepted as valid and normal under the abnormal circumstances of the event.

Signs and Symptoms Phase

The group participants are enabled to discuss specific signals of distress which they may have experienced, either during the incident, a short while later and at the time of the debriefing. These might include sleep disturbance, disturbing flashbacks or dreams, tears etc etc. By comparing their reactions the group is helped to realise that they and their reactions are normal.

Teaching Phase

This is an important opportunity for the debriefing team to teach stress survival skills to the group and to give information as to some of the normal reactions which may develop for people over the coming weeks. Many practical suggestions are made and personnel are encouraged to continue to take appropriate steps to manage their stress in the days which follow.

Re-entry Phase

Here future planning and coping are discussed particularly in terms of family and peer group support and fostering cohesion within the group. During this phase sources of further support will be mentioned and some guide-lines as to when members might need to seek further help.

The above is intended only to be a brief synopsis of the system of Psychological Debriefing. Debriefers should receive special training before doing this work but this need not be of long duration nor need the trainees be 'experts'. It is suggested that trainees have facilitation skills or counselling skills to enable them to deal with the emotional content of the debriefing.

Following the CISD organisations should make sure that one to one counselling is available for anyone who feels that it could be helpful and, again, the confidentiality of the whole process should be assured. Most people recover fully after the CISD though a small number may require some short term counselling to assist the process (About 1 to 4 sessions).

Long Term Support

Only in a small percentage of cases is long term counselling or treatment likely to be required because a person has developed the full blown Post Traumatic Stress Disorder. In this case intervention should be by properly qualified professionals. 'Ordinary' counsellors are not likely to have the skills or medical back-up to provide an appropriate level of help. PTSD is a difficult syndrome to treat once it become entrenched and the procedures outlined above can help in accelerating recovery and preventing the onset of PTSD.

23 Training for trauma: a real life study

John A. Connolly and Margaret Connolly
Solace International Emergency Management, Dublin

Simulated exercises have become more popular and common in recent years. They are viewed as a way of preparing staff to deal with the eventuality of disaster. Most Airline companies, as a matter of policy, schedule at least one major simulation per year. These will typically be airside events, such as fire or collision, or else a situation in which the incident is planned to have occurred at some distant point, and this simulation attempts to focus on events at the home Airport or base.

The authors believe that a number of factors or themes are common. Firstly, the attitude of the company involved is particularly relevant. Budgetary constraints, the relationship between the Airline and Airport Authority, and flight scheduling form a particularly important backdrop to what occurs. These issues tend to set the tone for the way in which the simulation is carried out, and therefore essentially determine its effectiveness.

Staff responsible for organising and managing the simulation tend to have ambivalent attitudes. On the one hand, their professionalism strongly advises them to keep their staff well trained and experienced through simulation, in order to reduce the putative effects of a catastrophic incident. The incidence of disaster is sufficient to keep this constantly in mind. However, the required annual simulation may also be seen as a chore, to be met with relief when completed, and a sense of duty having been done. Exercises may also be seen as a potential source of embarrassment.

Therefore, while the exercise may be planned diligently, it may be seen as an end in itself, and not used as effectively as might be to benefit company staff. Most exercises in practise will develop unexpected, chaotic or indeed very humorous aspects, and may be deviated or deflected from their expected course by unplanned external events. These are to be expected, and indeed may add to the reality of the simulation. However, relatively little attention has been given to the affect of the simulation on staff themselves.

They are not typically involved in pre-planning or developing exercises, probably in the mistaken belief that any exercise should be as unexpected and shocking in its occurrence as possible, and ideally should catch the staff unawares. The belief in this aspect of simulation is so strong that it tends to blind management to other aspects of pre-planning, where staff can indeed be involved to great effect. The preparation, evaluation and follow up with regard to groups not under direct company control, such as volunteers acting as meeters and greeters, is typically ignored.

In our opinion the experience of simulation can in fact be significantly disturbing for a large number of participants, who may feel disorientated, troubled and overly emotional both during and after the event. While one aim of simulation is to allow people the opportunity to experience a realistic enactment, it should not stop there, and while the simple shocking, distressing or confusing of staff may define the simulation as "very real", it may leave a legacy of distress, embarrassment and indeed anger among staff, if not developed appropriately and in context.

This paper refers to a company, SimAir, with 20 to 30 employees at an airfield and fuel supply depot, and an office in the local town, which has approximately 25 staff. The company policy is to use those staff directly to man the telephone response to an emergency. Staff are expected to man the phones dealing either with press or relatives.

A simulated exercise had occurred approximately nine months before the involvement of Solace. SimAir consultants had designed and implemented a simulated exercise, using the services of a large group of individuals. These were instructed to act as a hungry pack of media people, and a similar group representing relatives was also organised. On the day of the simulation the staff were informed of an oil storage fire and explosion, with resulting casualties, and thrown into a brilliantly simulated "real life' experience. The exercise was highly professional, well-constructed, and efficient, proceeding perfectly as the organisation had planned. Unfortunately, no preparation or input from staff was requested, and no debriefing or follow up occurred. In the months afterwards it became apparent that staff had been troubled by their experience, felt impotent at their perceived lack of competence during the simulation, and felt a degree of anger towards management, feeling in some way let down. Solace was asked to become involved and to develop an educational and training input of benefit to staff.

During an initial seminar with approximately 20 staff, a clear residual wariness and resistance was noted, so the seminar was allowed develop into an interactive session, with emphasis on the free exchange of information. The evaluation of cues from staff led Solace to emphasise the following points repeatedly:

1. Any further training would be organised and developed in conjunction with staff.

2. Staff needs and responses would determine how further input was constructed.

3. It was emphasised that SimAir positively wished to obtain staff input, and to satisfy their needs.

A number of questions were asked, in order to establish the attitude and belief system of staff. Almost three in four (72%) believed it was not normal to have complete co-operation among staff who were working under stress. Only 57% knew which individual would direct and manage their own section in the event of an emergency. There was very little agreement on what advance planning should be made, but staff observations were interesting, and confirmed that staff tended to rely on an external locus of control, rather than seeing themselves as active or controlling.

While the majority felt there were good reasons to be prepared for emergency, believing it improved performance, lessened panic and stress, and could save lives, few had any clear planning made in regard to their own family. One in four gave no comment, the same number thought home should be "informed", and some 37% thought vaguely that one should "make arrangements" or "have a plan".

All staff thought that it was possible to help each other at work after a disaster, 58% through talking, 13% through consoling, and 29% through group processes. 88% felt that debriefing was important, and a surprisingly high figure of 83% felt that counselling should be mandatory for all staff after an event. The benefit of this was explained as normalising staff (50%), reducing isolation or reducing anxiety (25% each).

It was seen clearly that the possible catastrophic effect of bad media coverage was apparent to staff, and they desperately needed further training and support in this area.

Following this first session another seminar was held for staff, with four declared aims, confidence building, an overview of emergency and disaster, outlining probable response to relatives and media, and effective coping.

Follow-up showed that the demand for increased training, both in counselling and handling relatives, had dropped from 36 to 4%, and the demand for more staff input from 13 to 0%. The staff displayed a more extensive understanding of what would be relevant, and were clearer in their demands, for example on issues such as needing a formal Director when they were working, and having more staff available. 22% specifically mentioned that debriefing should be made available after the exercise.
Active worry about a disaster happening had reduced, and a fully positive response to staff being involved in the aftermath was obtained. Positive responses increased from 50 to 100%

On both occasions 60% of staff felt they would be judged by the Company on their performance. However, after input they showed a clearer delineation of their task, and an alteration from strongly feeling their response should be "the best" (which is in fact very vague) to a clearer perception of how their co-operative and assured input will result in a professional presentation which is company favourable.

The vaguer need for understanding has dropped from 28 to 16%, and the more specific need for debriefing and counselling has increased from 26 to 37%.

Participants Response to Educational Input.

Staff were asked to give their response to the input they received. and were generally positive. When asked to specify 40% stated that learning about the probable problems of relatives, and the questions that they might ask, was most helpful, and 60% felt that the sharing of personal experience by Solace staff was the most helpful. The 'least helpful aspects were a variety of comments, such as staff disliking the slides, as they upset them too much, or preferring a video presentation of disaster, as it would be more vivid.

Relaxation exercises were too brief, and more practical examples of situations was also requested. It was remarked that no "policy makers" were present at the sessions (although it appeared that this had not been desired when the session was planned). One staff member complained that their peers did too much talking during the session.

Evaluation of input showed staff had become more specific and clearer about their needs, which is the first step in interactive education. As a final point, the participants were also asked to suggest what both Solace and the Company should next do, and requested Solace involvement in exercise debriefing, and that the company formulate and explain policy more clearly, set-up training programes and define counselling and debriefing access and availibility.

Specific non-company involvement is essential in debriefing and counselling, as it appropriately protects staff from management, as well as offering other benefits. The responses obtained confirms that such external input can be utilised positively by staff. It is clear from responses that staff have a strong need to know a company policy exists, and to have this explained clearly to them.

Discussion.

This paper describes the effect of a simple training and educational input designed to make Company staff more effective in the face of emergency or disaster. It argues that simulated exercises are useless, and indeed can be counterproductive and damaging, if not placed within an appropriate context of staff involvement, pre-training, setting of objectives, debriefing and follow-up.

Effective educational input demands clear objectives, appropriate preparation, learner involvement, and evaluation of the programme. Company staff can be a major resource when emergency arises. If abused or disregarded, poorly managed staff will effect a negative image on the Company and present with expensive and distracting problems for months or years afterwards. If used in a positive fashion however, the Company can use its experience of emergency to grow its own staff, to develop confidence, and in particular to present a positive profile to the World.

24 The ripple-off effect of aviation disasters on families and children

Margaret Connolly and John A. Connolly
Solace International Emergency Management, Dublin

"A pain which has not been understood inevitably reappears; like an unlaid ghost it cannot rest until the mystery has been solved and the spell broken.' (Freud 1909)

Airline disasters are not an everyday occurrence. but when they do occur the impact, not only on the families involved but on the general public, friends and neighbours, can be enormous. In the immediate post-impact stage the media-hype is tremendous and people around the world are shown scenes of the devastation.

However, very little is shown of the silent grief of people who may have known someone on board that particular flight; the elderly aunts and uncles who may be on the periphery of the trauma, but would be feeling as intensely as if they were involved in the drama; the newspaper man who may have handed the newspaper regularly to someone who had been on board that flight; the staff members with whom that person may have worked for many years; teachers who may be teaching that person's children currently, or indeed the teachers who may have taught that person many years ago.

The authors' mention but a few of the people who may be touched by the loss of one person in an airline disaster. Multiply this by two or three hundred, depending on the type of plane, and we have a huge ripple-off effect.

In the authors' opinion this ripple-off effect must not be ignored and health care workers and professionals need to become more aware of how to handle and support those people touched by such a large effect.

In order to understand the meaning of trauma the authors find Freud's (1920) definition is relevant, and leads us to a greater understanding of the helplessness of the ego. "The essence of a traumatic situation is an experience of helplessness on the part of the ego in face of accumulation of excitation, whether of external or internal origin. The ego is bereft and attacked both internally and externally. There is nothing to hold on to, it is as if the whole self is falling apart and splitting."

Comprehending this definition leads us to a glimpse of the bewildering state of helplessness and turmoil that one is thrown into after experiencing a traumatic event. One's own personal experience has to be called on in order to survive. Freud (1920) took into consideration the importance of certain life threatening external events in "Beyond the Pleasure Principle" "The notion of trauma implied an organization, that of the mind, invaded by stimulation so intense that normal psychic activity is devastatingly paralysed and reduced, since the mind's over-riding task is to muster all its available energy to immobilise the unmanageable quantities of excitation pouring through the breach in the protective shield". He is giving due importance to the shattering effect of certain life threatening external events.

It seems that Freud's descriptions encompasses the collection of symptoms for Post Traumatic Stress Disorder found in the diagnostic criteria in the DSM 3 R (American Psychiatric Association, 1987). It has to be remembered that, as yet, children have not been given a special category in the DSM for Post Traumatic Stress Disorder.

The behaviour of children involved in a traumatic incident, or indeed children whose families and friends have been involved in such an incident, demonstrates a different response to that of adults. Children appear to have better coping mechanisms than adults and they work through the trauma in their own way, depending on their age. How they react is not the way adults expect them to react, and adults often say: 'It seems like nothing has happened, my Tom just went out to play with his friends the next day.' Many adults find this shocking as they expect the child to react like themselves. What we have to remember is that this is the child's way of coping and it must be respected.

Children of different age groups also react in different ways. It has been found that pre-school and adolescent children cope less effectively than the child in the 5 - 11 year age group - the latency period. All the literature emphasises the importance of the way in which parents and carers cope with their own trauma and recommends they contain their own anxieties. This, however, places a huge burden on them.

The authors' were involved in therapy with a family who lost their father in a plane crash many years previously. The body was never recovered. There were six children ranging in age from 7 to 19 years. The themes which emerged in this case are similar to those mentioned in the DSM. However, at the time of the crash no-one was aware of these symptoms and they were not recognized as a particular syndrome or disorder.

However, life moved on and subsequently the family members left school, went to University and got married. They appeared to have coped with the traumatic event. Their own children were born.

Each mother explained, when asked by their own children where their grandfather was, that he was dead and had been killed in an aircrash. Very little was stated about the grandfather, but as the children grew, particularly from the age of about seven or eight, they began to ask questions. It was as if an unlaid ghost had to re-appear before finally resting. The mothers were now faced with the reality of what had happened and they knew it was important how they handled the answer, so they sought professional help to learn how to answer their children's questions.

A sample of questions asked by the children were: Why was there no body? How was my grandfather killed? What is an explosion? What does a bomb do to a plane? Surely if we went out now and went to the bottom of the sea we would find the bodies? Let's get the airline and give out to them. What did my grandfather look like? What colour was his hair? Was he tall? Was he kind? They had seen their own friends with grandfathers bringing them for special treats and this had to be coped with by the family. All of these seem macabre questions, but the children needed answers. The reality of this was the mothers now realised that, for the first time, they were able to talk openly about what had happened.

At a birthday party one of the grandchildren asked: Granny how did my Grandfather die? A huge irony for the mothers was that, after protecting their mother for so many years, here were their own children asking her blatant facts. However, it transpired that the grandmother felt it was important to tell the truth and faced all the questions with an openness which stunned her own children.

From then on as the questions came up they were answered in a manner that was appropriate to the age of the child. Each child's questions varied depending on the different age, and the positive thing that emerged was that the children felt free to ask questions at any time. It was also decided that an old video would be shown to the children so they could actually see what their grandfather looked like. The children felt safe enough to express their opinions and it appears they were contained and their questions could be answered honestly and truthfully.

One question continually asked by the children was could they see the monument which had been erected in memory of those killed in the plane crash. At present the families are hoping to go. Each mother stated that they personally felt they still needed to return to the accident site. They also stated they would go as individual families as even now they are not sure how they might cope with the hugeness of emotions if they all went together.

The therapist's question is:

Did the mothers, in some way, through their transference, shift their idolisation of their father, their memories, dreams and hopes, on to their own children.? Is this what happens to the children of children involved in traumas or is this an unusual case?

It is the authors' opinion that until this family return to the site and say their farewells the ghost will not be laid.

Interestingly in "Memorial Candles: Children of the Holocaust" Dina Vardi (1982) suggests "that the conflict and emotions relating to their devastation and losses become frozen in an emotional muteness, a zone of apathy in their personality". This is repeated in their children's inability to talk about their own feelings and their sense of being "dead" inside. Born into profound emptiness of their parent's emotional muteness, the children of survivors become a symbol of the security, belonging and continuity their parents had lost.

Is this also true of other types of disasters? Do the children of traumatized children all carry memorial candles and is this an expected pattern which emerges in the children of children involved in disasters. The answer to this question will emerge as research progresses but up to recently there have been surveys done on children of children and the effects trauma has on them and their family.

From the studies done to date it appears that some children develop emotional disturbance following traumatic experiences. In some cases the disturbances are short-lived but some may persist. It seems that stress reactions appear to be milder in childhood than adulthood, but pre-school and adolescent children are more likely to develop fears. Terr (1983) claims that children "do not usually show amnesia for the event, nor do they manifest psychic numbing, intrusive flashbacks. However, children become preoccupied with re-enactments of the events, nightmares and fears, and could be prone to reacting adversely to later, milder stressors, if these are similar to the previous ones."

These re-enactments and fears could, in the authors' opinion, in some instances be termed as flashbacks. As Yule (1990) stated he is "not convinced that children do not experience flashbacks."

In conclusion it must be emphasised that children are normally resilient and seem to cope with trauma better than adults. How well the trauma is handled will establish the child's coping mechanisms for the future. However, experience of our life threatening event will predispose to a more acute reaction in the future.

References

Freud, S. (1909) Analysis of a phobia in a five year old boy. S.E., Hogart, London.

Freud, S. (1920), Beyond the Pleasure Principle, S.E. XX, Hogarth, London.

Terr, L. (1983), 'Chowchilla revisited: the effects of psychic trauma four years after a school bus kidnapping,' Am.J.Psychiatry. 140, 1543-lSS0.

Vardi, D. (1992), Memorial Candles: Children of
the Holocaust, Tavistock/Routledge.

Yule, W. & Williams, R.M. (1990) Post Traumatic Stress Reactions in Children. J.Traum.Stress 3: 279-96.

American Psychiatric Association: Diagnostic and Statistical Manual of Mental Disorders. (Third edition, revised). 1987, Washington, D.C.

Part 4
CROSS-CULTURAL FACTORS

25 Cross-cultural aspects of Human Factors in a multi-national, multi-cultural airline

Capt. Majid Kabbani, Saudi Arabian Airlines

Introduction

Saudia Arabian Airlines (Saudia) is the flag carrier of the Kingdom of Saudi Arabia, and is the largest Airline in the middle East.

Its was founded in 1945 with a single McDonnell Douglas DC-3 devoted primarily to government use. Saudia soon developed into the primary means of transport within the vast areas of the Kingdom. As such, it has played a pivotal role in the astonishing development of the country.

The total number of its fleet stands at 111 including the Boeing series 707s, 737s, 747s (100s, 200s, 300, special performance and freighters); Airbus Industrie A300-600s, and Lockheed Tristar L-1011s. The fleet also includes Beechcraft A-100s, Cessna Citations, Grumman Gulf-Streams (G-IIs, G-IIIs and G-IVs), Piper Apaches, Piper Archers, a Falcon and a DC8.

Saudia employs approximately 24,000 personnel. The center of operations is in Jeddah, Saudi Arabia with offices located throughout the world. The part of the organization we will discuss is the Flight Operations Division, and its 2,300 employees.

We have nearly 1100 Flight Deck Crew, and more than 3,000 Cabin Attendants. The Cabin Crew falls under Marketing for all administrative purposes. However, Flight Operations is responsible for their Safety and Emergency Training and assumes responsibility for them while on duty. Because the airline has grown so fast, and continues to expand its routes and services, Saudia requires expatriate employees to supplement the Saudi members of the work force. Today, approximately 70% of the flight deck crews are Saudi Nationals. The remainder come from 39 different countries. The cabin crews are nearly 70% non-Saudi, coming from more than 50 countries.

The problems encountered

We at Saudia have been utilizing a multi-national work force since our foundation. Bearing in mind that linguistic differences represent only a minor part of the problems facing multi-national work groups, we have looked at the many problems we encounter and have tried to enumerate them.

Aviation, particularly for pilots, is an exacting profession which is not very tolerant of errors. Training must be thorough and standardized. Since the crews bid for their flights, they do not know who the other crewmembers will be until they arrive for the pre-flight briefing. As long as everyone has the same understanding of their job, the same training, and meet the same standards, everything works well. If, however, some fall short of the standards, or some are operating on a level which falls below that of their flight mates, a deadly situation can develop very quickly. Our job in the training department is to make sure the likelihood of this happening is reduced to a minimum.

To produce crews who meet exacting standards of both knowledge and performance when their backgrounds are homogenous is a difficult task. When presented with the situation we have, it becomes a daunting responsibility. People from the same culture are generally taught and learn in the same fashion. They have all grown up doing pretty much the same things and have a broad based platform of common traits, beliefs, habits, and customs. When an instructor enters a classroom, he or she can begin instruction immediately, paying little or no attention to the backgrounds of the trainees because all are very similar. However, in our classrooms the instructors begin their lectures with a totally different mind set. They are not looking for trainee assimilation of the material, rather they are looking for clues which will reveal the amount of knowledge the individuals possess. This can come through the type of questions asked, body language, side conversations between trainees on a break, or through the overall atmosphere in the classroom.

The instructor must make the evaluation quickly for the purpose is to modify his presentation on the fly. He must present certain core material within his fixed time. However, the way in which this is done can and must vary from class to class. Each one of the trainees in front of him could come from a different country. Each one has been in an educational system different from the others. Different things have been stressed by his former instructors, not only in aviation related subjects, but going all the way back to his time in primary school. As an example, the Western cultures tend to place emphasis on the scientific method from an early age. The Middle Eastern cultures do not, they place emphasis on memorization instead.

Taking this one step further, each individual learns in a way unique to himself. If there is a cultural or a nationality difference between two trainees, there will also be educational, educational methodology and life experience differences.

What works in one country with one nationality is not guaranteed to work in the same country with a different nationality, let alone in a different country with many different nationalities. Consequently instructors must learn almost infinite patience. They must be able to present the same material in hundreds of different ways in an attempt to get on the same wavelength as the trainee. They must be able to switch from high to low gear and from a presentation of the intricacies of an aircraft system back to the basics of that or a similar system without hesitation.

The knowledge level of the instructor in this environment must be far beyond that of his contemporaries elsewhere. He must have nearly the same experiences as the trainee to effectively relate to him and as importantly to generate a sense of trust and respect from the trainee. The most effective instructors are those who come from a broad aviation background as crewmembers themselves and who have been instructing for nearly all of their aviation careers. The background information and experience required to be successful in the classroom requires a person who is not only knowledgeable about his subject but is also knowledgeable about and able to present instruction on the basic concepts of it on a moments notice. He must use this flexibility almost daily in his attempt to meet the challenge; getting an equal footing for all the trainees prior to presenting any new information.

Once we have the trainees at the same knowledge and desired skill level, we still have not solved all our problems. Now we have the more conventional ones of dealing with different cultures, races and backgrounds in the work place. Unfortunately, our work place is a little more confined than most and if you get upset, you cannot go for a walk. Any situation that comes up must be dealt with. How this is done is extremely important both in the cockpit and the cabin.

If we look at the problems with a more global view one can see them from a different perspective. We are likely to experience multi-cultural, multi-national based difficulties in the cockpit, in the cabin, in flight dispatch and in our maintenance department. They are the same problems within each group. If a way is found to solve them for one group and then applied to the others, the internal problems of each group will be addressed. This leaves the problem of the interaction among the various groups.

The proposed solution

Over the past decade we have tried to develop a human resource training program that will work in our environment. We have looked at numerous Cockpit Resource Management courses but none of them went far enough toward solving our unique set of problems. By taking the basic ideas and concepts of the best of these, adding our own and tailoring this to meet the specific task at hand, we generated our own Crew Resource Management training program.

We also developed our own Flight Instructor Initial program integrating many of the concepts of the Crew Resource Management course. The intention of this is two fold. First we want to cover the technical aspects of flight instruction but we want it approached utilizing the concepts available in human resource training. Second, with the flight instructors trained first and using these new found skills not only with new employees but with seasoned ones as well, this type of training will catch on more quickly. It will be received much better if it is seen in operation prior to an individual being scheduled for a course on it.

Our plan is to have all of our cockpit crews go through the 3-day CRM program. We are extremely happy with the executive management level support we have received in allowing us to do this and to do it outside the Kingdom of Saudi Arabia so there are no day to day distractions to impede the progress of the trainees. The first courses have already been concluded. The trainee response was more than we hoped for. They were enthusiastic, actively participated in the exercises and drills and often stayed well after the formal end of the day with the instructors seeking additional information. At this stage we are in the process of observing the results during simulator training, line and proficiency checks. CRM Recurrent training will be included in future phases.

Once we have the problems of each group solved, we intend to continue conducting courses with cockpit and cabin crews in the same class. We hope this will be beneficial to both and allow us to overcome the cockpit-cabin communication problems we face.

Following this, the next step will be to get all four groups (Cockpit Crew, Cabin Crew, Flight Dispatch, Maintenance) involved in a single class. We feel that if enough are exposed to this, the attitude changes and communication enhancements will spread to all.

Conclusion

We hope that in identifying some of the problems we have, some faced by all carriers, some totally unique to our situation, we can conquer them with applied CRM concepts. The multi-cultural, multi-national work group might need a longer time for fruitful production than a culturally homogeneous group. But when multi-nationalities overcome problems and traditions interact, better results are achieved.

We also see the CRM training in our environment as a vehicle we can use to promote a more tolerant attitude both on and off the job for all who are not only working but living in this multi-cultural, multi-national, environment we call Saudia.

26 Applying the critical incident management model to intercultural cockpit/ATC communication: a case study

Dr Jan Meyer
Crisis Management Services, Minnesota, USA

There is an old proverb in Western culture which warns "Don't make a mountain out of a molehill." In the case of most modern airplane accidents, each contributing factor alone might appear to be small and/or trivial--a molehill. However, the cumulative impact of these details--if uninterrupted--is that they can become a mountain, as they did literally in the case of TG311 (31 July 1992 at KTM). It is common knowledge that most if not all accidents are now due to human factors; TG311 is no exception. It is the unseen cumulative effect of human factors that provides the danger.

Long before Flight TG311 on 31 July 1992, all involved parties were building a base on which decisions were made: storing experiences and knowledge into "deep mindsets." These mindsets, without conscious thought, become the set of "lenses" through which these individuals see the world. These mindsets determine their expectations of, and responses to, other people. At least six different mindsets were at work here: the universal cockpit culture, the corporate TG culture, the Thai culture, the universal ATC culture, the internal KTM ATC/ACC culture, and the Nepali culture. While some of these six may have shared "values," or expectations, more have different mindsets on many issues. And each culture has a previously determined expectation of the other cultures. At the outset of the flight, it can be assumed that the potential for miscommunication was high.

This fatal flight of TG311 from BKK to KTM proceeded normally until the first incident which was potentially irritating: the crew having to call KTM six times before being acknowledged. By itself, this is no cause for concern. But, there is a joke in Thai culture: "If you see a snake and an Indian at the same time, which do you kill first?" Everyone in that culture knows the answer, of course: "The Indian." Nepalese are seen to be like Indians by outsiders. So, when I ask Thai pilots the answer to that question, then read to them the lines from the cockpit/ATC recorder, I ask them to put these two things together: given the cultural "lens" through which Thai see Nepali--and vice versa--what would you feel when this (the recorded conversation) occurred? The answer is always the same: "we don't trust them to be doing their job." And the Nepali report similar expectations about the Thai. This is the first in a growing pile of incidents which, cumulatively, became a problem. And each of these incidents presented an opportunity for intervention.

The desired runway was first not available and then available, and the weather conditions were changing. These are incidents added to the pile. The flap fault problem also caused distraction. Several incidents of non-standard phraseology being used in the radio communications led to confusion, as did differing expectations of the role of the ATC/CC. Cumulative small problems--and prior assumptions based on cultural expectations--led to the Captain assuming too much of the workload, contributing to work overload on his part. A cultural norm for Thai is best described in the saying, "Put ten Thai people in a room and tell them to come out in order: it would take about ten seconds." Like many cultures, both Thai and Nepali cultures are hierarchical: this contributes to the gradient of authority in the cockpit *and* in ATC. Non-professional over-use of the radio frequency--RNAC to ATC--was distracting. Non-assertiveness on the part of both the Co-pilot and the ATC controller were contributing factors to the growing stack.

The Critical Incident Management Model (Meyer, 1993) provides a structure, or framework, to deal with this cumulative phase, both for prevention and response. The first part is a recognition of an individual's cultural make-up: three levels of consciousness are at work; two are "out of awareness." Then, it is important to put that individual into a context: many cultures contribute to the values, assumptions and expectations of that individual. Professor Howell at the University of Minnesota contributed another step for this framework by identifying Levels of Competence (we might substitute "aware or unaware" for "conscious and unconscious"): the unconsciously incompetent pilot isn't doing a good job but doesn't know it. An example would be the pilot who landed at the wrong airport; his co-pilot knew the error but wouldn't say anything due to the captain's negative and authoritarian leadership style..

The consciously incompetent pilot isn't doing a good job and knows it. An example of such a pilot might be the Northwest Express pilot who, in December of 1993, flew his plane and passengers into terrain in Hibbing, Minnesota in the U.S.

The unconscious competent pilot is the one who is following SOP's as appropriate, and does so automatically. On my first flight in a cockpit, I witnessed this type of competence: a warning went off, and before I could turn my head to see what it was, the Second Officer had "fixed" the problem. The consciously competent pilot is the one who is developing STS's (short term strategies) because SOP's do not cover the situation. His or her behavior is no longer automatic and has moved into his mental awareness. The super competent pilot is the one who continually assesses for situational awareness, and <u>communicates</u> SOP's or STS's to fit the situation.

Meyer's Model relates those states of competence to Levels of Decision Making. All work can be seen as on a continuum, with the potential for conflict, a critical incident, or sometimes an accident or disaster. The job of a commercial airline pilot is reported to be 99.5% sheer boredom and .5% stark terror. In this model, pilots are trained to use the lower levels--with less potential for problems--to identify worst case scenarios, playing the "what if" game with all parties involved, including the cabin crew. This creates a constant situational awareness. It also creates more effective time management since captains would conduct all appropriate briefings and debriefings at optimum points--"valley" times--during the flight and free up "peak" times for implementation rather than solution seeking or simply repeating unsuccessful SOP's. In the case of TG311, there was apparently no missed approach briefing which could have served to clarify the expectations of both crew members as to navigation points, etc.

Fixation and complacency are on opposite ends of the continuum of situational awareness. Both require "prompters," and all crew members--cockpit and cabin--along with ATC need to recognize the importance of these prompters. A prompter could be anything that happens, or needs to be done, which could serve as a clue to question whether or not there is optimum situational awareness, whether work is being properly distributed, or in the case of ATC, whether communication is clear. In the case of TG311, there were several things that could have been prompters. The most obvious is the "built-in" prompter of the GPWS. Cockpit crews need to continually be aware of what their automatic, or "conditioned," response is to the GPWS and if it is appropriate or not. While the GPWS sounded too late to save TG311, it is common to ignore it or to assume it is a false warning as these pilots did.

A question from the cockpit crew, from ATC, the cabin or even from a passenger to cabin crew could serve as a prompter, to "pierce the bubble" of fixation or complacency or frustration and bring situational awareness back into the conscious thoughts of the crew and the ATC. Another communication strategy which could be a prompter is recognition of the need to communicate any changes or deviations. In this case of TG311, the standard cabin announcement for landing had been made; no further announcements were made to the cabin. First, the obvious marketing reason for doing this is satisfied customers: since most such incidents end without mishap, we'd like our customers not to be left wondering why we started descent but obviously changed course. As one captain said, "We're not flying cargo back there, you know." Without an announcement, at best they would question our ability and tell others about their negative impression. Second, in a less severe mishap than this one, communication with the cabin can increase the likelihood that passengers could walk away. (The Sioux City, Iowa, UAL accident is a case in point: that any lives were saved has been attributed to the teamwork between the cockpit and cabin.) In this case, the need to communicate with the cabin early in the sequence of events might have served to cause the crew to divide up the workload, plan better Short Term Strategies, and clarify perceptions with ATC.

Both the ATC controller and the co-pilot in the case of TG311 needed to be more assertive, to take more active responsibility for a safe flight. There are several points at which the correct procedural question from ATC could have prevented the fatal crash; there are also many such points on the part of the co-pilot. This assertiveness would be aided by the identification of cultural assumptions: as identified above, there were at least six possible cultural mindsets contributing to the expectations of the parties involved in this accident.

Identifying those assumptions and the impact they may have on situations would help find optimal ways of overcoming any barriers erected by them.

Individuals take their personal styles of decision-making and conflict management behavior from the general patterns of the culture in which they grew up (Fisher, p. 27). As mentioned previously, the perceptions of one culture towards another, or of one sub-culture towards another, are in the "deep mindset" of every individual, and are driving decisions without his/her awareness. Another tool which needs to be utilized in every phase of the Critical Incident Management Model is that of a perception check: regularly taking "time out" to clarify if we all share the same perceptions of what is going on. In the green and yellow areas on the Levels of Decision Making, this would serve to solve problems before they escalate by avoiding many of the cumulative factors. At least as important, utilizing this Model throughout an organization would make total situational awareness (TAS) a constant habit.

This total situational awareness is especially true in industries which are vulnerable to accidents/disaster as part of their operations. Airlines, oil companies, and other similar organizations tend to focus their situational awareness on the airfield or the oil patch. They forget that they are also vulnerable in other areas, such as bomb threats, natural disasters, hostage-taking, etc. This does not contribute to what Barnaby (1986, p. 162) refers to as "crisis stability." And even worse, in the oil patch or on the airfield, the tendency is to focus on only those technical aspects of situational awareness, i.e., time, distance, speed, altitude, fuel. That is only one side--the task side--of the definition of situational awareness. The other side is the process side: the human factors. First, "human factors" has to be clearly defined, and that definition communicated, because human factors is not synonymous with human error. And, situational awareness needs to be re-defined to include all of the human factors such as those background areas of culture, etc., and the immediate factors such as recent stress, leaving on vacation, current relationships, etc. And, situational awareness needs to be a part of the total organization, making it simply a fact of every day life. Given the attention that is finally being given these phenomena, we are witnessing a major change, or a paradigm shift. As Volkan, et al, said, "we are standing on the bridge between one paradigm and the next" (1990, p. 9). A major contribution to that shift would be the clear definition of human factors and the expansion of situational awareness both to include the process side of the work, and an organization-wide application.

As noted above, there is no single cause in a human factors accident but there are several complex, interrelated contributing phenomena. The combination of these factors will never be the same in any two accidents, and we cannot be sure we have identified all of them. However, we have never identified any that are not preventable given careful attention! That is, they can be prevented if not perceived by technical people as unimportant, or no time to deal with them, because individual molehills can add up to mountains, as they did for TG31 1 .

Types of competence (adapted with permission of Wm. S. Howell

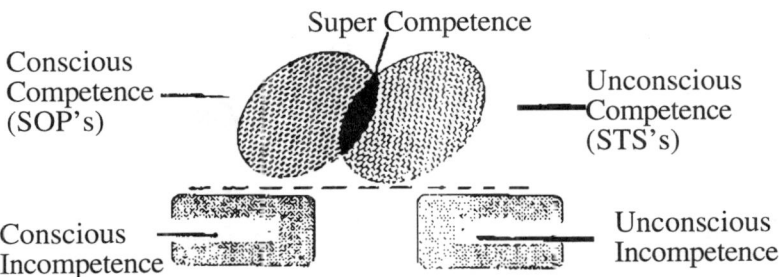

Levels of Decision Management

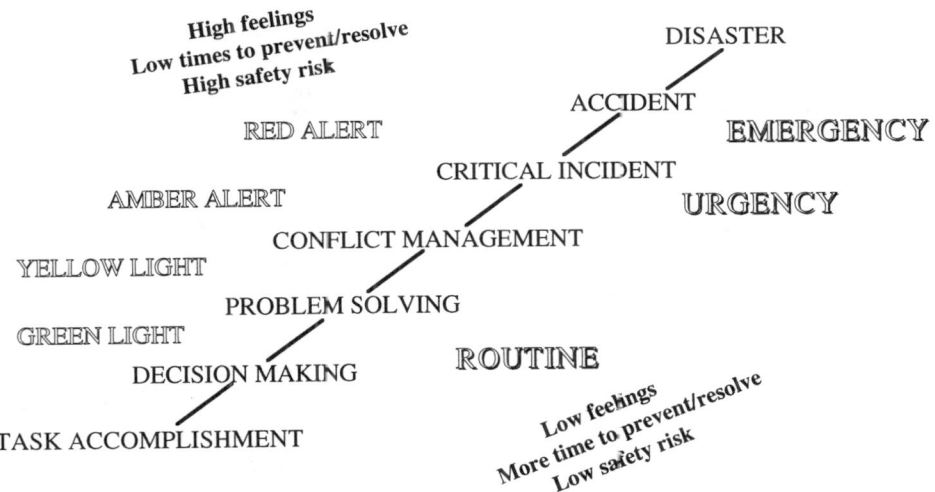

MEYER'S CRITICAL INCIDENT MANAGEMENT MODEL
(Meyer, in publication)

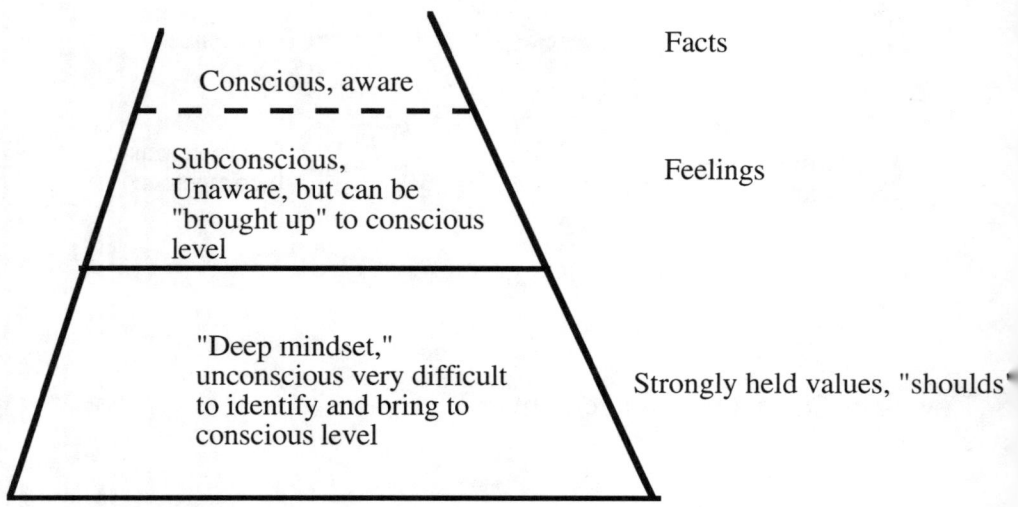

ORIGIN OF AN INDIVIDUAL'S CULTURE

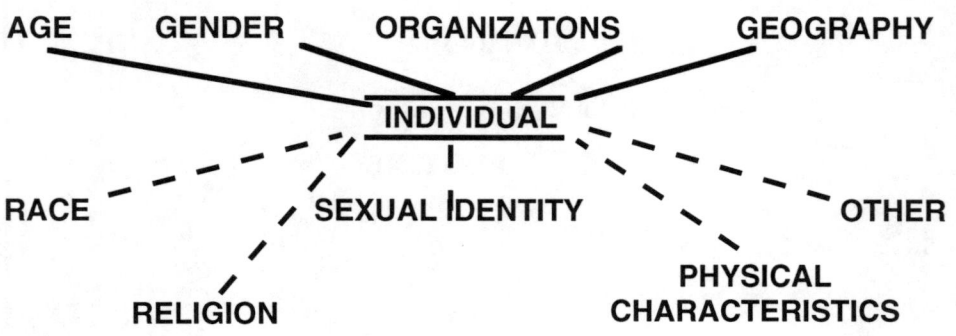

References

Barnaby, Frank (1986), *The Automated Battlefield,* The Free Press, New York, USA.

Dougherty, Devin (1992), *Crisis Communications,* Walker and Company, New York.

Fink, Steven (1986), *Crisis Management: Planning for the Inevitable,* American Management Association, New York, USA.
Fisher, Glen (1980), *International Negotiation: A Cross-Cultural Perspective,* Intercultural Press, Inc., Chicago.
Geertz, Clifford (1973), *The Interpretation of Cultures,* Basic Books, Inc., New York, USA.
Howell, William S. (1982), *The Empathic Communicator,* Wadsworth Publishing, Belmont, CA, USA.
Kluckhohn, Florence R., and Strodtbeck, Fred L. (1961), *Variations in Value Orientations,* Row & Peterson, New York, USA.
_____ (1992), *Human Factors Digest No. 7,* ICAO Circular 240-AN/144.
Mehrabian, Albert (1981), *Silent Messages: Implicit Communication of Emotions and Attitudes,* Wadsworth Publishing Company, Belmont, CA, USA.
Meyer, Dr. Jan (1993), *Critical Incident Management Model* in the Critical Incident Management Program, Bangkok, Thailand.
Meyer, Dr. Jan (in publication), *Crisis Management Through Total Situational Awareness.*
Volkan, Vamik D., Julius, Demetrios A., and Montville, Joseph V. (1990), *The Psychodynamics of International Relationships Volume I: Concepts and Theories,* Lexington Books, Lexington, Mass., USA.

27 The multi-national crew: verbal and non-verbal communication, with special reference to safety

Captain Arild Smith-Christensen, The Norwegian Civil Aviation Administration
Dr Fanny Duckert, The University of Oslo

The Power of Communication

In May 1895, the Norwegian explorer Professor F. Nansen left his ship which was stuck in ice. His intention was to cross the arctic on skis. Together with him was Lieutenant F.H. Johansen. The two men started the crossing, reaching the Frans Josef Island 12 months later. They were almost dead. However, it is interesting to note: while fighting for their lives, eating their dogs - raw meat, sleeping in one common sleeping bag in order to keep each other warm, the two crew-members kept their distance and addressed each other respectively as Professor Nansen and Lieutenant Johansen. They never addressed each other by first name. Never letting the communication create an informal atmosphere, they pulled through because neither of them was willing to give the other the victory of watching oneself give up. It must have been hell. However, this situation is not entirely unknown in some cockpits, but of course on quite a different scale.

By the way: Professor Nansen and Lieutenant Johansen never communicated on first name terms.

When communication problems exist, they are often less obvious in an uni-national crew - both to the participants and the outside observer. But basically there is no difference in the role of communication within a uni-national crew and a multi-national crew. When we have chosen the multi-national crew as basis for our reflections, it is because the communication problems are more easy to detect in the latter one. On the other hand communication problems in a uni-national, but heterogeneous, cockpit can be more painful as the communication participants have a larger repertoire of subtle meanings and verbal communication tools by sharing a mutual language.

Article 83 bis

The cockpit as a working place is identified by restricted space and a limited area of freedom, but also by the necessity of reciprocal cooperation. The future development in aviation will lead to increasingly heterogeneous and culturally complex air-crews. Cultural differences will be more prominent and must to a greater degree be taken into consideration as concerns the subject of safety.

The entry into force of the Article 83 'bis' to the Chicago Convention will materially advance the cause of global aviation safety. Leasing of aircraft (aeroplanes and large helicopters) on an international scale is already of considerable proportions, and will in the future become progressively extensive. Increasingly, the insurance companies will require an experienced crew (at least a captain), employed by the lessor, as a condition of the leasing agreement.

Scenarios

The cockpit scene is destined by the set of the actors. They will play out their individual differences, their languages, body odour, mimicries and postures, their tolerances and animosities, and their religions and cultural rites. In addition age, sex, and the social standing of the individual crew member will be important elements. These elements are at all times present in both the verbal and non-verbal communication which take place in the cockpit and also part of the social interaction during crew stopovers.

In this context there are many scenarios, which we will try to exemplify. These scenarios are based upon real experiences and observations.

What is felt as right at one time, will later, in afterthought, often become 'what was wrong at that time'.

"I remember very well when I crashed in the hills outside Geneva in Switzerland - killing myself, the rest of the crew, the passengers, and wrecking the aircraft. The only thing I don't remember from that accident was the newspapers headlines the following day. The explanation of this is that the dramatic fatal accident happened in a Comet simulator. (In those early days of the simulator, part of the scope was to illustrate the magnitude of the accident, rather than show how to avoid it. Furthermore, it had the effect of putting any cocky first officer in his place. This non-win exercise, measuring your burble point, was how the simulator was used in quite a number of training establishments. In some places they still are). Among the role-plays of the simulator-session was to put me - the F/O - into the role of the Pilot-in-command (PIC). When I took on the role as the PIC, I thought it was expected of me to role-play the 'Captain'. However, in this I was wrong. This subtle distinction was not easy to comprehend. But even if I did understand, I did not have a sufficient command of the language spoken by my superiors. Thus, I was not able to verbally behave in a way that was socially acceptable for a first-officer when put in the role of PIC.

Following the simulator sessions I played my act, sensing the importance to come along to the bar. I paid for numerous rounds of beer as compensation for having killed all of the crew and conceding that I merely was a alien first-officer knowing my place in the hierarchy. Not until late in the bar party I was unofficially told what was to be in the written report made up the next day.

Others of my 'foreign' colleagues did not fare that well. They failed the last test. They did not perceive that the visit to the bar was the real debriefing of the session. They proved themselves to be socially out of tune and remained aliens. And of course under the circumstances they were - as seen by their superiors, not joining the game of being 'a good sport', which implied reluctance to take part in the 'mason-ship' of the cockpit.

Persons unfamiliar with the rites are bound to face suspicion by their superiors and their peers.

The scenario just brought to you is not a picture of today. But as a description the scenario is still very much valid.

The Cornerstone of Safety

A) The instinct of survival will make every cockpit crew member have safety as a prime target.
B) Smooth communication in the cockpit is a prime prerequisite for safety.
C) In a socially harmonious cockpit, the communication becomes smooth.
D) When the communication is smooth, the cockpit becomes socially harmonious.

We do not know for sure whether C produces D, or D produces C. But, does it really matter? What matters is that the fulfilment of C or D is a prerequisite for the achievement of B. But in the context of A, it is of utmost importance that every crew member, every pilot, and every management of operations are made fully aware of B, C, and D.

Communication - A Fundamental Factor

The ability of communication is not something you can just take out of your flight bag, like a pair of sun-glasses, or the logbook. The ability to communicate is more like your spectacles. If you discover that you forgot to bring your spectacles along, your pilot-licence gets invalidated. Without your spectacles you are a hazard to flight safety. Similarly: without possessing adequate communication abilities you are a hazard to flight safety.

The ability to communicate is a fundamental human factor concept, clearly recognized and stated in the ICAO HUMAN FACTORS DIGEST NO 1. (HFD 1),and has from the 16th November 1989 been a part of the requirements for a pilot licence. This requirement is a 'standard' in ICAO Annex 1 Personnel Licensing.

Unfortunately, few National Licensing Authorities enforce the obligation to examine the applicants in their understanding of communication as safety factor, nor assess their command of communication skills. Worse, in a large number of countries, the topic of 'Communication' is not even a subject being taught in the flying schools/flight training organizations - if 'Human factors' are taught at all.

There is an unanimous agreement within ICAO that 'the art of communication' is essential for the safe operation of a flight. A fact substantiated over and over again by the accident investigation findings. Why is it so that many of the national CAAs omit to enforce these standards of the Annexes to which the Contracting State has reported compliancy? There are probably only three answers:

1) unwillingness, or
2) lack of funds/staff, or
3) incompetence.
4) - or could it be lack of communication?

'Aviation-English'

The English language has brought some informality in the communicational interaction between people. Many languages invite to 'power-distance'. This can for instance be observed in two of the other main European languages: The French have their 'vous' and 'tu'. Germans have the 'Sie' and 'du' - while the English just have the term 'you'. Or is it not that simple?
Captain B. Hutchinson of 55 years, and first-officer Claude Marou (26 years) will certainly communicate, addressing each other as Bob and Claude. However, under certain implicit defined circumstances, as part of the verbal rite, it might be expected from Claude that he should practice the address "sir" towards his superior.
By not having a mother-tongue in common, the participants in a social interaction feel each other to be strangers. This also increases the risk of mutual suspicion. Put yourself to test: Recall a situation when you have met someone speaking your mother-tongue with a heavy accent. Probably you did wonder: does this person also think with an accent? Such a reaction is not unusual, even if you are not a biased person.
Those who have 'advanced English' as their mother-tongue are often unaware that people to whom English is a second language frequently will be in difficulties when trying to grasp complicated messages: the subtle difference between being socially polite and that of inviting an informal friendly interaction may be difficult to perceive. Especially because there will be few non-verbal signals for the 'foreigner' to pick up. Unlike languages enriched by gestures when spoken, English is enriched by understatements.
In communities where English is not the basic language, many people have learned and practiced English as their daily language at work, i.e. in a multinational-cockpit. A limited vocabulary of English words constitutes a 'linga franca' enabling the crew members to fulfil their duties. However in such environments where only one or none of the crew members have English as their first language, the communication will mostly be limited to the necessities, thus making the cockpit atmosphere rather indifferent. Whether this will represent a hazard to safety is unknown. But such a cockpit is certainly not a stimulating workplace, and may create unnecessary boredom, which in turn is diagnosed as a safety risk factor. Therefore the issue of communication is not limited to verbal and nonverbal communication, but also to the absence of communication.

References

Caesar, H. *30 Years of Jet Losses - Conclusions Regarding Human Factors Research,* Proceedings, ICAO Human Factor Seminar, Leningrad, 1990.
Davis, P.J. East African - An Airline Story, Surrey, 1993.
Hofstede, G. *Culture's consequences - International Differences in Work Related Values,* Sage, 1984.
Jensen, R.S. *Aviation Psychology,* Gower Technical, Aldershot.
Roscoe, A.H. *An Operator's Human Factors Considerations.* Proceedings, ICAO Human Factors Seminar, Leningrad, 1990.

28 Culture and the cockpit in context: a situational perspective of behaviour in the cockpit

Roger Lambo and Richard Lambo
Aerosupport (Nigeria) Ltd

Introduction

Whether it be in relation to the compilation of statistics, or to behaviour in the cockpit, the context within which these activities occur, is central to the interpretations we give to them. In this respect, it can be said that nothing can happen 'out of context'.

However, the debate that revolves around the extent to which 'context', cultural or otherwise, either impinges upon, or is evoked by our actions, has divided major schools of thought within the social sciences. Any attempt to embark upon a regional comparison of air safety, or the cross-cultural study of flight crew attitudes and behaviour, must appreciate the interplay between these two principle notions of 'context'.

Africa's accident record: How really bad is it?

Where in fact does the truth lie as regards Africa's aircraft accident record? On the one hand, Nkosilathi Sibanda (1993) of Air Zimbabwe tells us that, "in 1987 there were 159 airline accidents, only three of which involved African airlines. Further on, he states that in 1991 there "was a world total of 1,082 passenger and crew fatalities, of which 10 involved African airlines, representing a meagre 0.9%".

On the other hand, Clinton Oster and his colleagues (1992), in their published account on why aeroplanes crash, tell us that in the period 1977-1989, "Africa had the worst safety record, with a death risk per flight of nearly 10.5 per million, almost twenty times worse than that of North America".

These statements by Sibanda and Oster and his colleagues are so contradictory, it is difficult to believe that they refer to the same phenomenon, i.e. the incidence of aircraft accidents in Africa.

Sibanda, in order to substantiate his argument against the inordinately high insurance premiums applied to African carriers, chose to use the absolute number of accidents which occurred within 1987 and 1991. Even if his analysis had covered the same period as that of Oster's, he would still have been able to show that North America experienced twice as many accidents and had almost 80% more fatalities than Africa. There is a certain logic to his analysis, for it is the actual number of crashes and of fatalities, that occur during any one period, that has the greatest impact on the public mind.

Oster and his colleagues, however, question the validity of any comparative analysis that fails to consider the different levels of activity of each airline or region. One measure that corrects for this, is the number of fatal accidents incurred, per the number of departures made. Thus, from 1977-89, although African airlines had 31 accidents as compared to the 63 accidents incurred by those in North America, the fact that they made 69 million fewer departures, meant that their safety record was about twenty times worse.

However, the absurdity of this kind of comparative analysis is brought home, when one considers, that even if all the African airlines had incurred only three accidents from 1977-89, their accident rate would still have been worse than that of the North American carriers. Similarly, even if the African airlines had managed to have only one pilot-induced accident, the rate would still have been worse, in spite of the 23 such accidents incurred in North America. Such absurdities invariably lead one to question whether it is at all valid to compare the two regions, given that their levels of airline activity differ so vastly.

The contradictory accounts made by Sibanda and Oster and his colleagues, serve to illustrate how raw data can be differently interpreted according to context. 'Context' being in this case the perspectives, orientations and motives of their users. Furthermore, it is essential that such subjective considerations be evaluated, when assessing the relevance of statistical data.

Neil Johnston (1993) has remarked that there is prima facie evidence that statistical analysis may be incomplete, and that "particular care is necessary when deducing the international incidence of CRM deficiencies".

In spite of such warnings, however, statistics are frequently invoked to support the hypothesis that variations in the crew-induced accident record, of the different regions and countries of the world, result from the impact that their respective cultures have on the behaviour of airline crew.

National culture and cockpit behaviour

When Captain Mack Eastburn of American Airlines first read the *Cultural Effects on Cockpit Communications* by S.G. Redding and J.G. Ogilvie, he was heard to exclaim: "For years I've been trying to discover why some countries' airlines have more accidents than others. Here's the answer" (J.M. Ramsden, 1985).

Geert Hofstede's (1984) classification of national cultures along the dimensions of individualism-collectivism, masculinity-femineity, power distance and uncertainty avoidance has had an impact on the recent study of cockpit behaviour. Redding and Ogilvie (1984) focused on the dimensions of individualism-collectivism and power distance in their cross-cultural study of the effect of hierarchy on crew communication. Asleigh Merritt (1993) likewise used Hofstede's dimensions in her study of the attitudes of flight crew with regard to CRM.

Although Johnston (1993) argues for the use of Hofstede's classification as a point of departure in the production of CRM courses, he does caution us of its limitations. All have, however, uncritically accepted Hofstede's definition of culture as "the mental programming of the mind which distinguishes the members of one group from another".

Hofstede's definition of culture subscribes to what has been termed as the 'bucket' theory of context, whereby the actions of the individual are constrained by the normative framework within which he or she participates. According to this perspective, individuals are reduced to 'judgemental dopes', blindly acting in accordance with the primordial values of their respective national cultures. No allowance what-so-ever is made for the individual's ability to stand back from, and reflect upon the normative foundations of their conduct, whether these be cultural, institutional or otherwise. The inadequacy of Hofstede's notion of culture to explain the dynamic, cognitive aspect of human activity, makes it imperative that, in our study of CRM, we search for other more suitable models of behaviour.

Increasingly, in existing CRM literature, the realization has been expressed that normative models of behaviour and decision making alone, do not sufficiently explain flight deck activity. In this respect, Judith Orasanu (1993) has called for the application of process criteria, so as to obtain a better understanding of "the practical reality faced by airline crews of having to make decisions in dynamic, time-pressured, action-oriented situations".

An African pilot is a pilot

It was the anthropologist, Max Gluckman (1961), who in the course of his work in southern Africa, stated that: "An African townsman is a townsman, an African miner is a miner". No longer could the behaviour of Africans in modern urban and industrial settings be solely explained in terms of their primordial ethnic identities. Africans in urban areas had now to be seen to be acting primarily within a field whose structure was determined by an urban, industrial setting.

Although urban Africans had not entirely abandoned their ethnic identities and relationships, these were now, along with the new identities generated by the urban environment, selectively used in the course of everyday interaction. This propensity for individuals to select amongst an array of identities and meanings, in the pursuance of their everyday activities, became a central feature in the study of both urban and industrial behaviour in Africa (Mitchell, 1987; Epstein, 1992; Kapferer, 1972; Soleye, 1967).

It forced a re-examination of the relationship between the individual and the context of his or her activity, and led to a much simpler, less constraining definition of 'culture', than that later proposed by Geert Hofstede. Thus Clyde Mitchell (1987) has spoken of 'culture' as merely being "extensive storehouses of meanings which people build up over time and to which they are constantly adding or from which they are constantly dropping elements". In this respect, culture becomes synonymous with language, in that, just as in the case of bilingualism and diglossia, an individual may alternate the use of different cultures, as is deemed appropriate to the situation.

In order to accommodate the cognitive dimension of human behaviour, Mitchell differentiated 'context' into two essential components - 'situation' and 'setting'. 'Situation' accounts for the interpretations that individuals give to the events and activities in which they participate, and to the behaviour of those with whom they interact. 'Setting' relates to the structural context in which social encounters occur, and is based on "the analyst's formulation of the more general circumstances which impinge on the actors".

Present-day discourse and conversational analysts, have likewise been preoccupied with the notion of 'context', and have proposed distinctions similar to those of Mitchell. Thus Emanuel Schegloff (1992) speaks of the "intra-interactional" and "distal" components of 'context' respectively. Aaron Cicourel (1993) distinguishes between the "narrow", locally negotiated interaction between actors, and the "broad", institutional settings in which that interaction occurs. Whatever definitions are given to the composite parts of 'context', all are agreed that the relationship between the actions of the individual, and the context in which they occur is 'doubly reflexive', in that each serves to shape the other.

By way of paraphrasing Gluckman, we should like to state that an African pilot is a pilot, in that the focus of our attention lies on his activity in the cockpit, and not necessarily on his African identity. The subject of our 'situational perspective' is the *interactional* activity of flight crew, and not on their individual cultures per se. National culture might very well have some unconscious impact on behavioural style. However, of greater significance to CRM, is the process by which crew members solicit and negotiate the use of elements of their national, ethnic, professional and institutional identities, while interacting with each other, for the joint purpose of conducting the flight.

The Situational Perspective and CRM

The unsuccessful transfer of American models of CRM to other parts of the world, has led to the recommendation that for cross-cultural training to be successful, it must acknowledge the presence of national culture and bend its intentions accordingly (Merritt, 1993). However, as rightly commented by Johnston (1993), this approach to cultural relativism poses what appears to be insoluble problems with regard to the establishment of universal CRM standards and principles (Johnston, 1993).

It is our contention that these problems derive, not so much from the process of applying CRM, as from the very definition that has currently been given to the notion of 'culture' and its relationship to the individual. As long as culture is defined in the terms advocated by Hofstede, cultural relativism will always be problematic.

We feel that the 'situational perspective' will enable us to overcome many of the problems that Hofstede's definition of culture poses for the world-wide application of CRM programmes.

Furthermore, in view of the increasing use of multi-national crew by major international airlines, we see the need for universal inter-cultural training programmes. Such programmes would be difficult, if not impossible to conceive under a culturally relativist approach to CRM. However, the 'situational perspective' should provide an adequate basis for the design and implementation of such programmes.

Finally, with its emphasis on the social actor as agent, the 'situational perspective' assures that the pilot, irrespective of culture, always retains control.

References

Cicourel, A.V. (1992), 'The interpretation of communicative contexts: Examples from medical encounters', in Duranti, A. and Goodwin, C. (eds.), *Rethinking Context: Language as an interactive phenomenon*, Cambridge University press, Cambridge.

Epstein, A.L. (1992), *Scenes from African Urban Life*, Edinburgh University Press, Edinburgh.

Gluckman, M. (1961), 'Anthropological problems arising from the African industrial revolution', in Southall, A. (ed.), *Social Change in Modern Africa*, Oxford University Press, London.

Hofstede, G. (1980), *Culture's Consequences: International differences in work-related values*, California, Sage.

Johnston, N. (1993), 'CRM: Cross-Cultural Perspectives', in Weiner, E.L., Kanki, B.G. and Helmreich, R.L. (eds.), *Cockpit Resource Management*, Academic Press, Inc., London.

Kapferer, B. (1972), *Strategy and transaction in an African factory*, Manchester University Press, Manchester.

Merritt, A. (1993), 'Cross-Cultural Attitudes of Flight Crew Regarding CRM', in Jensen, R.S. and Neumeister, D. (eds.), *Proceedings of the Seventh international Symposium on Aviation Psychology*, Ohio State University, Columbus.

Mitchell, C. (1987), *Cities, Society and Social Perception: A Central African Perspective*, Clarendon Press, Oxford.

Orasanu, J.M. (1993), 'Decision-Making in the Cockpit', in Weiner, E.L., Kanki, B.G. and helmreich, R.L. (eds.), *Cockpit Resource Management*, Academic Press, Inc., London.

Oster, V., Strong, J.S. and Zorn, C.K., (1992), *Why Airplanes Crash: Aviation Safety in a Changing World*, Oxford University Press, Oxford.

Ramsden, J.M. (1985), 'World airline safety audit', in *FLIGHT International*', 26 January.

Redding, S.G. and Ogilvie, J.G. (1984), 'Cultural effects on cockpit communications in civilian aircraft', in *Flight safety Foundation Conference, Zurich*, Flight safety Foundation, Washington.

Schegloff, E.A. (1992), 'In another context', in Duranti, A. and Goodwin, C. (eds.), *Rethinking Context: Language as an interactive phenomenon*, Cambridge University Press, Cambridge.

Sibanda, N. (1993), 'Why high premiums should be resisted' *African Airlines*, May-June, 1993.

Soleye, O. (1970), *An Arena for Negotiated Order - A Case Study of a Factory in an African Community*, Unpublished Ph.d. thesis, University of Manchester.

29 Cultural differences: flight deck reality and problems

David Johnson, Interaction Trainers Ltd

Introduction

Political, economic and social effects are producing an increased global mobility of flight deck crew in an industry already well known for its internationalism.

Airlines worldwide are operating with cockpit crews composed of individuals from a very wide mix of ethnic, social, cultural and language backgrounds. This paper identifies a number of areas of interest (and possibly concern) which the author and his colleagues have detected during fifteen years of training pilots and flight engineers in Crew Resource Management and in Instructional Skills, in many airlines and on all five continents.

The material presented is based upon personal, individual experience and anecdotal evidence rather than on formal research. It is intended to stimulate thought and discussion - to raise questions rather than to provide answers.

Areas of Interest

The following list identifies some of the inter-cultural areas which have raised problems on flight decks or in briefings and debriefings within the author's experience. The difficulties may be in the area of interpersonal relationships - simply 'putting someone's back up' - or may reflect a deeper concern for flight safety or operational efficiency. In many cases the event soured a relationship and distinctly affected the value of the training involved or the level of cooperation and coordination of the crew. The material is in no particular order of priority or importance.

Nationality   A pilot operating in his home country and airline resenting the presence of expatriates among his colleagues, and expressing the resentment either to the expatriates or to his co-nationals.

Religion   Careless comment about religious denomination or the effect of religious festivals or observance.

Military / Civil   Comment about one's own or a colleague's background in terms of the presence or lack of military experience. The comment may be totally well-meant; for example: "Of course, you didn't have the advantage of Air Force training, did you?" - intended empathetically but alas very differently received by a pilot struggling with a difficult training session and sensitive to any criticism.

Green / Non-green   Dispute generated by differing views on matters connected with conservation and the environment

Animal Rights / Hunter   Friction between individuals who differ markedly in their views on the status of animal species

Male / Female   Some male pilots (usually, but not exclusively, of older vintage) view flying as 'a man's world' and resent or are uncomfortable with females in the cockpit. On another level, one female captain with a major European airline recently expressed concern that male captains expected less of female copilots, or were more reluctant to give necessary corrective feedback to them. She believes that line-flying standards of the females are being eroded.

First Language / Second Language   Where a crew is composed of individuals who do not have a common first language, misunderstanding can occur because of differences of meaning, grammar and syntax. It may arise because of the misuse of colloquialisms, in the structure of sentences or simply because a single word (correctly translated) may have different meaning in the 'other' language. For instance, an expatriate pilot told often in his first language that his performance in type-training was *quite* good, resented the description until he discovered by accident that the word *quite* in his instructor's first language carried the meaning of *very* in his own.

Company Trained / Free Market There is a tendency amongst some company-trained pilots (possibly from 'cadet' schemes) to view incomers from the 'free market' as somehow inferior and lesser-qualified. There is a corresponding view amongst some free-market pilots that company-trained colleagues are to varying degrees arrogant and blinkered. The respective views are usually aired only among pilots belonging to one group or the other, but sometimes surface in mixed groups - generating much more heat than light.

Age / Youth Age's intolerance of youth ("They're not like we were") and youth's dismissal of age ("Doddering old fool") are well known and well documented - we've all been there! When either shows on or around a flight deck the results can be devastating for one or the other.

Smoker / Non-smoker Friction can readily arise between the committed non-smoker (often an ex-smoker) and the thoughtless smoker. The problem may arise on a flight deck, in a briefing or training room, or even in the bar.

Fitness Freak / Couch Potato Differing views on fitness, diet and exercise may occasionally generate some difficulty between individuals. The Fitness Freak may view the Couch Potato as dull, lethargic and unreliable. The Couch Potato may view the Fitness Freak as too intense and narrow-minded. The titles themselves are indicators of how each sees the other.

Automatics / Hands-on The pilot who loves to hand fly may be dismissive of the one who prefers the use of all the 'automatics' at his disposal. Equally, the automatics buff may consider his colleague's manual-preference as inefficient or an affectation.

Politics The word politics is used here in the sense of liberal or conservative - in both cases with a lower-case initial. The source of potential dispute may for instance be social (perhaps an expression of views on 'Law and Order') or operational ('sticking to the book' versus 'flexibility').

Pro-CRM / Anti-CRM Crew Resource Management, in various forms and with various titles, is now widely trained and widely accepted as a subject area fully integrated (hopefully) with technical training. However, some individuals regard it as an unnecessary imposition and some even resist its principles. Their view has been expressed as "We don't need all this psychological rubbish, it's only a question of common sense and airmanship". Such a view, expressed to an individual who sees great value in CRM principles and training, can lead to considerable mutual mistrust and friction.

Summary

The possible impact of cultural differences ranges far beyond the obvious one of ethnic grouping, powerful though that may be. Many of the factors which from time-to-time affect human relationships and operation lie in more subtle and less-easily recognised areas, and may produce disruptive or destructive attitudes and behaviour.

This paper has illustrated only a selection of items which have been observed by the author and his colleagues to produce problems between people; it has not attempted to present any answers.

It does perhaps illuminate an area which all CRM training should address.

30 Cross-cultural assessment of flight crew behavior styles

Dr Neil A. Johnson and Dennis J. Sullivan
Arnautical Training Center, Inc.

Effective crew resource management programs offer training on a variety of topics relevant to safe flight operations, for example, decision making, communications and situation awareness. Ultimately though, the application of these skills to the flight environment is largely influenced by attitudes and behavior styles. It is in this realm that CRM trainers should understand some basic psychological truths.

All human actions are motivated. It is not difficult, however, to easily assume that some people are unmotivated because we do not understand what is motivating them. Flight crew members do things for their own reasons, not ours. Therefore, in CRM courses or on the line, we cannot, "motivate" flight crew members; we can only work to create conditions which will encourage them to motivate themselves in desirable ways. If we wish to influence the behavior of flight crew members in ways that promotes safe flight operations, we must understand what motivates the individuals.

Two people can perceive the same situation in very different ways. Flight crews become more effective when they understand and appreciate the differences in each individual crew member's behavior style. Unless we learn to recognize and accept these differences, they become a barrier to cooperation and thus a barrier to crew coordination. One of the main objectives of any CRM course should be to overcome these barriers by discussing them. However, when working across cultures, or in a culturally mixed environment, the challenge is to find an objective way to do that.

The objective assessment of behavior styles becomes a problem when implementing CRM training cross-culturally, because most of the existing instruments used for assessing personality characteristics have no scientifically established validity for use in multiple cultures. Availability in multiple languages is also a major problem. It is presumptuous to assume that because English is the international language of aviation, it is also the international language of personality assessment.

The Personal Profile System™

A notable exception to these problems is the Personal Profile System™. In working to solve the problem of how to individualize learning and increase self-awareness, Dr. John G. Geier, extending the work of William Moulton Marston developed the Personal Profile System™ (PPS) in 1969. The model divides behavior into four main dimensions: Dominance (D), influencing (i) of others, Steadiness (S), and Conscientiousness (C). Figure 1 depicts the relationship between the dimensions.

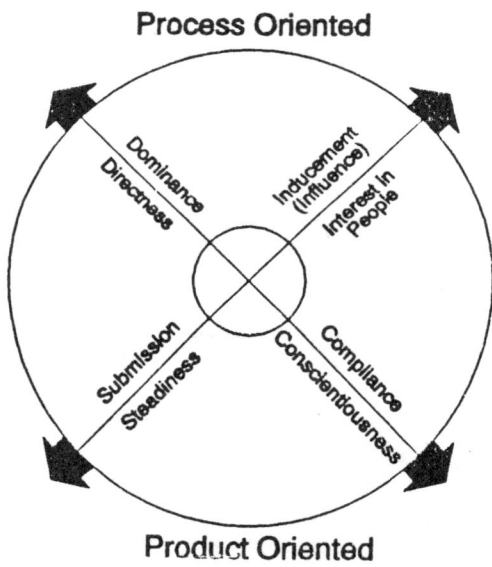

Figure 1 The PPS two-axis model

Process versus product

The PPS differs from other models, such as Managerial Grid, in that it does not put people in numerical "boxes" but rather accounts for complex human behavior by showing how individuals are a blend of four different behavior styles. In different situations we may use any one or a combination of the styles. The frequency and intensity with which we use certain styles develop a core behavioral style for each of us.

High D and High i individuals tend to be more interested in the process. They want to shape the environment according to their particular view. They focus on "what" and "who," respectively, These individuals continually test or challenge the limits set by the group or organization.

High S and High C individuals tend to be more interested in the product. They focus on "how" and "why," respectively. These people may often need encouragement to go beyond limits set by the group or organization.

High D's are task-oriented and interested in action that gets results; High i's are people-oriented and interested in accomplishing their goals through other people; High S's are people-oriented and interested in maintaining a stable, predictable environment; High C's are task-oriented and concerned about their personal competence and the correctness of a task. Human behavior would be easier to understand if each individual was one pure style or another. However, everyone is a combination of these four tendencies, but some tendencies will usually be stronger than others.

Cross-cultural data

As reported by Johnston (1992), Hofstede differentiated national cultures across four dimensions: Power Distance(PDI), Uncertainty Avoidance(UAI), Individualism (IDV), and Masculinity (MAS). He then grouped data from 50 countries into culture groups as indicated in Figure 2.

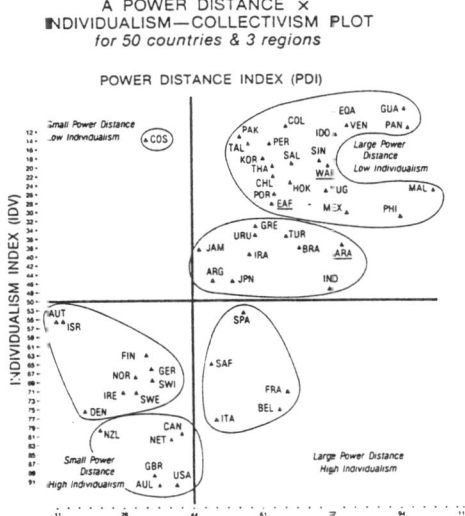

Figure 2 Hofstede's culture areas

Rieger and Wong-Rieger (1988) and Redding and Ogilvie (1984) have endorsed Hofstede's findings, albeit, cautiously. In particular both studies note the presence of "status consciousness in high power distance cultures and that this contributes to perceiving no barriers to communications due to status" (Johnston, 1992).

Johnston (1992) states that the most potent source of CRM problems seems likely to be in high power distance cultures. He notes that "junior crew members are more likely to fear the consequences of disagreeing with leaders and possibly, with good reason. Leaders are likely to feel comfortable with paternalistic behaviour and leadership by directive." Johnston implies a similar potential for CRM problems in low power distance/high individualism cultures. This latter situation brings the potential for operations whereby each individual performs their job without the perceived need to coordinate or communicate with others.

Practical results

Over the past two years Arnautical Training Center, Inc. has conducted CRM training for military and commercial airline crews in the United States, Mexico, Brazil, Portugal, Germany, Ireland and Turkey. Although not intended as a research project, using the Personal Profile System™ we have collected behavior style data on 612 cockpit crew members. By chance we have PPS data from 7 of the countries included in Hofstede's research.

In high power distance/low individualism cultures such as Brazil, Mexico, Portugal, and Turkey, the predominant behavior styles recorded for cockpit crews were also grouped together, in this case as task-oriented (Dominance and Conscientiousness). In small power distance/high individualism cultures such as Germany and Ireland, the predominant behavior styles recorded for cockpit crews were grouped together as people-oriented (influencing and Steadiness).

Although supportive of the previously cited research, this data was collected as part of CRM training, not as a carefully constructed research project with all the necessary scientific controls. We therefore cautiously offer the major finding here as the apparent, validation of the Personal Profile System as a useful tool for CRM training in a variety of cultural applications.

Application of the PPS

The Personal Profile System can be self-administered and self-scored to provide behavioral data on ones self or, it can be used by a group to assess each other. It takes approximately 30 minutes to administer and score. Depending on the particular culture, the results may then be used in a wide variety of ways.

We have, through practical experience, learned that group functioning and leadership are viewed in widely divergent ways as one moves across cultures. Ultimately, the success of any program will rest on how well you communicate with your group and how well you can get the group to communicate among themselves. We have found that by providing a culturally sensitive vehicle to generate discussion, we can focus the group on CRM issues specific to their particular culture. In a collectivist society, for example, the self-administered, self-scored PPS allows individuals to see a profile of their on-the-job behavior without becoming confrontational. It allows them to see how their particular behavior style can be most effective, how it can be ineffective, and how to improve performance. It will allow, as Johnston (1992) suggests, for societies "where highly effective working groups are natural," to discuss "effective cockpit leadership" or, for high power distance groups to discuss how to "constructively ameliorate the excesses of abrasive leadership."

Conclusion

Although certainly not the end-all answer to the problems of implementing CRM training across cultures, the Personal Profile System has proved to be an effective tool for discussing behavior styles. It is available in numerous languages and has been adapted and validated worldwide. Unlike some instruments, we have found the PPS to be very popular with both military and civilian flight crews.

The bottom line for Arnautical Training Center has been that we have numerous clients worldwide for whom we are providing CRM training. We needed an instrument that was available in numerous languages and which had adaptability in terms of how it could be applied. Our cross-cultural data, although not scientifically derived, indicates that the instrument is sensitive to cultural issues, and in practical terms, it has been extremely successful.

References

Johnston, Neil (1993) CRM - Cross-cultural perspectives. In, E. Wiener, ,B. Kanki, and R. Helmreich, (Eds) Cockpit Resource Management.

Redding, S.G., and Olgilvie, J.G. (1984) Cultural effects on cockpit communications in civilian aircraft. Flight Safety Foundation Conference, Zurich. Washington: Flight Safety Foundation.

Rieger, F. and Wong-Rieger, D. (1988) Model building in organizational/cross-cultural research: the need for multiple methods, indices, and cultures. International studies of management and organisation, 18 (3), 19-30.

Part 5
THEORY AND HISTORY

31 'A predisposition to cowardice?': cultural influences on aviation psychology

Allan D. English
Royal Military College of Canada and Queen's University,
Kingston, Canada

Aviation psychology today encompasses many different disciplines, but certain practitioners have come to dominate particular fields. This paper will highlight some cultural influences, both organizational and national, on the development of the diagnosis and treatment of military aviators by British Commonwealth psychologists and psychiatrists in the first half of this century. The reliability of psychiatric opinion, what data were accepted as evidence, and the evolution of theoretical concepts, are among the issues examined.

The effects of stress on aviators is the key issue in this account, and it begins by tracing how this problem was handled from the earliest days of powered flight. The second part of the paper uses the controversy over "lack of moral fibre" (LMF) as a vehicle to study the effects of different national and organizational cultures on policies governing the treatment of psychological disorders in aircrew serving with the Royal Air Force (RAF), particularly Bomber Command, from 1939 to 1945. National cultures played a significant part in this story, because by the end of World War II almost one half of the pilots in the RAF came from the Dominions, and one quarter of Bomber Command's crews were Canadian (Terraine, 1985; Carter, 1991). While, strictly speaking, the label LMF was based on a complex administrative procedure, in reality it was founded on assumptions about human behaviour current in Britain and the air force, and many of these assumptions had their origins in the scientific community.

From its beginnings, the importance of the psychological aspects of aviation were recognized. These problems were originally studied by a variety of medical doctors with an interest in aeronautics. Despite their efforts, aviation psychology grew slowly until stimulated by the demands of World War I, but at its end a significant body of knowledge was emerging on the topic.

Experts recognized that most psychological breakdowns were caused by stress induced by fear, "a normal reaction to a very abnormal environment." While different individuals could tolerate varying degrees of stress, it was concluded that the best treatment for what was called "flying stress" involved sympathetic conversations with a Medical Officer (MO), and simple measures to relieve physical symptoms. Other, more complex regimes, including Freudian-based psychotherapy, showed little promise in the treatment of aviators for flying stress (Birley, 1920, p 1150).

One of the leaders of post-war aviation psychology was James L. Birley, a prominent British neurologist, who had served with the Royal Flying Corps and RAF in France from 1916 to 1919. In a series of lectures given just after the war, he further refined the concept of flying stress. He suggested that aviators went through three successive stages: the periods of inexperience, experience, and stress. He noted that 70 percent of casualties occurred during the period of inexperience, especially in the first three months of active service. Once past this stage, the aviator was at the "zenith" of his effectiveness. This was followed by the period of stress when the flier became "stale" or burnt out. Birley believed it was the MO's job to prolong the second stage as long as possible by resting the aviator "at the critical moment," before burnout occurred (Birley, 1920, p 1149).

Thus by the end of the First World War, many of the basic principles for the treatment of flying stress had been grasped and recorded for posterity. However, post-war economies stifled research between the wars, and in some countries, such as Canada, defence cuts arrested the study of aviation psychology completely.

One of the few books on military psychology written during the inter-war years was Frederick C. Bartlett's Psychology and the Soldier. Bartlett, a distinguished psychologist, was a founding member, in 1939, of Britain's Flying Personnel Research Committee (FPRC). His book stressed that those who suffered mental breakdowns caused by fear were "weaklings" with temperaments unsuited for military service. An alternate, behaviourist, view advanced by the American, J.B. Watson, that fear was mainly a learned response that could be subsequently unlearned, was explicitly rejected by Bartlett (Bartlett, 1927).

However, views like those expressed by Bartlett did not appear to influence RAF medical opinion until after Birley's death, in 1934. It created a void which neuropsychiatrists filled. These specialists, while following the general lines laid out by RAF doctors with wartime service, advanced explanations for psychological breakdown similar to those found in Bartlett's writings. This signalled a significant departure from previous RAF practice, and a new medical doctrine was enunciated as official policy in an RAF publication distributed before the outbreak of war.

The "Notes for Medical Officers on the Psychological Care of Flying Personnel," emphasized the importance of character defects in interpreting most psychological breakdowns. According to this publication, those with "strong characters" were able to display "patriotism," "tenacity of purpose," and self-sacrifice, while those with "weak characters" were described as "vacillating," "undependable," and "ineffective" (Air Ministry, 1939, pp 5, 8, 9, 19).

The opinions expressed in this publication were consonant with those current in psychology and psychiatry in Britain at the time. Hereditarian and Freudian views stressed a person's predisposition to breakdown due to a combination of "breeding," and experience in childhood and early adolescence. The possibility of modifying an individual's predisposition by training was largely ignored, based partly on the Freudian concept that the individual's early experiences had essentially defined his personality, and partly on the belief that temperament was primarily dependent on inborn tendencies (Gillespie, 1942).

This went beyond the experience of World War I, but in a largely theoretical manner, and the policies based on these assumptions led to many British Commonwealth aircrew being labelled cowards, or LMF, when their behaviour could have been explained in other ways.

Once World War II began, the RAF relied on the advice of its senior consultant in neuropsychiatry, Group Captain (later Air Vice-Marshal) Charles P. Symonds, and he, more than any other, defined RAF medical policy on aviation psychology during the war.

In an attempt to capture the RAF medical branch's understanding of psychological disorders in aircrew, Symonds co-authored a seminal report in the first four months of 1942. In it, the existing literature on psychological disorders in flying personnel was reviewed, and it was concluded that the field had not been properly worked since it had 'escaped the notice of trained psychiatrists" and been left mainly to non-specialist physicians. The report found that the "most important single predisposing cause of psychological breakdown in flying personnel [was] fatigue," that the main cause of fatigue was fear, and that "of particular importance is individual predisposition to fear, [which is] largely dependent upon temperament" (Symonds and Williams, 1942, p 5, 8).

From a scientific point of view, the greatest weakness in these wartime studies, was that they were almost exclusively based on the examination of persons already diagnosed as suffering from a psychological disorder. There was very little research done to estimate how many of those who were predisposed did not break down. To avoid this touchy issue, some psychiatrists used the term "validity of personal experience" to obviate the need for rigorous scientific method. They acknowledged that their samples were small and that no control groups were employed, but they justified their findings on the basis of their extensive professional training and clinical experience (Ironside and Batchelor, 1945, p v).

The weaknesses of this methodology were highlighted by F.C.R. Chalke, a Canadian psychiatrist, who reviewed some of the data after the war. Chalke's work questioned some of the basic assumptions of conventional psychiatry. He stated that, as a result of wartime experiences, he "was painfully aware of [the] present lack of basic scientific information..." on such important subjects as what comprised the "'constitutional' components of the tendency to develop mental illness," and, among the predisposed to psychological breakdown, how to distinguish between those who coped and those who did not. These comments called into to doubt the very foundations of contemporary psychiatric practice (Chalke, 1954, p 290).

World War I scientists had agreed that assessing flying temperament was a nigh impossible task. However, RAF neuropsychiatrists in World War II believed they could succeed where others had failed. But a report, published in October 1944, examining "the reliability of psychiatric opinion in the Royal Air Force" came to a different conclusion. It identified "disturbing disagreements" between psychiatrists which could "have far-reaching results," and found that nearly "half the assessments of severe predisposition [to neurosis] made by one psychiatrist were not confirmed by the other..." In other words, there was considerable risk that an individual could be incorrectly diagnosed, and discharged from the service without just cause (Hill and Williams, 1944, pp 1, 11).

The greatest challenge to RAF methods of dealing with flying stress and LMF cases came from the Dominions, especially Canada. This issue had come to the fore when "it became apparent that RAF medical standards and attitudes" were different "in many respects from" Canadian ones, and that a number of

Canadian aircrew were being unfairly labelled LMF. At first this challenge was pursued through political channels, because in Canada the professional psychiatric community did not become involved with these issues until the spring of 1943. When it did, one of its "immediate objectives" was "[t]o review and modify the concept of 'lack of morale fibre'" (Feasby, 1953, Vol. 1, pp 354 and Vol. 2, pp 96-7) However disagreements over diagnosis and treatment persisted, and this problem was not resolved to the satisfaction of Canadian authorities until the war was almost over.

Perhaps the most serious shortcoming of the RAF Medical Branch in its treatment of aircrew psychological disorders was that it had forgotten almost all the lessons of World War I. Furthermore, "...one of the most serious deficiencies on the part of psychiatry as a whole [in World War II] was its emphasis on the individual, almost as an isolated unit independent of group dynamics, and its relative neglect of 'social psychiatry'" (Ahrenfeldt, 1968, p 177).

However, RAF authorities did recognize many of the effects of social and morale factors, but they chose to concentrate on medical and psychoanalytical treatments because many of the solutions based on group dynamics could have seriously affected operational capabilities.

What I have tried to show here is that attitudes towards psychological disorders among British Commonwealth aircrew in World War II were dependent to a large extent on the national and organizational cultures of the specialists advising the RAF. The Dominions, especially Canada, because of their neglect of these areas of study, were forced to accept the judgements of others concerning the psychological fitness of their nationals, even though they found these decisions inappropriate in a number of cases. Canada only resolved this issue when its government, under pressure from public opinion, committed resources to the study and practice of aviation psychology.

Acknowledgement

Presentation of this paper was supported in part by the Dean of Arts, Royal Military College of Canada and the School of Graduate Studies and Research and the Department of History, Queen's University, Kingston, Canada.

References

Ahrenfeldt, R.H. (1968), 'Military Psychiatry', in MacNalty, A.S.

and Mellor, W.F. (eds), *Medical Services in War*, Her Majesty's Stationary Office, London.

Air Ministry (Great Britain), (1939), 'Notes for Medical Officers on the Psychological Care of Flying Personnel', Air Ministry Pamphlet [AMP] 100, Public Record Office [PRO] AIR 2/8591.

Bartlett, F.C. (1927), *Psychology and the Soldier*, Cambridge University Press, London.

Birley, J.L. (1920), 'The principles of medical science as applied to military aviation, Lectures I,II,III', *Lancet*, **1920**, 1147-51, 1205-1211, 1251-57.

Carter, W.S. (1991), *Anglo-Canadian Wartime Relations, 1939-1945, RAF Bomber Command and No. 6 [Canadian] Group*, Garland Publishing, New York.

Chalke, F.C.R. (1954), 'Psychiatric screening of recruits', *Department of Veterans Affairs Treatment Services Bulletin*, **9**, 273-292.

Feasby, W.R. (ed) (1953), *The Official History of the Canadian Medical Services 1939-1945*, 2 Vols., Queen's Printer, Ottawa.

Gillespie, R.D. (1942), *Psychological Effects of War on Citizen and Soldier*, W. W. Norton, New York.

Hill, B. and Williams, D. (1944), 'Investigation into psychological disorders in flying personnel: the reliability of psychiatric opinion in the RAF', FPRC Report 601, PRO AIR 57.

Ironside, R.N. and Batchelor, I.R.C. (1945), *Aviation Neuro-Psychiatry*, Livingstone, Edinburgh.

Symonds, C.P. and Williams, D. (1942), 'Psychological disorders in flying personnel, section 1. A critical review of published literature," FPRC Report 412(c), PRO AIR 57.

Terraine, J. (1985), *The Right of the Line*, Hodder and Stoughton, London.

32 Behavioural theory and behavioural technology in the design of safe systems

Julian C. Leslie, University of Ulster

The rate of development of psychology in the last thirty years has been remarkable, and this has been reflected in the number of academic journals, the increasing number of students in training, the increasing impact on many professions, and, in the British Isles at least, the high profile of psychology in the communications media. The developments have been very diverse and are thus hard to characterise, but arguably they have centred on a huge growth in the applications of psychology. This involves the application of a growing number of empirical, quantitative methodologies and a rapidly expanding number of areas. Those related to aviation include behaviour in the workplace, organisational behaviour, health-related behaviour, stress and coping, road transport, crowd behaviour, instrument design, and human-computer interaction. These are a small subset of a large class of areas of applied psychology.

Inspection of the methodologies used in applied psychology reveals huge variation: only a limited set of tenets unite them. These commit psychologists to using procedures that are replicable because they specify clearly the environmental events involved and the means of measuring observable behaviour to be used. These means often include verbal reports of otherwise unobservable behaviour. As a general rule, there are no constraints on the number or type of intervening and unobservable processes that can be invoked by psychological theories. Of similar importance in the present context, standards of measurement are no more stringent than the simple ones mentioned. Thus, a questionnaire measure, for example, may be said to measure a personality characteristic even though a careful interpretation of the available data suggests that the proposed underlying characteristic accounts for only a small percentage of the variability in the data. At worst, the liberality of current standards leads to the reification of commonsense notions. For example, I might suspect that "hard-heartedness" is a characteristic of, say, senior managers, then proceed to construct (and publish) a scale that may be reliable, but only accounts for a small proportion of the variance in the responses of the target group, and conclude that I have discovered a personality characteristic.

To the extent that my negative comments on contemporary psychology and applied psychology are fair, there is evidence that the whole rapidly growing edifice is unsoundly based and might collapse. However, it is routinely said that the type of criticism I have been making is not sustained because there is another, more important, justification for psychological research studies. On this view, the central precept is that studies should test theories, rather than be the simple, or unfocussed, collection of data. Then, the argument runs, the fact that a particular study demonstrates only a weak relationship between independent and dependent variables is not necessarily significant. Rather, the important issue is the long-term one of theory testing and development. An alternative view is that if there are few constraints on theory construction, then theory-testing is of limited value. At the moment, researchers are eagerly modifying "miniature theories" in innumerable subareas. This process is not rendering the whole edifice that is contemporary psychology any more sound. I would like to commend an alternative approach that I believe will underpin psychology more successfully (this is not a novel suggestion: cf. Sidman, 1960).

The key principle is the apparently simple one that methods or techniques of proven effectiveness should be employed. The rapid growth of psychology has occurred not because of recent theoretical developments in the discipline, but because of the availability of a range of psychological or behavioural technologies, some of which are highly effective in specific areas. We should exploit this sound base, but do so in a systematic way. This means that when a new problem is addressed, we should initially adopt and adapt methods that have been shown to be effective in an apparently related area, but we should also proceed to evaluate their effectiveness in the area of the new problem. Taken together, the two aspects of this recommendation imply that we must have standards by which to judge the use of any psychological methodology and we must apply them on every occasion on which that methodology is applied. This will in turn have implications for experimental and other "non-applied" areas of psychology: there will be a considerable onus on researchers to refine techniques so that, at least when they are used in favourable conditions (for example, those that prevail in a laboratory), they are highly effective. Our overall research agenda should give higher priority to doing things well, and, in particular, to continually extending our capacity to predict human behaviour through systematic replication of well-established phenomena.

I believe that this critique is relevant to aviation psychology for a number of reasons: firstly, those in the aviation industry are more aware than ever that human resources and human factors are of critical importance as they strive for greater efficiency and effectiveness; secondly, such critical consumers of psychological technology are only interested in the most effective tools for their needs; and thirdly, as indicated below a review of the current state of aviation psychology and related areas of applied psychology indicates that some opportunities for application of technologies found to be effective elsewhere are not being exploited.

As noted earlier, and illustrated by the wide range of topics addressed at this conference, very many areas of applied psychology have aspects relevant to aviation psychology. However, Fuller (1994) lucidly argues that application of behavioural analysis, which itself derives from the behaviourist tradition, is being neglected in favour of developments that relfect the current cognitive *zeitgeist*. This deficiency stems, at least in part, from the narrow research agenda of those working in the field of applied behavioural analysis. For the last twenty five years, the *Journal of Applied Behavior Analysis* has been the main publication for research that is concerned with the whole range of human and social problems approached from this perspective. However, it has included virtually no papers directly relevant to aviation and very few concerned with transport and accidents (an honourable exception here is that by Fuller,1991). Fuller (1994) points out that this neglect is regrettable because there are many possible straightforward applications of the key concept of the three-term relationship, or contingency, between antecedent conditions (A), required behaviour (B) and consequence (C), to the maintenance of safety in an aviation environment. He gives the example of a contingency that applies to ramp workers, whose accidents cost the industry $20,000 per worker each year. When they encounter the flashing anti-collision lights on an aircraft (A), they must change their behaviour (B), sufficiently to avoid collision and other undesirable consequences (C). Clearly, this does not always happen, but behavior analysis can suggest many ways in which the contingency could be made more effective.

Another cause for concern at the neglect of behavioural analysis in aviation psychology arises from the critique of applied psychology given earlier: applied behavioural analysis has a remarkable track record of providing effective intervention techniques across a huge range of areas of human activity, and we are consequently obliged to consider whether it has contributions to make to aviation psychology. What began as behaviour therapy for clinical problems now embraces many other areas where human behaviour is a problem in many other senses (see Bellack, Hersen, and Kazdin, 1982, for a wide-ranging review of areas of application). One long-term industrial application, involving the introduction of a "token economy" for safety practices, lead to annual savings at each of two open-pit mines of $300,000, which would seem to justify that innovation (Fox, Hopkins, and Anger, 1987).

Where behavioural analysis has not been the technique of choice for intervention in a particular type of problem, this has generally been because it lacks face validity in that case. A lack of face validity of applied behavioural analysis usually occurs either because it appears too simplistic for the matter in hand, or, relatedly, because it is seen as too manipulative in a context which is normally construed as involving a considerable amount of human judgment and decision making. Both factors may be operating in the immensely complex human-machine interactions that are a feature of modern aviation and related fields. A recent symposium at the Royal Society in London on human factors in hazardous situations provided a state-of-the-art account of how psychologists conceptualise some such problems (Broadbent, Reason, and Baddeley, 1990), and it will be useful for present purposes to review the aviation-related contributions.

Considering the prevention of accidents in complex systems in general, Rasmussen (1990) notes that we are primarily concerned with establishing good practice by operators at a high level, rather than with specifying particular acts. Relatedly, Rasmussen says "the trick in the design of reliable systems is to make sure that human actors maintain sufficient flexibility to cope with system aberrations, i.e., not to constrain them by an inadequate rule system. In addition,...actors...[should] maintain contact with hazards in such a way that they will be familiar with the boundary to loss of control and will learn to recover." (p. 10). He relates human error closely to adaptation and learning, and does not believe that it can be treated as separate class of behaviour. In a similar vein, Reason (1990) emphasises the importance of "latent failures" in complex systems. These are actions that affect the organisation and management of a system that later combine with other actions to produce disastrous results, and he includes the Challenger disaster amongst a list of recent and colossally expensive disasters that he attributes to latent failures. In Figure 1 he identifies key elements in the system that generate the accidents, and notes that while feedback loops 1 and 2, between accidents and incidents or unsafe acts and fallible decisions that occur earlier in the system sequence, are usually available and sometimes effective, loops 3 and 4, between psychological precursors of unsafe acts and line management deficiencies and those fallible earlier decisions, are not generally used. A feedback loop is formally identical to a three-term contingency, and Reason is saying that while some contingencies are effective, other important ones are not implemented and thus do not change the behaviour of the operators of the complex system.

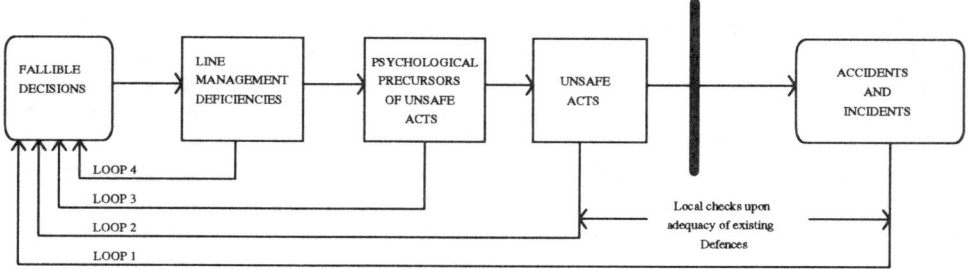

Figure 1 Features of Reason's model.

We can compare Reason's model with another recent account of psychological aspects of aircraft accidents. Diehl (1989) provides a model of factors involved in accident generation, investigation and prevention. He notes that four types of measure can be treated as accident prevention elements, each of which modifies the relationships between the behaviour of the operators of the system and the functioning of the system. In order of proximity to the incident and accident, and beginning with the one furthest away, these are: (i) elimination of hazards (such as banning dangerous practices or components of systems); (ii) incorporation of safety features in aircraft design and manufacture; (iii) provision of warning devices to signal, for example, engine failure; and (iv) establishment of procedural safeguards, such as training programmes and standard operating procedures. Importantly, he notes that the consequences of accident investigations tend to be modifications of the procedural safeguards and the warning devices, rather than the deeper-seated, but more remote, accident prevention elements.

While the models proposed by Reason and Diehl contain some different elements, and were devised in slightly different contexts, both writers are clearly seeking to indicate the importance of what are called contingencies in behavioural analysis: these are relationships, within a defined context between actions and significant consequences. Furthermore, the analyses of Reason and Diehl come to similar conclusions. They find that while complex systems involve the interaction of multiple factors, and many factors operating at different stages and levels may contribute to accidents, there is a tendency to seek to remedy problems only by altering the more proximal factors. Thus, following a major accident it is less likely that a hazard will be eliminated (on Diehl's model) or a line management deficiency dealt with (on Reason's model), and more likely that procedural safeguards are introduced or those who committed unsafe acts on the flight deck are identified. These observations are consistent with many other findings showing that we are more likely to be responsive to short-term contingencies than to long-term contingencies, although the latter may be far more significant (see Logue, 1988, for a review of relevant studies).

Returning to the Royal Society symposium, Broadbent (1990) is concerned with the relationship between a person's knowledge of a system and their ability to control it. He reviews a series of experimental studies that show that verbal accounts people give of their mental processes may not concur with their actual task performance. He concludes that, amongst other things, it is not safe to rely on classroom instruction for training operators of complex systems, nor can the knowledge of operators necessarily be assessed by written tests or verbal interviews. So-called on-the-job training, or "sitting by Nellie", will therefore retain an important role. This is consistent with the commitment in applied behavioural analysis to examining, and devising, environment-behaviour relationships.

Finally, Green (1990) examines human error on the flight deck, which accounts for more accidents than other factors. His report derives from extensive databases in the United Kingdom on the reporting of aviation accidents and incidents. He concludes that, consistent with the views of Rasmussen and Reason noted earlier, we should not seek to identify a special psychology of human error, but rather employ psychological knowledge of many types to deal with failures that occur at all levels of the aviation system.

To summarise, there seems to be a consensus that addressing human factors will be very important in making systems safer or ensuring a high degree of safety in ever-more complex systems, including those of aviation; that this requires an understanding of how human operators interact with all levels and aspects of complex systems; and that training operators in good practice is more important than trying to eliminate specific examples of error. There may indeed be no typical errors because human factors can combine, and operate through different levels of the system, to generate previously unseen and unforeseen problems. However, prevention of accidents will be enhanced by specification of a greater number of feedback loops which link inappropriate behaviour to consequences at various levels in the system. Finally, good practice must be defined largely in terms of on-task performance, rather relying on verbal accounts of that behaviour.

This summary suggests that applied behavioural analysis, which is primarily concerned with the specification of feedback loops or contingencies, in the sense of identifying a relationship between a class of behaviour and its consequences for the purpose of maintaining or modifying that behaviour, should be a strategy of choice in aviation psychology. Five characteristics of the implementation of this strategy will be: (i) that often the contingencies will already exist in some form within the system being examined but require to be made more salient to effectively modify the operator's behaviour; (ii) generally the behaviour that requires to be strengthened will be members of a class constituting good practice, rather than narrowly defined categories; (iii) sustaining good practice by these means will be more important than the direct elimination of instances of inappropriate behaviour - the focus of attention must be accident prevention; (iv) the strategy of enhancing the salience of contingencies that contribute to safety must be applied to all operators within the system, and thus from the chief executive downwards; and (v) means must be found to ensure that it is actions that are changed, rather than knowledge about possible actions.

This is a substantial agenda, but on the one hand support for its implementation may come from the aviation industry's growing, if tardy, realisation that psychological factors are crucial for its sustained success (Hawkins, 1987), and on the other hand there is a huge repertoire of techniques in applied behavioural analysis that may well be successfully adapted for aviation applications.

References

Bellack, A.S., Hersen, M., and Kazdin, A.E. (Eds.) (1982), *International Handbook of Behavior Modification*, New York: Plenum.

Broadbent, D.E. (1990), Effective decisions and their verbal justification. In D.E.Broadbent, J.Reason, and A.Baddeley (Eds.), *Human Factors in Hazardous Situations*, pp. 45-54, Oxford: Clarendon Press.

Broadbent, D.E., Reason, J., and Baddeley, A. (Eds.) (1990), *Human Factors in Hazardous Situations*, 145 pp, Oxford: Clarendon Press.

Diehl, A.E. (1989), Human performance aspects of aircraft accidents. In R.S. Jensen (Ed.), *Aviation Psychology*, pp. 378-402, Aldershot: Gower Technical.

Fox, D.K., Hopkins, B.L., and Anger, W.K. (1987), The long-term effects of a token economy on safety performance in open-pit mining, *Journal of Applied Behavioral Analysis, 20*, 215-224.

Fuller, R.G.C. (1991), Behaviour analysis and unsafe driving: warning - learning trap ahead! *Journal of Applied Behavior Analysis, 24*, 73-75.

Fuller, R. (1994), Behaviour analysis and aviation safety. In N. Johnston, R. Fuller, N. MacDonald (Eds.) *Aviation Psychology in Practice*, Aldershot: Avebury.

Green, R. (1990), Human error on the flight deck. In D.E.Broadbent, J.Reason, and A.Baddeley (Eds.), *Human Factors in Hazardous Situations*, pp. 55-63. Oxford: Clarendon Press.

Logue, A.W. (1988), Research on self-control: an integrating framework, *Behavioral and Brain Sciences, 11*, 665-709.

Rasmussen, J. (1990), Human error and the problem of causality in analysis of accidents. In D.E.Broadbent, J.Reason, and A.Baddeley (Eds.), *Human Factors in Hazardous Situations*, pp. 1-14. Oxford: Clarendon Press.

Reason, J. (1990), The contribution of latent human error to the breakdown of complex systems. In D.E.Broadbent, J.Reason, and A.Baddeley (Eds.), *Human Factors in Hazardous Situations*, pp. 27-36. Oxford: Clarendon Press.

Sidman, M. (1960). *Tactics of Scientific Research*. New York: Basic Books.

33 Opening up ATC work: behavioural, cognitive and sociological perspectives

Liam Bannon, University of Limerick
Dan Shapiro, Lancaster University

Introduction

This paper is intended to set the scene for a discussion of how different disciplinary perspectives can contribute towards our understanding of complex human-computer interaction situations, specifically focused on air traffic control (ATC). While the title of the Symposium "Psychological versus Sociological Approaches to ATC Work" might appear unnecessarily combative and divisive, the intent is to open up a direct debate about strengths and weaknesses of different approaches. Here we concentrate on developing the third, and probably least discussed to date - namely the sociological approach[1]. It is important to note that a variety of different sociological approaches could illuminate ATC work, and what we represent here is mainly just one form of contribution, namely that of ethnomethodologically-inspired ethnography. All 3 papers in this session involve members of a group of sociologists originally at Lancaster University who have carried out a study on ATC in the UK (Hughes et al, 1992)[2]. Our purpose in this introductory paper is more to open up the discussion, and put it in a larger context of current debates within the general HCI and CSCW community.

The Context: Evolving HCI Research

While the field of HCI is itself perhaps best viewed as an arena in which different disciplinary viewpoints vie for attention, the cognitive science perspective has been the most dominant in recent years. This approach has come up against a number of problems, both in terms of its research agenda and the usability and utility of its empirical results (Bannon & Bødker, 1991). For example, many experimental studies tend to analyse the individual without reference to their community, or their history, performing on a task designed by the experimenter in an unfamiliar environment. Performance is measured relative to a certain "ideal", rational model of problem-solving, and the deviations of subjects from rational action is noted. In an influential book, Lave (1988) provides a strong critique of both the theoretical underpinnings of the mainstream approach and the experimental manipulations often associated with it, arguing that "Cognition observed in everyday practice is distributed -stretched over, not divided among- mind, body, activity and culturally organised settings (which include other actors)". There is a call for changes, of a more or less radical kind, in the conceptual frameworks employed, the kinds of research undertaken, and methods used, in HCI.

The critique of the general HCI field, as exemplified by work appearing in such flagship conferences as the ACM CHI series, needs to be moderated by a number of important factors as we turn towards HCI work in areas such as process-control or aviation, where there has been a somewhat different research tradition. For example, the exemplary work of people like Hollnagel and Woods (1983), Rasmussen (1986) and others in the "cognitive engineering" perspective is of particular importance to our present concerns. Such work takes the features of the task domain as vital to an understanding of human-system interaction. So the nature of the work is factored into their models. Secondly, they usually employ skilled operatives in their studies, in very realistic situations, if not conducting actual on-site studies, so this diffuses further some of the criticisms noted above. However, emphasis has still tended to focus on the individual user's model of the task, the actual behaviour of each user, their errors, etc. This is adequate for certain purposes, yet the uncritical acceptance of this situation as the norm in the field has meant that the everyday needs of people to communicate with others both *around* and *through* the computer system have received insufficient attention. Current concerns in HCI, and in the emerging CSCW (Computer Supported Cooperative Work) field, are on extending the focus of concern from the human-computer dyad to larger groups of people and machines engaged in collaborative tasks[3].

It is specifically on this issue that there has been interest in alternative concepts and methods. This focus has lead to the need for extensions to existing conceptual and methodological frameworks as well as the search for more appropriate frameworks from other disciplinary areas. While more traditional sociological and anthropological concepts - division of labour, issues of power and control, symbolism, etc. are of importance, there has been particular interest in studies of an ethnomethodological nature. The emphasis in these studies is on the work that members do in order to make their work accountable to themselves and each other, focusing on the "working division of labour" as distinct from viewing the division of labour as an analytical category. Even within the cognitive science tradition, we see an extension of the basic conceptual apparatus in a number of directions, e.g. examining the role of artifacts in human cognition (Norman, 1991), and the way cognition is distributed among people and artifacts -"distributed cognition" (Hutchins, ms)[4]. Another alternative conceptual framework that has been applied is the Russian tradition of socio-cultural or activity theory (Kuutti, 1991). While the conceptual apparatus of this framework is difficult to apply directly, its focus on the concept of activities, which are inherently collective, not individual, phenomena, and on mediation of activity via instruments, tools, procedures, methods, etc. make it quite *apropos*.

The Case of ATC Work

Air Traffic Control (ATC) is a very complex work activity, involving a variety of tasks that must be interleaved, with obvious time constraints, including communication and cooperation not just with cockpit crew, but with other controllers on the ground. Given the safety critical nature of the activity, there has been a strong interest in understanding and either automating or supporting the work of the controllers with computer aids for many years[5]. Simplistic automation strategies will not work (Harper, Hughes & Shapiro, 1991). A more considered, evolving piecemeal strategy for supporting the work of ATC officers with technology is now developing among a number of researchers in the area. There remain however serious questions about human-machine task allocation in the design of the supporting technology systems, for ATC, just as for other areas involving intense monitoring of workflows and processes. Reducing the involvement of controllers in the actual controlling activity through automation can have the effect of making them less competent as controllers when in fact a system malfunction requires them to intervene and assume direct control for a period (Bainbridge, 1983).

The work of air traffic controllers (ATCs) has been the subject of study for many years by human factors (HF) researchers. As the work involves a high degree of expertise, it has been evident for some time that extrapolation of simplified laboratory studies to the world of work is deeply problematic in this area, so there has been a tradition of performing studies in as rich a setting as possible, and using experienced people in the studies. The conceptual frameworks employed in such studies have been varied. On the one hand, in an effort to eschew conceptual confusions, some researchers have adopted an extremely behaviouristic task analysis approach, focusing very much on identifiable tasks, and overt behaviours required of individual ATC's. This was the norm in most ATC studies until 10 years ago. Then, the influence of cognitive psychology (mentioned above) led to a different approach, going beyond simple behavioural studies. In particular there has been an interest in what has been termed "cognitive task analysis" (CTA). This differs from traditional task analysis, which tends to focus on behavioural performance and training objectives, by putting more emphasis on the cognitive processes involved in producing behaviour and on the nature of the learning process. As noted by Redding & Seamster (in press): " CTA focuses on decision making and mental models, learning and skill development, the interrelationships among job concepts and task elements, and group performance as well as individual differences." They claim that most CTA's identify the following: 1) the key job components, 2) the knowledge and skills required for similar job components, 3) important knowledge and skill differences between novices, (perhaps intermediates) and experts, or between good and bad performers and 4) the conditions which best facilitate learning. While it is generally claimed that cognitive and behavioural methods ought to be complementary, it is not always easy to discuss them in such a manner, as the categorisations and concepts may not mesh neatly.

We can add a further development, or perhaps note a parallel development, where more sociological methods have been applied. There has been an increased interest recently in studies that focus more explicitly on the *socially organised character* of ATC work, and the effects that new technology might have in supporting or indeed hindering this collaboration. Much of this work has been reported within the area of CSCW - Computer Supported Cooperative Work, and is often identified with an *ethnographic* approach to studying ATC work, *in situ*. This is quite distinct from the individualistically-oriented task-analytic studies done in laboratories, as often found in traditional human factors work, and while as we shall see, there are overlaps between this approach and CTA, there are also quite large differences in approach. As expressed by Hughes et al., 1992: "There is no one method of ethnographic analysis. ... The field workers immersed themselves in the work by spending several months observing activities on and around the suites, talking to staff, and discussing with them the researchers' developing understanding of what controllers do. While attempting to avoid prejudices and to allow the work situation to 'speak for itself' as much as possible, researchers cannot claim to address it innocent of any theoretical orientation; and their results would be much impoverished if they did. The purpose of an ethnographic approach is not so much to show *that* work is socially organised (which is rather easy) but to show *how* it is socially organised."

The ethnographic studies note, for example, how much individual work done by ATC officers is also done in a way so as to make available to other ATC officers information as to the state and conduct of the task, without requiring overt messaging between officers. In any attempt to "improve" the tools of the ATC officers, they point out how great care must be exercised so that the current, often non-obvious, fluid use of artifacts and signs to communicate the state of affairs in the airspace to all in the control room are not disturbed by new technology. The technology may, while making specific tasks easier, have the undesirable side-effect of occluding some vital information about the state of affairs to others. An example that has been studied in this regard is how properties of the physical flight control strips are used to make available information about the state of affairs to others in simple yet undemanding ways that would be difficult to replicate in simple electronic replications of such strips.

Comparing Approaches

While any attempt at direct comparison of approaches is bound to be difficult, perhaps in some sense impossible due to the incommensurability of different perspectives, from the point of view of systems design it would appear reckless if one did not at least try to utilise all the concepts and results available, from whatever disciplinary background, or research method, so as to develop appropriate technology to support ATC's. While such comparative studies are rare, there has been an initial attempt to investigate the complementarities of certain approaches in a recent paper by one of the authors (Shapiro, 1993) which we will briefly refer to here as a pointer to the kinds of studies that may be fruitful. The paper contrasts two studies undertaken from different disciplinary perspectives but with exactly the same subject matter: the use and possible electronic replacement of the paper flight progress strip in en-route air traffic control. One involves an ethnographic method and an ethnomethodological theoretical perspective (Hughes et al., 1992). The other involves an experimental behavioural study undertaken in the US by O.U. Vortac et al. (1992).

Shapiro notes the obvious problems with an exercise of this kind which takes just two specific studies as its basis. We should also note that several of the 'standard' criticisms of task analysis either do not apply or only partially apply to the Vortac et al. study. While the study did take place using a training simulator 'experiment' rather than a real-world setting, that is not intrinsic to the method and an equivalent real-world study is perfectly feasible. While the study used ATC instructors rather than real current controllers, that too could be corrected provided a sufficiently unobtrusive means of observation could be devised, which again should not be insuperable. It looks only at individual controllers, in communication through the simulator with 'ghost' pilots and a 'ghost' controller, but the researchers recognise this as a problem and describe their intention to study a pair of controllers co-operating at a suite. Commenting on the study, Shapiro suggests that the approach needs a much more purposive and directed means of initially choosing and then refining what are the pertinent units of activity to observe. He complains that while it was possible to conclude that strip use was important; it was not able to determine the implications for the possible automation of this function, or how it should be done. Finally, Shapiro notes: "the sociality of the work, which is so fundamental to the ethnographic account, is entirely missing from the task analysis, and it is not easy to see how it could be recovered". At the same time, he is aware of limitations of the ethnographic-ethnomethodological account concerning the degree of independence between data and interpretation.

What would be of interest now is if we could have a comparison exercise between an ethnographic account and a cognitive task analysis of similar activities. CTA methods include such methods as observation and interviewing, protocol analysis, psychological scaling, cognitive and performance modelling, and error analysis of different forms. As noted above an ethnographic account would also encompass some of these methods: observing and interviewing in particular. At least at this level, the kinds of material produced might be comparable. While the ethnographic account does not develop models of "internal cognitive processes", it does try to explain observed behaviour by recourse to concepts which describe the nature of the work from the point of view of those carrying it out. While one might expect vast differences here, we can detect, at least tentatively, some interesting commonalities in terms of what the different views call attention to in the work of ATC.

For example, in an overview of CTA, Redding & Seamster claim that 2 key findings emerging from such studies are that the 2 key tasks for ATC's are: to maintain Situation Awareness & to develop and revise the Sector Control Plan. Let us note one of the key features of ATC work as identified by Hughes et al(1992) from their ethnographic work - "getting the picture". To quote them directly on this: " Controllers 'build a picture' of the state of the sector by relating traffic within it to a 'schematic' of that sector's characteristics. ....'Getting the picture' therefore means working out what proportion of flights fit the scheme and what proportion are exceptions; assessing these for the kinds of control actions that will be required, and planning for those actions; and issuing the instructions to create an appropriate current order, and make the traffic flow." At least as a first pass, there seems to be some agreement on what the key aspects of ATC work are. Exactly what is involved in "getting the picture" would seem to be an interesting exercise to explore and develop within different approaches. Even more so, in thinking about system design, how could one support ATC's in this demanding task? Whether one refers to something going on "in the head" of the ATC, in terms of mental models or such like, or whether one prefers a phenomenological account, both kinds of reports would seem to indicate the need for support tools to provide some form of Gestalt to help controllers follow the air traffic in a sector.

In conclusion, the purpose of this paper was to open up a discussion on the variety of ways that one might study ATC work, and note some features of each approach. While they are not directly comparable, certainly there should be scope for collaboration across the disciplinary divides.

References

Bainbridge, L. (1983) Ironies of Automation. In G. Johannsen & J. Rijnsdorp (Eds.) *Proceedings of IFAC/IFIP/IFORS/IEA Conference on Analysis, Design & Evaluation of Man-Machine Systems*, pp 151-8, Baden Baden Pergamon.

Bannon, L. & Bødker, S. (1991) Beyond the Interface: Encountering Artifacts in Use. Book Chapter in J.M. Carroll (Ed.) (1991) *Designing Interaction: Psychology at the Human-Computer Interface*, pp.227-253. (New York: Cambridge University Press)

Harper, R.R., Hughes, J.A., & Shapiro, D.Z. (1991) Harmonious Working and CSCW: Computer technology and air traffic control. In J. Bowers & S. Benford (Eds.) *Studies in Computer Supported Cooperative Work. Amsterdam: North-Holland.*

Hollnagel, E. & D.D. Woods. (1983). Cognitive Systems Engineering: New wine in new bottles. *International Journal of Man-Machine Studies,* 18, 583 600.

Hughes, J. A., D. Randall & D. Shapiro. (1992) 'Faltering from Ethnography to Design', in *Proceedings of "CSCW '92: Sharing Perspectives"; the*

Fourth International Conference on Computer Supported Cooperative Work, Toronto, 2-4 November 1992, pp 115-122.

Hutchins, E. (ms) *How a cockpit remembers its speeds*. University of California, San Diego.

Kuutti, K. (1991) The concept of activity as a basic unit of analysis for CSCW research. In Bannon, L., Robinson, M. & Schmidt, K.(Eds.) *Proceedings of the Second European Conference on CSCW - ECSCW'91* (Dordrecht: Kluwer).249-264.

Lave, J. (1988) *Cognition in Practice*. (Cambridge: Cambridge University Press).

Norman, D. (1991) Cognitive Artifacts. In J.M. Carroll (Ed.) (1991) *Designing Interaction: Psychology at the Human-Computer Interface*, pp.17-38. (New York: Cambridge University Press)

Rasmussen, J. (1986). *Information-processing and human-machine interaction: An approach to cognitive engineering. New York: North-Holland*.

Redding, R.E. & T.L. Seamster (in press) Cognitive Task Analysis in ATC and Aviation Crew Training. To appear in N. Johnston, N. McDonald & R. Fuller (Eds.) *Aviation Psychology in Practice*. Brookfield, VT: Ashgate Publishing Co.

Shapiro, D. (1993). *Ferrets in a sack? Ethnographic studies and task analysis in CSCW*. Paper presented at Workshop on CSCW Design & Groupware, Austria, June 1993.

Vortac, O.U., M. Edwards, J. Jones, C. Manning & A. Rotter, '*Analysis of Flight Progress Strip Use by En Route Air Traffic Controllers*', Project Report–Observational Study 1.2, Department of Psychology, University of Oklahoma, Norman, OK 73019, USA. ('O.U. Vortac' represents the collaborative research efforts of F.T. Durso, S. Lewandowsky & S.D. Gronlund).

---

[1] The other approaches are evident in a number of ATC-related sessions at this Conference.

[2] The contribution of the remaining author (L. Bannon), who comes from a psychological background, has been in helping to explore the limitations of different frameworks, and the possibilities for their cross-fertilisation.

[3] In this context, within the aviation area, it is interesting to see the current emphasis on Crew Resource Management (CRM).

[4] This latter approach is of particular interest due to its concern with mediated communication and the use of representational artifacts in such settings as ship navigation and the aircraft cockpit.

[5] Of course, organisational-political factors also affect this work, although we do not focus on this issue here.

34 Cooperative work and technological support in Air Traffic Control

D. Randall
Department of Interdisciplinary Studies, Manchester Metropolitan University
R. Harper
Rank Xerox EuroParc, Cambridge

Air Traffic Control as a safety critical domain

There is general agreement that the ATC system is, as it were, under some 'strain' as a result of the effective doubling traffic in the airways during the course of the last ten years or so, although accidents remain rare.[1] The demands on the system are to an extent contradictory in that on the one hand the needs of both airlines and passengers for a cost effective and time-efficient system must be met, while at the same time there is the overarching requirement that overall safety levels be maintained and where possible enhanced.

It is hardly surprising, therefore, that a great deal of research effort has gone into the provision of technical support for Air Traffic Controllers (ATCOs) which would enable levels of both safety and expedition to be maintained whilst dealing with higher levels of traffic flow. At the same time, new technologies for use in ATC have not proved wholly successful historically.[2] Indeed, ATC in the UK can still be characterised as a 'low tech' endeavour where paper both exists in abundance and seems still to be an instrument of routine ATC work. While doubting that technology by itself can provide solutions to the problem of safe transportation at higher capacity levels, we believe the potential for greater capacity and enhanced safety requires attention to the relationship between technology and the character of work in a domain such as ATC.

Safety critical systems often require highly skilled operatives to work together in complex ways. The nature of the 'skills' that operatives in such domains deploy, however, while potentially crucial for the maintenance of safety, is often both subtle and elusive. Moreover, the degree to which the relevant skills should be characterised as 'individual' or 'collective' in terms of their consequences for systems design remains contested. Much research, the large part of it under 'cognitive' auspices, has been undertaken on the

223

work of controllers (examples abound, but see Wise et al (1991), etc.) Nevertheless, studies of co-operative orientation to potentially hazardous situations are rare. If ATC is to remain a "High hazard/ low risk" system in La Porte and Consolini's (1991) terms, the need to examine the relative merits of considering the work of controllers in individualistic and collective terms is paramount.

Concepts such as cooperation and co-ordination which have evolved from the interdisciplinary field of Computer Supported Co-operative Working (CSCW) give an alternative characterisation of what we would argue are inherently 'social' features of work (Hughes *et al.*, 1991), and furnish us with the opportunity for a fine detail rendering of how those concepts are manifested in the social organisation of work through the use of ethnography. Such approaches provide us both with a detailed understanding of current work practices and potentially with a vehicle for identifying their relationship with technological innovation. The purpose of this paper, then, is to examine how new technologies in the domain of ATC may be developed which will prove relevant to the dual requirements of safety and expedition through an understanding of the work as co-operatively constituted, and to suggest design features which will render incorporation less problematic.

Controlling work, the 'trustability' of paper and the culture of support

The focus of our studies, encompassing two lengthy periods of ethnography at the London Air Traffic Control Centre (LATCC), was on controlling activity as teamwork in a 'working division of labour' (Anderson *et al.*, 1989). In this respect it was at the outset a specifically sociological study, which contrasted with the cognitive psychological perspectives that had previously been brought to the domain.

There is a considerable literature from these latter perspectives which focuses on various areas of interest, notably error generation (Reason, 1987; Stager and Hameluck, 1988) and in many instances argues the case for their relevance to issues of automation. In this paper, the emphasis will be on the distinctive quality of an interest in error *handling* from within sociology. Attention to cooperation and co-ordination as features of the relevant and skilful work of ATCOs constitutes one of the ways in which sociology can proffer insights into their importance for safe working and the possibility of their attenuation by allocation of these functions to technological components. The analysis focuses on two aspects of the social organisation of work which we believe have consequences for automation and safety. Firstly, we show how it is in and through the collective attention to paper based information that errors are handled, and safe working in general is manifested 'on the suite', and secondly how in and through active co-ordination, the culture of support that acts as a guarantor of 'inter suite' attentiveness is maintained.

For the individual radar controller the primary responsibility is sectoral, including the maintenance of separation standards within the sector, and the co-ordination of that traffic in and out of the sector as aircraft are 'passed'.

The controller's scheduling problem involves receiving a steady stream of traffic into the sector must organise and make orderly the flow of that traffic so as to avoid mishap, and with due recognition of the need for flights to be expedited as effectively as possible. Available to the controller are both a set of rules governing procedure as laid down by the Manuals of Air Traffic Services, and a number of information sources. The latter can be described as taking three forms. Information is available directly from the radar screens and the printed paper strips, and indirectly and more intermittently from other operatives, including those 'on the suite' by word of mouth, those on other suites through, most frequently, the telephone, and from pilots via the R/T.

Both the radar and the paper strips present information from database processing applications which in the case of the radar provides a 'real time' representation of the relative positions of aircraft, and on the printed paper strips a substantial amount of other information about route, etc. It is important to realise that necessary though radar data is, it is by no means sufficient to the task of controlling. It depicts only the 'current state of play'. The strips, which are produced from original Flight Plans submitted by the airlines also have a significant role to play. They are, indeed, a vital resource for controlling work.

Strips are updated manually either as aircraft pass over reporting points or as new information is input at the suite. They are quickly overlaid with varied written information, including changes in flight levels, times, etc., the writing being done as instructions are given or as new information becomes known. One quickly discovers also that not only are strips written on, but that *anyone can write on them*. They serve to provide the controller and his/her colleagues with a history of events, a record of intentions, and act as a resource for deciding 'what must be done next'. As each instruction to an aircraft is given, the controller records the change in pen on the strip. When co-ordination is effected, again the fact is recorded. New information about changes in estimated times can be appended by any member of the team. In addition, *anything can be written on a strip*. While standard formats exist for much standard information such as flight levels, it is normal to see a variety of signs, squiggles, written comments, and so forth, all of which are attention getting devices for the controlling team. Further, the strips are regularly moved around by different members of the team, as when a 'chief' for instance will place two strips in adjacent positions an cock them out with the comment, 'watch these two ...'. In a nutshell, the strips are the physical counterpart to the flexible working of the controlling team. They are robust, flexible, and publicly available 'at a glance' to all members of the suite. They represent a highly informal 'working division of labour', where 'things to do' are allocated among the personnel on the suite according to principles that are determined from 'work in hand'.

Moreover, as the cognitive literature shows, 'slips' and 'errors' are not uncommon in ATC and may be to a degree inevitable, although as Stager and Hameluck (1988) point out, such errors may be categorisable in a variety of ways. While some of this may be a result of inattention, poor decision-making and so on, it is also clear that the inaccuracies of database information can produce problems. As one controller put it: "If you assume the information you're getting is wrong more times than its right, you'll be right more times than you're wrong." Thus, and for instance, radar faults can arise and the paper strips can fail to arrive at 'timely' moments or contain incorrect information, faults which must both be recognised for what they are and dealt with. That is, the information is not in itself reliably trustable. Trustability, we find, is arrived at through the medium of the interpretative work done by co-operating personnel on and across the suites, even in the case of what appears to be the most routine of the activities such as those performed by the 'wings', through checking of, for instance route structure. It is through the constant checking of data by all members of the team, by the various means used to 'draw attention to' significant changes, and above all by constant mutual attentiveness that database information comes to be reliable. It is the strips as a public site of team activity that make this possible.

Attention to co-ordination also demonstrates the importance of mutual attentiveness. The need for the active co-ordination of aircraft across sector boundaries[3] is without question a time consuming activity and has led to considerable attention being paid to the possibility of reducing it. At the same time, it is somewhat puzzling that it does not appear to reduce in direct proportion to declining levels of traffic. We believe that this can be explained through attention to the social aspects of co-ordinating work. Whereas task orientation to co-ordination might lead one to presume that it is in the interests of everyone that such communications are kept to the necessary minimum, a sociological orientation suggests that rather more than task completion is in fact at stake when co-ordination work is done. Our observations suggest that background conversation during co-ordination work, including apology for inelegant work, explanation of decisions, and justification of solutions serves the important function of maintaining attentiveness to other people's problems. All in all, it is a constituent feature of the passing of information by co-ordination that it is done *actively*. Attention to that information is therefore guaranteed in and through that activity. In passing, it should be noted that similar conversations saturate controlling culture, and are to be found in data which encompasses not only work activity but also coffee breaks, talk around the suite, late night 'war stories', and so on. All of these things feed into the culture of support in important ways. In any event, for the controller working within such a culture, the relevant issue is as much whether errors will be noticed as it is whether they will be made. To an extent, mistakes are part of the 'routine troubles' of work. The culture of support manifested in co-ordination work and so on can be recognised as a means of minimising the consequentiality of error in that oversights, incorrect level allocations, etc. are routinely detected and pointed out by people who are not necessarily responsible for the section of sky in which they take place.

Designing relevant technologies

There is a *prima facie* case for better technological support for controlling work. However, the history of innovation in ATC has occasioned some cynicism by controllers. Their arguments, while of course self interested, are also claims for safety and effectiveness predicated on the very teamwork we have described above. Their reservations about new technologies reflect their concern that such innovations should be relevant and geared to their practices as currently constituted.[4]

Our research concern was to inform the design of a prototyping facility for an electronic version of the paper flight strip which would be relevant to controlling work (Bentley *et al.*, 1992). There can be no doubt that an electronic version would furnish a number of useful functionalities, including a more effective conflict alert facility, closer links between RDP and FDP and thus between the radar and the strips, and a reduction in the number of strips which require displaying. Additionally, it can be argued that it would open up the possibility of semi-automated co-ordination procedures (see Shapiro *et al.*, 1991 for a fuller account). At the same time, without careful consideration of the issue of teamwork there is a serious risk of attenuating the public availability of information. To return to a point made earlier, technological innovation should not occur in isolation from working practices. Electronic display will not eradicate information error, and thus there is a strong case for arguing that such a facility must allow for the mutual attentiveness and 'checking' we have described, possibly by re-distributing work among 'tactical' and 'strategic' controllers. Regardless, important decisions will have to be made concerning the number of screens available and the way in which data is to be shared between them. Equally, the fact that automated co-ordination is technically feasible should not obscure the fact that reducing co-ordination may have the unintended effect of reducing other co-operative activity.

It may well be true that at some point in the future new technologies may provide pilots with information resources and decision support facilities that will obviate the need for the culture of support and mutual attentiveness. Then, controlling work may indeed become more individualistic and nonetheless as safe as it is at the moment. The near future in our view, however, requires an incremental approach which retains the principle of public availability 'under glass'. It is our view that the process of change cannot be safely managed by presuming a 'jump' to radically new technology and practices. Rather, it should be recognised that as these changes work through the system, a means must be found of ensuring that each innovation can be *trustably* incorporated into controlling work. Because current practices are the way in which safety levels are maintained, it is important that innovation does not radically intervene in those practices. It is unlikely that this will be done if the means by which this trust is managed is attenuated by those very technologies.

Notes

[1] Controllers report that, despite recession, levels of air traffic are higher this year than ever before.

² The British experience has been that various new facilities, most notably that of 'RD3', have been underused (see Hughes *et al.*, 1988; Harper *et al.*, 1991).
³ Not all aircraft have to be actively coordinated. Those passing sector boundaries 'straight and level' at agreed levels laid down in the manuals can be handed over 'silently'.
⁴ It is by no means the case that controllers are hostile, or even indifferent to, all technological support. The conflict alert facility is an example of a facility that has become trustably incorporated.

References

Anderson, R. J., Hughes, J. A. and Sharrock, W. W. (1989), *Working for Profit: The Social Organisation of Calculability in an Entrepreneurial Firm*, Avebury, Aldershot.

Bentley, R., Rodden, T., Sawyer, P. and Sommerville, I. (1992), 'A prototyping environment for dynamic data visualisation', in *Proceedings of the 5th IFIP Working Conference on User Interfaces,* Ellivuori, Finland, 10-14 August.

Harper, R. R., Hughes, J. A., Shapiro, D. Z. (1991), 'Working in Harmony: An Examination of Computer Technology in Air Traffic Control', in Bowers, J. and Benford, S. D. (eds), *Studies in Computer Supported Cooperative Work: Theory, Practice and Design*, Amsterdam, Elsevier, North Holland.

Hughes, J. A., Shapiro, D. Z., Sharrock, W. W., Anderson, R. J., Harper, R. R., Gibbons, S., (1988) The Automation of Air Traffic Control, SERC/ESRC Research Report, GR/D/86157.

Hughes, J. A., Randall, D. W., & Shapiro, D. Z. (1991), 'CSCW: Discipline or Paradigm ?', in Bannon and Robinson (eds.), *ECSCW '91: Proceedings of the 2nd European Conference on Computer Supported Cooperative Work*, Kluwer Academic Press, Amsterdam, Netherlands, 25-27 Sept.

La Porte, T.E. and Consolini, P. M., (1991) 'Working in Practice But Not in Theory: Theoretical Challenges of 'High Reliability Organizations', *Journal of Public Administration Research and Theory,* **1**, pp 19-47.

Reason, J. (1987), 'Generic Error Modelling System (GEMS): A Cognitive Framework for locating common human error forms' in J. Rasmussen, K. Duncan and J. Leplat (eds), *New Technology and Human Error*, Chichester, Wiley.

Shapiro, D. Z., Hughes, J. A., Randall, D. and Harper, R. R. (1991), 'Visual Re-representation of Database Information: The Flight Strip in Air Traffic Control', in *Proceedings 10th Interdisciplinary Workshop on Informatics and Psychology: Cognitive Aspects of Visual Language and Visual Interfaces*, Scharding, Austria.

Stager, P. and Hameluck, D. (1988), Factors associated with air traffic control operating irregularities: an analysis of Fact Finding Board reports, Report prepared under Transport Canada Contract No. AP-0264 for Air Traffic Services Branch, Evaluation Division, Ottawa, Canada.

Wise, J. A., Hopkin, V. D. and Smith, M. L. (eds) (1991), *Automation and Systems Issues in Air Traffic Control*, Springer Verlag, Berlin.

35 The organisational context of an interface: the case of ATC

R. Harper
Rank Xerox EuroParc, Cambridge
D. Randall
Department of Interdisciplinary Studies, Manchester Metropolitan University

The essence of the argument we put forward in "Cooperative work and technological support in Air Traffic Control" (this volume) is that a large number of errors within ATC socio-technical systems are solved, avoided, and dealt with through the social interaction of controllers and attendant control staff, the chiefs, the wingmen, and the assistants. This interaction has its particular focus in the paper-based flight progress strips, which are central to the collaboration on and around particular control suites, and in the work of achieving "clean" handovers between sectors. The achievement of these handovers often involves quite rich interactions between the respective personnel, who may discuss not only the detail of some particular ATM, but more general concerns relating to current ATC decision making. This social interaction is at once (a) a semi-formalised feature of current ATCO work at LATCC, being partly represented in some of the protocols of controller liaison; (b) taught as "techniques of the trade" when controllers are validated; and (c) a manifestation of what may loosely be described as controller culture, wherein cooperation, helpfulness, endeavouring to explain one's purposes, and reasoning for the mutual benefit of one's colleagues are part and parcel of a value system.

One consequence of social interaction having such importance in ensuring the fail-safe nature of the ATC system is that developments in either the organisation of work or in the technology that supports it can reduce the socio-technical systems' effectiveness. This can occur if those developments interfere with, restrict, or block this interaction. A particular example of this can be found in some of those systems that have been developed and or trialled with the purpose of reducing "coordination work" between controllers. In some cases — but not all — instead of reductions in such work lessening the incidence of error, the paradoxical consequence has sometimes been an increase in the difficulty of the problems individual controllers have to deal with. This can lead to a related increase in the amount of errors they make. Ultimately, this can result in a reduction in the ATC system's capacity. In other words, instead of increasing the total number of ATM's, such developments can have the opposite effect.

Now this argument is, we think, rather more complex than it would at first appear. It can be easily misunderstood. It is not being said that ATC systems should always preserve as much interaction between human operatives as possible; nor, complimenting that, is it being argued that technology should have a minimal role in ATC, or rather a role that ensures that people, and hence their intercourse, should stay central to the socio-technical environment. (Although there might be some interesting arguments to that effect). What is being argued is that any system development must bear in mind the subtle but crucial role that social interaction currently has in some ATC systems, and LATCC provides a notable case of this.

We want to underline the strength of the argument by way of using a somewhat extreme example. We want to show how the structural impediments for effective interaction between military and civil operations at LATCC result in problems, delays, confusions and sometimes safety threatening situations. By structural impediments we have in mind a range of matters that result in there being differences between civilian and military controllers in the following areas:

1) in knowledge about particular ATM's;
2) in perspectives and preferred options for sets of ATM's;
3) in the working culture of collaboration vis-a-vis pilots and vis-a-vis other controllers.

These impediments mean that there is minimal interaction between the military and civilian controllers. This does not result in a reduction of the workload at the "interface" of civil and military operations, as it increases the potentially problematic nature of those relations. Put another way, these structural impediments restrict what may be described as efficacious coordination interaction.

Some evidence

Space obviously precludes full analysis of this phenomenon. But here are some transcripts of coordination work at LATCC which give some idea or indication of the "problematic" in question.

Transcript 1

Controller	What's he up to? [Pointing to a Military plane]
Controller to observer	See this plane here? See this one? It looks like he's gonna come in.[i.e. enter the airways] He's going to come in, isn't he? And I'm climbing him [points to a plane in the airways] to 20 telephone time ..[he calls the military]

Transcript 2

Controller on phone to Military Ops	Got a problem. See that Speedbird? [A British Airways aircraft]
Military Controller	Give me a moment ...
Controller	Just before Malby ... one of your boys is there [i.e. a military plane] at 16 and I wanna know where he's going.
Military Controller	Oh right .... no, don't worry, he's turning away.
Controller to observer	There we go again.

Transcript 3

Controller on phone to Military Ops	This one [referring to a military plane] .. looks as if he's going to do a crossover.
Military Controller	Which one?
	<2 seconds silence>
Military Controller	Ah, no ... I see which one you mean ... no ... I'll check ...
	<60 seconds silence>
Military Controller	You're OK ... he's waiting, I've got a couple more for him ... from Yeovilton.

These scraps of dialogue show a number of things. One is an apparent tardiness on the part of the military controllers in recognising concerns of mutual interest to themselves and their civilian colleagues: the civilian controllers draw attention to some problem, but the military controllers don't see it straight away. They have to "find it". At a deeper level, what one can see is a lack of mutual understanding as regards the specific matters in hand. Somehow, there is a failure of each to recognise or understand the position of the other. So, although decisions are made, there is a sense in which the actual decisions are delayed.

Now, although these transcripts do not provide sufficient proof, we think it not unreasonable to contend that what they show is a failure to achieve efficacious decision making. This can be further underlined if we contrast the above transcripts with the following one.

	Transcript 4
Controller on phone to TMA controller	What are you going to do with Dover? [referring to a departure from Heathrow]
TMA Controller	Can I send it out at 12?
Sector Controller	Fine

Here there is rapid recognition of the issues, of the plane(s) in question. The individuals concerned recognise the other's "problem" or "interest" and "reason" for making the call. Here we have Schutz's "assumption of the reciprocity of perspectives" made manifest in the practical world of a socio-technical system (Schutz, 1962). The sector controller can see and understand *in advance* what the TMA controller's position is, and can help the latter achieve the goals that they both have: safety and expiditing of air traffic.

This last transcript is of controllers in the Civilian Operations room; the first set of civilian controllers contacting their equivalent in the Military Ops room. The reason for these differences, differences which can be glossed as the smoothness or the roughness with which coordination and collaboration can be achieved, reside in structural impediments.

Let us specify some features of these impediments.

1) In knowledge about particular ATM's

The civilian and military operatives are presented with distinct representations of airspace movements both on their radar screens, in the associated flight progress strips, and in the R/T.

Thus, in military ops, all UK airspace is divided by a line between Anglesey and the Wash. The controllers' radar screens display either half of, or all of this airspace. To contain all this, the radar screens are 8 inches in diameter. But to prevent the clutter that could arise given the scope of the airspace covered, only those aircraft that are currently under control have data blocks presented beside their blips. All else remain unidentified. Furthermore, unique frequencies for any particular controlling operation mean that military controllers only hear the pilots they are dealing with.

Contrast this with the information the civilian operatives have. To begin with, their airspace, their sector is much smaller. But their radar screens are twice the size. Nearly every target on these screens will have data blocks beside them. Hence civilian controllers have RDP information not only about all their own aircraft (in this they are like the military controllers), but also all the aircraft that in one way or another are in the vicinity of those they are controlling. All this means that civilian controllers have a much finer grain of understanding about the particular circumstances of specific ATM's than do military controllers.

2) In perspectives and preferred options for sets of ATM's

Partly for the reasons just noted, civilian controllers "know" more about their particular domain of airspace than do military controllers and hence have a better, richer perspective of ATC circumstances and preferred courses of action. They can see which aircraft are about to come into their sector and which they need to bear in mind; what will be the impact of some aircraft they are just about to hand off, and even how busy or hard-worked their neighbours are.

In contrast, athough military controllers can find out information about aircraft other controllers are managing1, their system does not provide this constantly and "at a glance". Information about other aircraft is systematically hidden from their view. Moroever, they cannot find out the busy-ness or difficulty that their colleagues may be facing, and hence alter their controlling decision accordingly, without potentially adding to the difficulties their colleagues face. This is because the only way they can find out how to help is by calling their colleagues, and hence making them even busier. It is unsurprising, therefore, that military controllers rarely have much contact with one another. In short, military controllers find it difficult to pre-empt or helpfully coordinate aircraft under their own control with those under the other controllers.

3) In the culture of cooperation vis-a-vis pilots and vis-a-vis other controllers

Civilian controller culture celebrates and rewards cooperativeness and mutual help. There is the obvious instantiation of this in the thanks that one often hears expressed when controllers consult with one another over their headphones. But there is also the informal rituals of celebrating helpfulness in "work talk" over tea, at lunch, and of course, down the pub after work. There is also the denigration and various ways of punishing those who are not "helpful". Controllers will complain about having to work side by side "so and so" if that person has a reputation for being unhelpful. There is also some leeway for controllers to select who they work with on the shift schedules. This can sometimes result in certain persons being without a place when the rosters are near completion, and Watch Managers can find themselves having to negotiate with the chiefs about getting an "awkward customer" on to the suites. When this happens, the informal stigma attached to individual controllers becomes a semi-formal feature of work organisation being reflected in management decision making.

Military controller culture has a whole range of different features which do not result in the same premium being placed on cooperativeness. To begin with, because of the nature of their work, military controllers have very little to do with one another. There are few handovers, few agreements to be struck, no need to keep an eye on what "next door" is up to. For another, and related to the piecemeal nature of their work, military controllers will often have little opportunity to have breaks with one another. One will have completed his or her "job" at just the time his or her colleagues are starting theirs. Finally, military controllers rarely work nights, or periods when it is very quiet, which might afford opportunities to get to know one another. Civilian controllers, especially on nights, can often have many hours to while away when nothing happens in the airspace except for an occcasional reported sighting of a UFO[2].

Conclusion

It must not be thought that military controllers are any less able than their civilian counterparts or that there are any simple ways that these differences in perspective could be remedied. What limits military controllers have on their understanding, made so graphic in their sometimes tardy responses to civilian controllers' requests, are we argue a reflection of the structural conditions in which they find themselves. This causes the interface between military and civilian operations at LATCC to be one that often causes concern. It constitutes a restriction on what we have wanted to suggest is efficacious, coordination interaction.

Notes

[1] The data block beside any military plane subject to control indicates the number of the "consul" being used for the controlling activities. Other controllers can dial this consul and hence the controller in question.

[2] Because of the way radar data processing works, UFO's will not appear on radar screens. But it is not unusual for pilots to describe over the radio the unknown objects they see in the airspace. These reportings, mostly at night, break up the monotony of night duty for controllers.

References

Schutz, A. (1962), *The Problem of Social Reality: Collected Papers I*. The Hague: Martinus Nijhoff.

Part 6
PERSPECTIVES ON CREW RESOURCE MANAGEMENT

36 Extending Crew Resource Management: an overview

Brent Hayward, Qantas Airways Ltd, Melbourne, Australia

Introduction

Over the past 15 years, the development and acceptance of the principles of Crew (formerly Cockpit) Resource Management have been major advances for advocates of the role of human factors in aviation. One of the prime protagonists of the period, Dr John Lauber of NASA Ames and now US NTSB fame, defined CRM as "the effective utilization of all available resources - information, equipment and people - to achieve safe and efficient flight operations" (Lauber, 1984). While that baseline definition remains appropriate, it is now apparent that the initial focus of CRM training, the cockpit crew, was too narrow, and that it is and in fact always was necessary to extend the principals of CRM beyond the cockpit door to include other integral components of the aviation system.

Industry Developments

In recent years this realisation has resulted in the development of training packages which have extended the scope of CRM training to include and in some cases to blend groups such as cabin crew, air traffic controllers, ramp, dispatch and maintenance personnel. One of the first groups included in the extension of CRM principles to non-cockpit crew were cabin attendants. This signalled belated recognition from our industry that an aircraft's crew included all who flew, although it must be observed that this recognition is as yet far from global. Indeed, some carriers have changed their course *title* from cockpit to *crew* resource management, but little else.

The recognition of flight attendants as an integral component of a flight's operational team received additional impetus following two major accidents in 1989 where it became apparent that vital information possessed by cabin attendants was not communicated to or was not effectively utilized by the cockpit crew. The British Midland B737 accident at Kegworth, England, and the Air Ontario F-28 accident at Dryden, Canada (Moshansky, 1992), are now classic case studies of the perils of ineffective utilisation of all available resources, and have themselves been used as powerful argument for the integration of emergency procedures (EP) training for all flight crew (Baker & Frost, 1993). A video on "The Dryden Accident", produced for the Australian Airlines integrated EP course (Hayward, 1993) is now in widespread use with international airlines and training organizations.

Regulatory Response

The recent revision of the US Federal Aviation Administration's Crew Resource Management Advisory Circular 120-51A (FAA, 1993) provides formal redefinition of a flight's operating crew. It states that: "A more modern definition includes not only the cockpit crew but also all other groups that routinely work with that crew and are involved in decisions required to operate a flight safely. These groups include but are not limited to: (1) dispatchers; (2) cabin crewmembers; (3) maintenance personnel; (4) air traffic controllers" ... "several air carriers have found it useful to extend CRM training ... to other operational groups. The goal of such training is to improve the effectiveness of these groups themselves and the quality of interactions between them and cockpit crews". Also noteworthy is the direction taken by the currently proposed changes to the FAA's Federal Aviation Regulation Part 135/121 requiring CRM training. This regulation will mandate CRM training and set compliance minima and training timetables for all US cockpit crew, cabin attendants and dispatchers.

Extended Training Applications

America West Airlines were amongst the pioneers of attempts to include flight attendants in initial CRM training efforts, and did so with a degree of innovation, also using flight attendants as specially trained facilitators for the components of their course which were restricted to cockpit crew (Vandermark, 1991). At about the same time, Australian Airlines hit on a novel method for imparting CRM principles to cabin crew via joint EP training. While the company had been running its Aircrew Team Management (ATM) programme for technical flight crew since 1985, approval for funding was not forthcoming when attempts were made to extend this training to include all flight attendants. However, as described by Baker and Frost (1993), the airline went on to develop a two-day integrated emergency procedures training course for all aircrew, which has been in operation since 1991. This course has a strong human factors foundation, includes annual ATM recurrent training, and as such has served as de facto CRM awareness training for flight attendants, in addition to providing a vehicle for strengthening communication and understanding of role responsibilities amongst all crew members. Chidester and Vaughn (1994) report that American Airlines have employed a similar strategy by including flight attendants in CRM recurrent training sessions since 1990.

In recent years maintenance crews have been the recipients of extensive and highly successful CRM-style training efforts at several US carriers, most notably via the Pan American MELD programme (Taggart, 1990), and Continental Airlines' ongoing Crew Coordination Concepts (CCC) training (Fotos, 1991; Taylor, Robertson, Peck & Stelly, 1993). Dispatchers have also been involved in innovative extensions to CRM training to varying degrees at a small number of US-based carriers, including American Airlines (Chidester, 1993) and Southwest Airlines (Taggart, 1993).

There have also been attempts to develop "Controller" Resource Management programmes for the training of Air Traffic Controllers in CRM principles (Helmreich & Sherman, 1992), in addition to ad hoc efforts to integrate controllers into CRM programmes run by airlines primarily for flight crew (e.g. Australian Airlines' ATM programme).

We have also witnessed the development of CRM programmes tailored to assist the adaptation of employees to specific events in their life and work environments. These have included the advent of teambuilding workshops to help disparate flight crew and their families adjust following a major and prolonged industrial dispute (Hayward & Alston, 1991), efforts to facilitate adjustment to the harsh realities of airline mergers (Richardson, 1994), and courses such as the team skills workshop introduced to facilitate the preparation of new captains at Southwest Airlines (Taggart, 1993). The new captains' course is of particular interest in that it involves flight attendants, ground operations agents, mechanics, maintenance supervisors, dispatchers, and FAA representatives in working with the upgrading pilots on a variety of problem solving exercises.

Does CRM Training Work?

Any management asked to approve funding of the magnitude required to introduce an effective CRM programme is entitled to expect a worthwhile return on training investment. So, does CRM training work? While the question is straightforward, the answer is not. The qualified response is that well designed CRM programmes, with appropriate management support, allowed to operate within an appropriate organisational context, tailored to fit both organisational and national culture, and given quality reinforcement through sound recurrent training, do work.

However, CRM training does not lend itself easily either to standardization or regulation. There is no perfect training design which will be appropriate for all organizations, nor is there any guarantee that a particular application of CRM training principles will prove successful in a given environment. There are however some critical factors which can affect the success of any CRM programme. A non-exhaustive list includes: the motivation for CRM programme introduction, the quality of training design, the training objectives, the budget for development of materials, training methods employed, training facilities, training personnel, course implementation, the effective marketing of CRM principles, ongoing reinforcement of those principles via quality recurrent training, and the amount of real support the programme receives from divisional and company management.

It follows then that there are a number of items which can be addressed in order to optimise the effectiveness of a CRM programme. Helmreich (1993) proposes a set of axioms regarding factors which may enhance or reduce the impact of CRM training programmes. One of these is that "effective CRM programmes are not off-the-shelf, but are designed after research into the culture of the organization and reflect the national culture". This underscores the importance of well-researched training design. Byrnes and Black (1993) provide an excellent overview of items to be covered to ensure quality of training development and implementation.

Helmreich refers to the consideration of national and organizational culture in training design. The work of Hofstede (1980, 1991) has been extrapolated to the aviation environment (Johnston, 1993; Merritt, 1993) and has provided for fascinating debate on the relevance of culture to training, and vice-versa. Individuals who have been submerged in the turbulence of a corporate merger will testify to significant observable differences in organizational cultures even when the new partners are from the same national culture, let alone when there are national cross-cultural barriers to negotiate as well. By way of illustration, when Japanese banking powerhouses Dai-Ichi and Nippon Kangyo merged to form the leviathan Dai-Ichi Kangyo, a team of managers from both sides were assigned to develop a 200-word glossary explaining what each bank meant when using exactly the same words (Fisher, 1994). As employees began to work together, they searched their dictionaries like tourists in a foreign land asking for directions to the nearest toilet (bathroom; restroom...).

Another Helmreich axiom is that "management, check airmen and instructors play a critical role in determining the effectiveness of CRM training". This refers to Hackman's (1987, 1993) concept of the "organizational shell", where process, structure and context interact to influence a flight crew's performance. As Hackman observes, "new skills learned in training are like the sprouts of plants that emerge in the spring. If the climate is unfavourable, or if someone inadvertently steps on them, they do not survive ... A full-fledged CRM program also must ensure that the organizational context supports rather than undermines the use of resource management skills" (1993, p. 62).

A third axiom is that "without reinforcement, the impact of CRM training decays". Helmreich and his colleagues at the NASA/University of Texas/FAA Aerospace Crew Research Project stress the pivotal role played by check airmen and instructors as primary role models and agents of reinforcement in contributing to CRM programme acceptance. The NASA/UT group have conducted extensive studies on the effectiveness of CRM training (see Helmreich & Wilhelm, 1991), and have evolved benchmark methods for the collection of both attitudinal and observational performance data, the most useful tools for evaluating training effectiveness. The Flight (formerly Cockpit) Management Attitudes Questionnaire (FMAQ, Helmreich, Merritt, Sherman, Gregorich, & Wiener, 1993) and the Line/LOS Checklist (Helmreich, Wilhelm, Taggart, & Butler, 1994) have been utilised for the collection of data in many airlines and across many cultures. One major finding from these data indicates that initial CRM training constitutes only an awareness phase and that continuing, high quality reinforcement is essential in order to produce long term attitudinal and behaviour change.

The Next Generation

Through the many advances made in research and training, the 1980's may in retrospect be viewed as a watershed period for human factors in aviation. Bob Helmreich suggests that we may now be at the end of our *Iron Age* and the dawn of our *Renaissance*. However, he also cautions that "we should avoid self-satisfaction and remember that the Renaissance was a period without indoor plumbing when transportation was in sailing ships and horse drawn conveyances. We have a long way to go to bring our training and evaluation into the space age" (1993, p. 77).

One move in the right direction is the growing recognition that in order to achieve the management support that is so essential for the success of a CRM programme, a strong emphasis on "organizational outcomes" may become the focus for the *next* generation of CRM training. One result of the merger of Qantas and Australian Airlines is that we are now working towards implementation of the next generation of CRM training for the new Qantas group, a process which has involved the integration of two culturally distinctive approaches to human factors training. Using an expanded EP course vehicle, the new training will focus not only on traditional CRM goals, but will also aim to enhance the commercial success of the airline through the addition of several organizational outcomes to our course terminal objectives. They include the blending of the cultures thrown together by the merger, the removal of barriers to more effective communication and coordination amongst crewmembers, enhanced teamwork, a sharper customer focus, increased ownership of company product, and a greater commitment to the competitiveness and commercial success of our new airline. Our belief is that through the addition of these tangible benefits this form of extended CRM training can become an indispensable tool for organizational development and culture change.

References

Baker, R.L.A., and Frost, K. (1993). Australian Airlines' integrated crew training. In B.J. Hayward and A.R. Lowe (Eds.), *Proceedings of the 1992 Australian Aviation Psychology Symposium*. Melbourne: AAvPA.

Byrnes, R.E., and Black, R. (1993). Developing and implementing CRM programs: The Delta experience. In E.W. Wiener, B.G. Kanki, and R.L. Helmreich (Eds.), *Cockpit Resource Management*. San Diego: Academic Press.

Chidester, T. (1993). Role of dispatchers in CRM training. In *Proceedings of the Seventh International Symposium on Aviation Psychology*. Columbus, OH: Ohio State Uni.

Chidester, T., and Vaughn, L. (1994). Pilot/flight attendant coordination. *The CRM Advocate*, **94** (1), 8-10.

FAA. (1993). *Advisory Circular 120-51A: Crew Resource Management*. Washington, DC: Federal Aviation Administration.

Fisher, A.B. (1994, Jan 24). How to make a merger work. *Fortune*, 58-61.

Fotos, C.P. (1991, Aug 26). Continental applies CRM concepts to technical, maintenance corps. *Aviation Week & Space Technology*, 32-35.

Hackman, J.R. (1987). Organizational influences. In H.W. Orlady and H.C. Foushee (Eds.), *Cockpit Resource Management Training: Proceedings of a NASA/MAC Workshop* (NASA CP-2455). Moffett Field, CA: NASA Ames.

Hackman, J.R. (1993). Teams, leaders, and organizations: New directions for crew-oriented flight training. In E.W. Wiener, B.G. Kanki, & R.L. Helmreich (Eds.), *Cockpit Resource Management*. San Diego: Academic Press.

Hayward, B.J., and Alston, N.G. (1991). Team building following a pilot labour dispute: Extending the CRM envelope. In *Proceedings of the Sixth International Symposium on Aviation Psychology*. Columbus, OH: Ohio State University.

Hayward, B.J. (1993). The Dryden accident: A crew resource training video. In *Proceedings of the Seventh International Symposium on Aviation Psychology*. Columbus, OH: Ohio State University.

Helmreich, R.L. (1993). Fifteen years of the CRM wars: A report from the trenches. In B.J. Hayward and A.R. Lowe (Eds.), *Proceedings of the 1992 Australian Aviation Psychology Symposium*. Melbourne: AAvPA.

Helmreich, R.L., Merritt, A., Sherman, P., Gregorich, S., & Wiener, E.L. (1994). *The Flight Management Attitudes Questionnaire*. Austin, TX: NASA/UT/FAA ACRP.

Helmreich R.L., and Sherman, P. (1992). *Controller Resource Management Presentation to the FAA: Draft*. Austin, TX: NASA/UT/FAA ACRP.

Helmreich, R.L., and Wilhelm, J.A. (1991). Outcomes of crew resource management training. *International Journal of Aviation Psychology*, 1 (4), 287-300.

Helmreich, R.L., Wilhelm, J.A., Taggart, W.R., and Butler, R.E. (1994). *Reinforcing and Evaluating CRM: The Revised Line/LOS Checklist* (LLC Revision 4). Austin, TX: NASA/UT/FAA ACRP.

Hofstede, G. (1980). *Culture's consequences: International differences in work-related values*. Beverly Hills, CA: Sage.

Hofstede, G. (1991). *Cultures and organizations: Software of the mind*. Maidenhead, UK: McGraw-Hill.

Johnston, A.N. (1993). CRM: Cross-cultural perspectives. In E.W. Wiener, B.G. Kanki, and R.L. Helmreich (Eds.), *Cockpit Resource Management*. San Diego: Academic Press.

Lauber, J.K. (1984). Resource management in the cockpit. *Air Line Pilot*, 53, 20-23.

Merritt, A. (1993). *The Influence of National and Organizational Culture on Human Performance*. Paper presented at the Australian Aviation Psychology Association Industry Seminar, Sydney, October, 1993.

Moshansky, V.P. (1992). *Commission of Inquiry into the Air Ontario Crash at Dryden, Ontario: Final Report*. Ottawa: Canadian Ministry of Supply and Services.

Richardson, G. (1994). Human factors climate after reorganisation. In *Human Factors in Aviation - Proceedings of the IATA 22nd Technical Conference*, Montreal, October, 1993. Montreal: IATA.

Taggart, W.R. (1990). Introducing CRM into maintenance training. In *Proceedings of the Third International Symposium on Human Factors in Aircraft Maintenance and Inspection*. Washington, D.C: Federal Aviation Administration.

Taggart, W.R. (1993). Captain upgrade CRM training: A new focus for enhanced flight operations. In *Proceedings of the Seventh International Symposium on Aviation Psychology*. Columbus, OH: Ohio State University.

Taylor, J.C., Robertson, M.M., Peck, R., & Stelly, J.W. (1993). Validating the impact of maintenance CRM training. In *Proceedings of the Seventh International Symposium on Aviation Psychology*. Columbus, OH: Ohio State University.

Vandermark, M.J. (1991). Should flight attendants be included in CRM training? A discussion of a major carrier's approach to total crew training. *International Journal of Aviation Psychology*, 1 (1), 87-94.

37 Assessment of non-technical skills: is it possible?

Patricia A.M. Antersijn and Marieke C. Verhoef
KLM Flight Crew Training Centre

As you all know, airlines must start assessing non-technical skills in the near future. But is it possible, and how should we do it? At KLM we are convinced that, before you are able to assess non-technical skills, you have to make sure that your training in non-technical skills is adequate and sufficient. And that the people who will coach your cockpit crew on non-technical skills (and in the near future will assess them), have the right tools to do so. In this presentation, I would like to give you some insight into KLM's approach to deal with this problem.

This presentation will cover the following topics:
1. The philosophy behind KLM's training approach.
2. Implementing a new training tool: the Feedback and Appraisal System.
3. First results of the try-out of the Feedback & Appraisal System in KLM's A310 and DC-10 division.

1. KLM's Training philosophy

If you take training seriously, it is important to regularly evaluate your training package and training approach. At the end of 1987 KLM's Flight Crew Training Centre came to a major conclusion: All important training items to ensure a good working cockpit crew were covered, but there was still something missing. We had our skill training, LOFT training, Crew Management training, a training in Public Address techniques, our KHUFAC, but they were all separate courses or subjects; there was no real relation between the technical and non-technical training. Subjects taught during, for instance, the Crew Management Course, were not reinforced during simulator training. The instructors did not have a tool to do this. As a consequence the instruction of non-technical skills within KLM was not as effective as it could be.

The missing part was A STRUCTURALLY INTEGRATED TRAINING APPROACH OF TECHNICAL AND NON-TECHNICAL TRAINING.

When this conclusion was reached at the end of 1987, the Flight Crew Training Centre was confronted with the question where to start. Non-technical training was up to then, a once in a lifetime activity. And instructors didn't have the tools to give effective feedback on non-technical performance of the cockpit crew.

To find out where to start, it was first necessary to map out the existing training process. For KLM it pointed out that the main area's, were: - job description,
- selection,
- the training itself,
- the process of data collection and comparing this to the norm,
- and the organizational structure for monitoring and controlling part.

Notwithstanding the importance of the items, I will focus the second part of my presentation on the development of a tool for instructors. A tool to help them in the process of non-technical data collection and to help them to compare this data to the norm. We called it the Feedback & Appraisal System.

2. Implementing a new training tool: the Feedback and Appraisal System

The Feedback and Appraisal System, in short FAS, consists of two parts: a terminology part and a reference part.

When dealing with non-technical skills, it is important that both the instructor as well as the crew, know what they are talking about. That they speak the same language. Miscommunication, misunderstanding and misinterpretations are fatal for effective counselling or debriefing. Especially the acceptance of the crew of the instructors feedback is important. The quality of the feedback can be just as good, but if the acceptance is zero, the effect of the debriefing is zero. This demands a carefully planned debriefing tactic from the instructor.

A frame of reference is important so that everyone knows what KLM expects. In training and assessment situations, it gives the instructor a tool to be as objective as possible. Of course, it is very difficult to describe a kind of norm for non-technical skills. The behaviour of a crew depends on the situation and on the individual crew members themselves, or does it?

If we want to assess non-technical skills, it is important that this be done as objectively as possible. At KLM we have been working on the Feedback and Appraisal System for 4 years now.

The strength of the Feedback and Appraisal System is that it describes in clear terminology the work of our cockpit crew; Clearly visible for everyone and with no psychology, at all. This is because it was developed from on-the-job situations. More than 60 interviews with instructors, pilots and flight engineers resulted in over 600 cases where non-technical aspects play an important role in the safety of the operation. In the end, all these on-the-job situations were divided into five main categories, with the acronym WILSC:
    WORK ATTITUDE
    INFORMATION MANAGEMENT

LEADERSHIP
STRESS MANAGEMENT
CO-OPERATION

There are 14 sub-categories.

A short definition is given of each sub-category and underneath the matching behavioural components that play a role in this category.

See for instance one of the sub-categories of Work Attitude: Exercise of self-criticism. The definition of this sub-category is Being critical in relation to one's own functioning. With behavioural components as:
- evaluating one's own performance
- willing to discuss one's own functioning
- being open to criticism from others

and / or
- asking others for information about one's own functioning

All definitions and descriptions are available to the instructor as well as to the pilot and/or flight engineer. So the instructor as well as the person who receives feedback in the debriefing, know what is meant by certain terms, how this is translated into observable behaviour and what KLM expects from her crews. This approach and set-up is one of the most important points if you want to get acceptance for implementing a new tool. In order to gain acceptance from the users, it should be practical, visible for everyone and deal with their job, no hocus-pocus or amateur psychology. The users must be part of the development of the system.

At KLM we started in July 1992 by trying out the Feedback and Appraisal System in our A310 and DC-10 Divisions. To introduce the system to all the pilots and flight engineers of these two divisions, we developed a special Type Recurrent program. Instead of studying parts of the AOM at home, the crew was asked to read the information about the feedback and appraisal system.

In the briefing there was one hour to show a 15 minute video about FAS, to do a short exercise on non-technical behaviour and to discuss questions on this subject. The simulator session was a real LOFT session. And during the debriefing, the non-technical performance of the crew was discussed according to the new system.

To prepare our instructors we made sure that every instructor went to an advanced instruction training in which they learned how to use the feedback and appraisal system and in which a refresher of instruction techniques took place. An instructor was not allowed to give the Type Recurrent as long as he had not taken the course.

In our instructor training we teach the instructors to use the feedback and appraisal system in a very practical way. We use cases, video-analyses and debriefing role-plays. But first of all we let them think about the meaning of the main categories for themselves.

For instance, what do you think that the category INFORMATION MANAGEMENT means?

In the discussion that follows things come up like: getting information, using resources, deciding on priorities, planning, taking decisions, updating plans, structuring information.

After this, we looked at the definitions used in the system. The sub-categories of INFORMATION MANAGEMENT are:
- Information analysis
- Planning and Anticipation
- Decisiveness

With for instance behavioural components of Information analysis as:
- actively and systematically searching for relevant information
- using available resources
- involving proposals and suggestions of others
- classifying information into main issues and side issues / cause and effect
- penetrating to the heart of a matter
- keeping an overview by continuously comparing new information to the actual information

The instructors had to conclude for themselves that the definitions matched their own thoughts, that the Feedback and Appraisal System really deals with their work and is in fact not something completely new but just an agreement on the terminology used when talking about non-technical performance. In short: that it is a tool for them to make their job easier.

3. Results of the try-out of the Feedback and Appraisal System in KLM's A310 and DC-10 division

What are the results of the try-out of the Feedback and Appraisal System in our A3 10 and DC- 10 division so far. The main questions were:
- Will the system be accepted by instructors as well as pilots and flight engineers?
- Is the feedback and appraisal system really a helpful tool to assist instructors in coaching crew members in their non-technical performance?

and
- Is the system complete, are parts missing or superfluous?

To get information to answer these questions, we asked instructors and crews to fill out a questionnaire after every Type Recurrent. In the period July to December this resulted in a total of 118 instructor questionnaires (a response of 99%) and 194 questionnaires from pilots and flight engineers (a response of 87%). Some results:

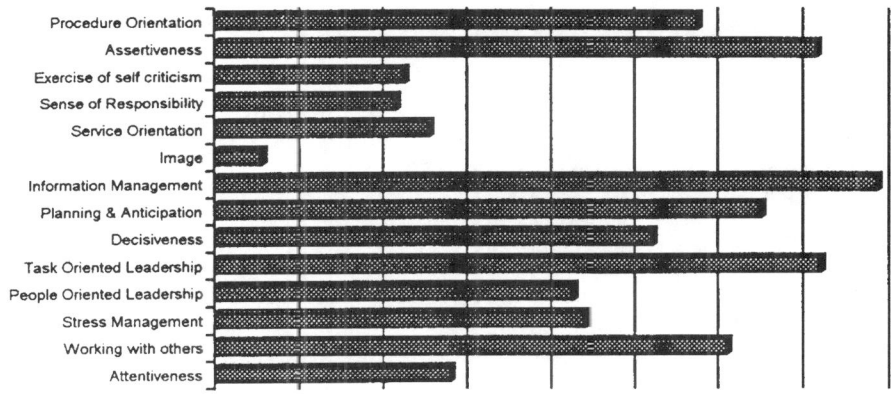

Figure 1: What categories are used during the debriefing?
- Instructors

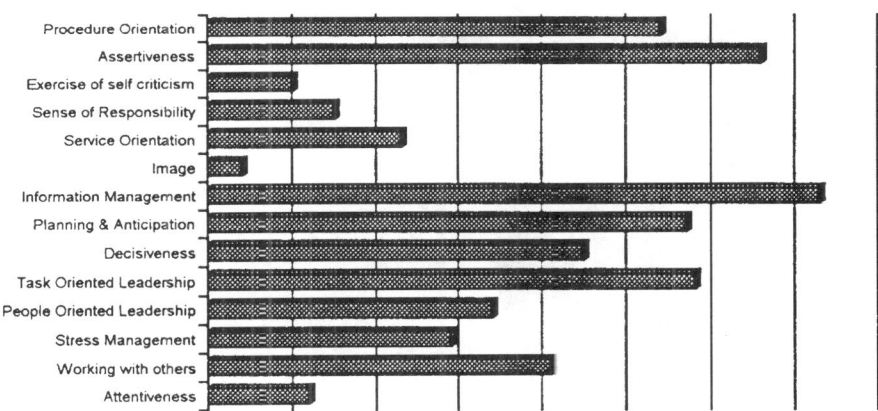

Figure 2: What categories are used during the debriefing? - Pilots/ Flight Engineers

The responses of the instructors and pilots / flight engineers were more or less the same as expected. All categories were used but the 5 most used categories were:
- procedure orientation
- assertiveness
- information analyses
- planning and anticipation
- and task oriented leadership

and the 5 categories used less:
- exercise of self-criticism

- sense of responsibility
- service orientation
- image
- and attentiveness.

The explanation can be found in the fact that the 5 less used categories are categories which are more visible during normal line operation and not during a simulator session. This contrasts with the 5 most used categories which are necessary skills to solve abnormals or emergencies trained during simulator LOFT training.

Other questions concerned the quality of the debriefing.
For the instructor:
- Were you able to discuss the items you wanted to debrief ?
- and Was FAS a useful tool in this?

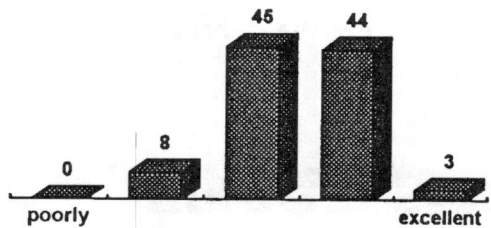

Figure 3: **Were you able to discuss the items you wanted to debrief?**

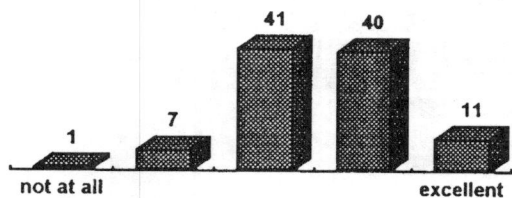

Figure 4: Was FAS a useful tool?

47% of the instructors were able to discuss the items they wanted to in a positive to excellent way. 45% were neutral, which means that there was no difference with the past. Over 50% was convinced that FAS was a very good tool to help them. 41% were neutral. Further research showed that the main reason for their neutrality was a lack of experience with FAS.

Concerning this subject we asked the pilots/flight engineers:
- If the debriefing was clearer because of the use of the FAS?
- and if the use of FAS helped them to gain more insight into their performance?

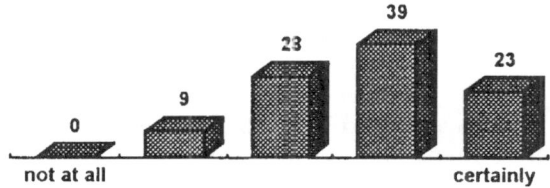

Figure 5: Was the debriefing clearer because of the use of FAS? (1%: no opinion)

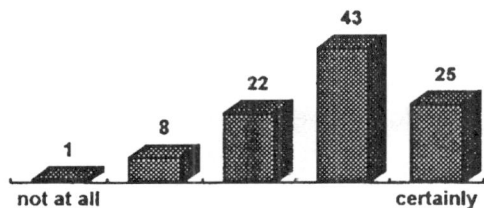

Figure 6: Did the use of FAS help you to gain more insight into your performance? (1%: no opinion)

Over 60% of the pilots and the flight engineers were of the opinion that the debriefing was more clear because of the use of FAS, 28% was neutral. And almost 70% found that FAS was a good to excellent tool for giving them more insight into their performance.

To check the acceptance of the System, we asked the instructors:
- What is your opinion about the use of the FAS as a tool to debrief non-technical skills?

and the pilots and flight engineers:
- If they would recommend the FAS to other colleagues?

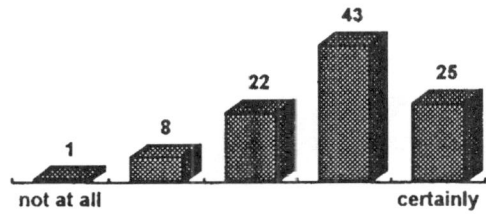

Figure 7: Instructors: What is your opinion about the use of FAS as a tool to debrief non-technical skills?

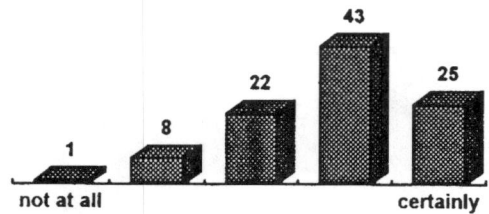

Figure 8: Pilots/Flight Engineers: Would you recommend the FAS to other colleagues? (3%: no opinion)

99% of the instructors were neutral to very positive toward the use of FAS as a tool. And 71% of the pilots and flight engineers would strongly recommend it to other colleagues, 20% were neutral.

Although these figures are rough indications, they show a clear trend that we are on the right track. At KLM we have concluded that the try-out of the Feedback and Appraisal System is a success. And we have decided to start implementing the system in our other divisions.

To come back to our main questions:
- Will the system be accepted by instructors as well as pilots and flight engineers?

The answer for the A3 10 and DC-10 division is YES.
- Is the feedback and appraisal system really a helpful tool to assist instructors in coaching the non-technical performance of crew members?

The answer again is YES. But experiences of the last few months show that coaching the instructors is very important until the use of the Feedback and Appraisal System has become second nature.
- Is the system complete, are parts missing or superfluous?

We have the idea that, although more research is necessary especially during route training, that YES, the system is complete. Some categories are more useful during route instruction on normal flights while others are more important during simulator training.

But what about assessment?

Can the feedback and appraisal system be used to assess non-technical behaviour? We believe that we have now developed a very strong tool in training and coaching crews in a structured way. And most important of all, the try-out proves that the system is acceptable. If you want a system to assess non-technical skills then acceptance is an essential condition.

We are convinced that when instructors and crews are used to work with it in training situations, the Feedback and Appraisal System is a strong basis on which non-technical behaviour can be assessed.

38 An operational model for the evaluation of Crew Resource Management (CRM) skills in Line Operations Simulation (LOS)

Thomas W. Houle, Air Line Pilots' Association (ALPA), USA

Background

In the years since the first Ruffel-Smith study much progress has been made in the area of CRM. The concept of Crew Resource Management is by now well documented, supported and incorporated in airlines around the world. We have clearly defined the problem and what needs to be done to address the issues. The injury has come up with an excellent definition of CRM. This was first stated by the Hon. Dr. John Lauber and now is listed in the FAA AC121-52.

Crew Resource Management refers to the effective use of all available resources; human resources, hardware, and information. A current definition includes all other groups routinely working with the cockpit crew who are involved in decisions required to operate a flight safely. (AC121-52)

The other major achievement of this initial research was the establishment of some behavioral markers (AC121-52). These markers basically defined what was considered good CRM. These have been modified from AC121-52 to put them into a more operational useful categories.

1. Briefings
2. Inquiry/Advocacy/Assertion
3. Crew Self Critique
4. Conflict Resolution
5. Decision Making
6. Team Building and Maintenance
7. Workload Management
8. Situational Awareness

The majority of commercial carriers have by now recognised the need for at least some type of human factors training. This early form of training usually consisted of a one to four day seminars facilitated by line pilots on and off campus location. This is normally referred to as Phase One training. Phase Two is to consist of practice and feed back. This would be an annual simulator ride in which to practice these new CRM skills. Phase Three would be some type of a annual refresher training in some aspect of human factors. As of today, the majority of commercial carriers are moving in this direction.

One of the driving factors in moving in this direction is the FAA'S Advanced Qualification Program (AQP). This is a new concept in airline training. Instead of the regulatory agency defining the minimum number of hours per course of instruction the carriers will present a curriculum of train to proficiency. Theoretically, each student would progress at their own rate. This should by itself save the airlines money and at the same time improve the quality of instruction. Another goal of the program is to use the lowest level of simulation appropriate for the lesson objective. If the lesson objective can be met with a device in the classroom there will be no need to go into a full motion simulator to teach the objective.

Each carrier that applies for AQP will be required by the FAA to have a complete human factors program in place. This would also include some way to evaluate CRM. This program will even include the concept of evaluating CRM skills in the simulator and on the line. The problem is that as of today Crew Resource Management is not an exact science, therefore the idea of evaluating these "soft" skills is very difficult.

When the initial research was being conducted the researchers were very aware of this limitation. But at the same time they felt that it was important that the line pilots were able to practice these new concepts in an environment that was free of recriminations. They, therefore, created a new category of training called the non jeopardy LOFT. The idea was that since the concepts were not completely transferable into skills that could easily be taught the best that could be achieved in the short term was just practice of the concepts.

The field of research has not yet progressed to the point yet where the instructors can tell the pilot if you do these three things you will be completely situationally aware. In the present state we are a long way from measuring CRM as easily as + or - ten feet as we do on practice steep turns.

That does not mean it is not possible to measure CRM at all. Most check airman will tell you that they know good CRM when they see it. But that is extremely subjective. What we need is a good model for evaluating CRM on a objective level

Limitations of the Model

The first limitation of the model is that not every behavioral marker will be evaluated every year. It is entirely too cumbersome and not necessary to observe and or evaluate every single CRM behavioral marker each year.

The second limitation is that only those behavioral markers that can be translated into a skill that can be taught and used in the cockpit will be evaluated. Unless the behavioral marker of decision making can be translated into a specific skill or model that can be used in the cockpit it will not be evaluated. That does not mean that it cannot be taught or discussed in the classroom or practiced in the simulator. Only that the concept will not be evaluated in the simulator.

The third limitation of this specific model description is that it is only limited to five specific skills. These are the only skills that I am currently aware of. If there are other skills available they can easily be put into the model

Model Description

The model is a synergistic approach to Crew Resource Management evaluation. This means that we look first at the entire concept and decide what is the end objective. The end objective of CRM is a safer flying environment. But defining what a safer flying environment is a very nebulous concept. Therefore, we focus on what we can measure.

Then the end objective becomes evaluating CRM in a LOS ride. This is accomplished by teaching specific CRM skills that can be observed, defined and measured. The entire program is built around this one objective of evaluating these skills. The ideal situation is that you take it even one step further and you develop now the lesson plan for handling a failure in any one of your defined skills. This is helpful in keeping you focused on teaching the correct skills. But first you must define what skills can be observed, defined and measured.

In this example we have selected five skills from the behavioral markers. These are no means the only skills that can be taught. But each one of these skills can be directly backed up with research and therefore it was felt that there were the strongest and most important to date. It is not so important to argue or discuss the specific merits of these skills but rather that you pick something very specific. As stated earlier the most important thing is that these skills are observable, definable and measurable. These skills are

1. Crew Briefing's (Initial, take-off, approach, debrief)
2. Inquiry and Assertion
3. Decision Review Process
4. Situational Red Flags
5. Announcing intentions (I plan to....)

Now that you have defined your skills you are prepared to develop the classroom material. It is useless to teach any course in CRM until you have completed these steps. You would be wasting valuable time and energy discussing innumerable CRM concepts that would not directly translate into the simulator.

Once the classroom material is completed you are then ready to develop the LOS scenario. The idea now is develop specific scenario's around current operations topics keeping in mind how you are going to evaluate each skill.

The scenario is built so that a specific point the Check airman either observes the correct skill or he did not observe it. If he observed the behavior it would automatically be given a score of 1 to 5 based on previous beta testing of the scenario.

An example would be the full mission simulated flight at NASA-AMES Research Center (Foushee, Lauber, Baetge, & Acomb,1986). The better pilots and crews paid much more attention early on during low work loads of the deteriorating weather (Orasanu 1990). These crews briefed the entire scenario as conditions changed. This greatly increased their shared mental model so that during high work load situations communications were only focused on the most important items. This greatly reduced errors and improved the decision making capabilities of these crews.

The second group of Captains briefed the entire scenario as part of their initial approach briefing versus the initial pre-departure briefing. These crews are outlining contingency plans during low work loads times. This again creates the shared mental model and allows much more time for contingency planning. Therefore, any one who did this would get a two. Anything higher than a four is considered passing. The instructor/check airman would obviously have the capability to add any additional behaviors observed for instructional purposes.

The third group of Captains did the least amount of preplanning. Their approach briefing was minimal with very little contingency planning or additional discussion of the deteriorating weather. This group successfully handled the problem but during the high workload time there was considerably more conversation due to the lack of planning. They had no shared mental model. This was the majority of line pilots. Therefore, anyone that came in for a LOS ride and did that would meet standards and would get a three on a 1 to 5 scale.

This method does several things. The most important thing is that it quantifies the grading system in a objective manner. Any score can be rationalized and discussed with scientific data to back up the grading. The important thing that it does is that it removes a large amount of subjectivity off the shoulders of the check airman. They either observe the behavior or they do not and they have a specific grade to give the crew. If the crew completes the required action at the recommended time the grade is fixed and definable. This relieves the check airman to observe the big picture of this crew. There maybe seven to ten points to observe during a four hour simulator period of CRM intersection points and the other time the check airman is globally observing the crew. These global observations are only used to increase skill level. Nothing observed outside the observation points cannot be used against the party involved.

Summary

The model revolves around five basic concepts:

1. The behavioral markers are the best indicators of CRM effectiveness
2. There are specific skills associated with the behavioral markers.
3. These skills are observable, measurable and definable .
4. The LOS scenarios can be built so that there are specific points during the session at which these skills can be measured
5. The LOS scenario can be tested on large enough population to give you a five gradation (1 to 5) break out.

The most difficult aspect of the proposal is the testing of the scenarios. They must be tested on a large enough population to ensure that you can get true graduation. Companies with similar equipment could share scenarios from year to year This would be especially useful in small carriers where there is not enough of a population to get a good database. This would be beneficial to both parties and would not be difficult to accomplish. Even the training committees of the pilot's associations or the trade associations (Airline Transport Association/ICAO etc.) could be responsible for compiling the data. This would be an invaluable resource and would give the developer a rich library from which to draw.

In the past developers got too bogged down in the detail of trying to interject evaluation into every single manoeuvre in the simulator. This method was doomed to failure because it was incredibly time consuming for the check airman to grade and also it allowed too much of the evaluation to be subjective on the check airman.

The check airman also did not like it because it was almost impossible to get a quantitative answer why one crew was better than another. Nothing is more embarrassing than showing a group of check airmen a video of an excellent trip only to have half of them argue that the individuals should fail. Under this method most of that subjectivity is removed.

This method is very time consuming and costly on the short run. But I think it is the only rational approach to CRM evaluation given the state of the art research into CRM skills.

39 Work group multitasking in aviation

Mary J. Waller
NASA/University of Texas/FAA Aerospace Crew Research Project

Although the performance of work groups in dynamic situations is often critical to overall organizational performance, researchers have typically neglected the study of how work groups *multitask*, or perform multiple tasks in realistic, dynamic environments under deadline conditions. At the same time, our own experiences in and observations of real work groups indicate that groups in dynamic environments often encounter situations in which they must perform several tasks in a limited amount of time.

Examples of multitasking behavior in work groups abound in aviation organizations, and include behavior in airline flight crews, ground operations crews, cabin crews, air traffic control crews, and countless other groups. A flight crew, for example, may be faced at once with the tasks of communicating with air traffic control, managing a hydraulic failure, negotiating a course deviation with a dispatcher, gathering weather information, and operating the aircraft.

While crew resource management (CRM) principles implicitly subsume group multitasking behavior under the topic of workload management (Helmreich & Foushee, 1993), neither the CRM literature nor the literature concerning workload transition (see Huey & Wickens, 1993) elaborate on specific *processes* used by time-pressured groups to manage and perform tasks. Likewise, previous small groups research has focused on single individuals performing single tasks (cf., Chesney & Locke, 1991), single individuals performing multiple tasks simultaneously (Wickens, 1989, 1991), multiple individuals collaborating to perform a single task (cf., Hewett, O'Brien, & Hornik, 1974), or, at best, multiple individuals performing a string of sequential tasks (Saavedra, Earley, & Van Dyne, 1993), but *not* on the performance of multiple tasks by multiple individuals under time pressure. Given the disparity between multitasking behavior in real work groups and the existing groups research, this paper accordingly develops a general model of work group multitasking behavior, explicates the group-level processes contained under the CRM rubric of workload management, and suggests future empirical investigations of multitasking in aviation work groups.

A Model of Work Group Multitasking Behavior

While no general model of group multitasking behavior has been offered in previous literature, two areas of prior work are helpful in developing such a model: small group literature addressing task-oriented processes, and the literature concerning individual-level multitasking behavior. Concerning the former, the work on coordination processes in groups suggests that resource allocation in groups is an important factor in overall group performance (cf. Shiflett, 1973). Similarly, the research concerning group task characteristics suggests that information about the tasks a group performs is vital to the group performing well (cf. Hackman, 1968). Group development research suggests that autonomy (Buller, 1986), time (Gersick, 1989; McGrath & Kelly, 1986), and performance feedback (Klein, 1989) all affect groups' processes and performance.

The research addressing individual-level multitasking behavior suggests two specific mechanisms which individuals use to perform multiple tasks (Wickens, 1989: 72). First, time sharing occurs when an individual actually simultaneously performs more than one task, and involves sharing cognitive processes and motor skills among the tasks. Second, time swapping occurs when an individual does not perform more than one task at a time, but instead sequentially switches his or her attention and resources among several tasks. These individual-level mechanisms may be useful in describing group-level behavior as well. These mechanisms, in concert with the group literature concepts of resource allocation, task characteristics information, autonomy, time, and performance feedback, suggest the necessary elements for a model of work group multitasking behavior.

The subprocesses in the model proposed here are also informed by models of decision making behavior. Many individual-level (cf., Wickens, 1992: 260) and organization-level (cf., Simon, 1956; Mintzberg, 1973: 78) models follow the same three-step pattern of information acquisition, information evaluation, and derivation of final outcome from the first two steps -- all preceding actual task performance. Based on this previous work, it seems reasonable to believe that work groups facing multiple tasks may follow a similar three-step pattern of actions. This three-step pattern is represented in the proposed model by three subprocesses: information gathering and interpretation, task prioritization, and resource allocation. The overall model of work group multitasking behavior is depicted in Figure 1. Included in this model are assumptions of time constraints, dynamic environment, static group membership, group autonomy, and group self-regulation. The two feedback loops illustrate the cybernetic nature of the model, and allow for work groups to adjust their behavior according to the performance feedback they interpret.

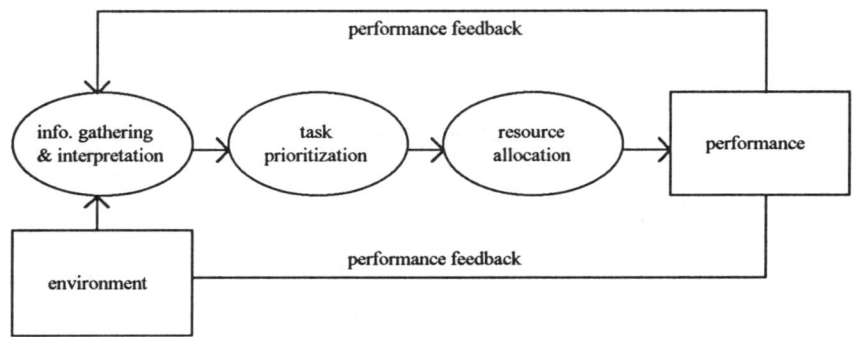

Figure 1 Model of Work Group Multitasking Behavior

Multitasking Model Subprocesses

Information Gathering and Interpretation Before deciding how to perform tasks, a work group must, either implicitly or explicitly: (1) identify the group tasks it needs to perform to achieve a group goal; and (2) receive or collect information about those group tasks (see Saavedra, 1990: 368). Work groups may receive task and goal information from the environment through two separate channels (see Saavedra, 1990: 375). First, work groups may proactively seek out information from the environment regarding tasks awaiting performance, the state of tasks being performed (e.g., whether a task has been performed to the satisfaction of others outside the group), or organizational factors such as prioritization, resources, and deadlines. Second, work groups may passively (or reactively) receive information from the environment regarding task performance. For example, an airline flight crew may learn from the cabin crew that a passenger has become seriously ill during the flight, and emergency ground transportation must be coordinated.

After task and goal information from the environment is received by the group via reactive or proactive means, it may also pass through individual or group perceptual filters. Individuals may filter, weight, or categorize information by using, among other things, functional background or other past experience (Dearborn & Simon, 1958). Information may also be filtered or coded based on shared group experiences (Gersick & Hackman, 1990).

Task prioritization During this subprocess, work groups form an implicit or explicit shared understanding of which tasks are more important than others. The specific basis for the subprocess proposed here stems from the individual-level multitasking process of task prioritization -- the "implicit or explicit assumption that the optimal task manager will possess a mental priority scale that can provide the basis for appropriately shedding tasks when workload becomes excessive and resuming (or assuming) tasks when workload is relieved" (Huey & Wickens, 1993: 221). Obviously, task prioritization in work groups differs from individual task prioritization in that the workload is shared among group members; however, the same task prioritization process as a whole may occur within work groups.

The work group task prioritization process compares tasks awaiting performance to other tasks on a number of different dimensions. These dimensions, based on a synthesis of previous group and multitasking literature, include: (1) the familiarity of the task and its relative difficulty; (2) the source of the task, if identifiable, and the relative status, power, or immediacy attached to the task by that source; (3) the task deadline; (4) the status of the task in terms of its potential completion (e.g., it may already be 75% finished); (5) the sequence of the task in terms of any interdependence among the tasks being prioritized; and (6) the cooperation requirements of the task. Following this comparison process, the group implicitly or explicitly arrives at a ranking of tasks by performance priority.

Resource allocation Huey and Wickens recently concluded that "team effectiveness depends heavily on effective resource management; that is, personnel within the team share information effectively and are appropriately coordinated in their monitoring and task performance responsibilities" (1993: 231). The resource allocation subprocess concerns the application of work group resources to the prioritized tasks awaiting performance; as such, this subprocess represents the core of work group coordination efforts. Work group resources are both human and physical, and include attention, time, labor, and material resources within the group. Individual-level cognitive workload literature indicates that, given the autonomy, individuals adopt different strategies for task performance depending on the characteristics of a particular task combination (Huey & Wickens, 1993: 61). It seems logical to believe that work groups also adopt different strategies as well -- namely, group-level time sharing and time swapping strategies.

Implications

The testing of the proposed model of work group multitasking behavior will help identify, describe, and measure complex group processes in motion as groups work. This identification is a necessary step in the responsible development of multitasking training interventions. Too often, training interventions are developed prematurely, before the behavior to be adjusted is fully described or measured. Such interventions often result in scattered success and failure, and produce little generalizable knowledge.

Given the complex and dynamic situations they continually face, flight crews and air traffic control crews provide an excellent research venue for the study of work group multitasking in action. Consistent with the model presented here, the investigation of multitasking behavior in such groups should be firmly based in observational research methods, using either field or simulation studies to test and inform the model. Future work in multitasking behavior research should focus on examining differences in multitasking behavior between low- and high-performing crews, and developing multitasking training interventions based on those differences.

Considering the dynamic nature of aviation groups' environments, future research should also examine differences in multitasking behavior under *shifting* deadline conditions. The management of such timing and planning interruptions could have important consequences for effective multitasking behavior. Finally, future research should investigate the linkage between situation awareness and the multitasking component of workload management. As alluded to by the addition of the information gathering and interpretation subprocess of the model, this linkage could prove to be vital in triggering desired multitasking behavior in aviation work groups. This idea suggests that crews may be proficient in separate situational awareness or workload management/multitasking activities, but that these proficiencies may not necessarily predict the translation of gathered information into appropriate multitasking behavior.

References

Buller, P.F. 1986. The team building-task performance relation: Some conceptual and methodological refinements. Group and Organizational Studies, 11: 147-168.

Chesney, A.A., & Locke, E.A. (1991), Relationships among goal difficulty, business strategies, and performance on a complex management simulation task. Academy of Management Journal, 34: 400-424.

Dearborn, D.C., & Simon, H.A. (1958), Selective perception. Sociometry, 21: 140-144.

Gersick, C.J.G. 1989. Marking time: Predictable transition in task groups. Academy of Management Journal, 32: 274-309.

Gersick, C.J.G., & Hackman, J.R. 1990. Habitual routines in task-performing groups. Organizational Behavior and Human Decision Processes, 47: 65-97.

Hackman, J.R. 1968. Effects of task characteristics on group products. Journal of Experimental Social Psychology, 4: 162-187.

Helmreich, R.L. 1991. Strategies for the study of flightcrew behavior. In R.S. Jensen (Ed.), Proceedings of the Sixth International Symposium on Aviation Psychology, 1, 326-367. Columbus, OH: Ohio State Univ.

Helmreich, R., & Foushee, C. 1993. Why crew resource management? Empirical and theoretical bases of human factors training in aviation. In E. Wiener, B. Kanki, and R. Helmreich (Eds.), Cockpit resource management, San Diego: Academic Press.

Hewitt, T.T., O'Brien, G.E., & Hornik, J. 1974. The effects of work organization, leadership style, and member compatibility on the productivity of small groups working on a manipulative task. Organizational Behavior and Human Performance, 11: 283-301.

Huey, B., & Wickens, C. 1993. Workload transition: Implications for individual and team performance. Washington, D.C.: National Academy Press.

Klein, H.J. 1989. An integrated control theory model of work motivation. Academy of Management Review, 14: 150-172.

McGrath, J.E., & Kelly, J.R. 1986. Time and human interaction: The social psychology of time. New York: Guilford.

Mintzberg, H. 1973. The nature of managerial work. New York: HarperCollins.

Saavedra, R. 1990. Beer sales and delivery teams. In J.R. Hackman (Ed.), Groups that work and those that don't. San Francisco: Jossey-Bass.

Saavedra, R., Earley, P.C., & Van Dyne, L. 1993. Complex interdependence in task-performing groups. Journal of Applied Psychology, 78: 61-72.

Shiflett, S.C. 1973. Performance effectiveness and efficiency under different dyadic work strategies. Journal of Applied Psychology, 57: 257-263.

Simon, H.A. 1956. Executive performance and leadership. Englewood Cliffs, N.J.: Prentice-Hall.

Wickens, C.D. 1989. Attention and skilled performance. In D. Holding (ed.), pp. 71-105, Human skills. Chichester: John Wiley & Sons.

Wickens, C.D. 1991. Processing resources and attention. In D. Damos (ed.), pp. 3-34, Multiple-task performance. London: Taylor & Francis.

Wickens, C.D. 1992. Engineering psychology and human performance. New York: HarperCollins.

40 Women's learning and leadership styles: impact on CRM

Mary Ann Turney
Dowling College, Oakdale, New York

It has been more than a decade since Texas International, United Airlines and KLM began classroom programs to address Crew Resource Management (CRM) issues (Charles, 1991). Early CRM training was narrow and focused primarily on the role of the Captain. Current CRM has broadened to include the flight crew and the aircraft crew. CRM training applies human factors principles. One particular principle is interpersonal skills.

Flight crews are predominately male and hierarchical in nature. The ideal pilot image portrays a dominant male figure with "the right stuff." (Nagel & Wiener, 1988). There are those who believe that doing the job in the cockpit does not include interpersonal skills. However, the paradigm has shifted in aviation. In today's cockpit, job performance means having effective interpersonal skills. At present, "the world's 2000 or so women transport cockpit crewmembers are helping to erase the perception that aviation is a 'man's world.'" (Gilmartin, 1992, p.62).

Concepts regarding command, leadership, communication style, decision-making and shared authority have different meaning for women and men. In order to promote the functional effectiveness of every member of the crew team, learning and leadership styles that do not conform to the past paradigms must be addressed. These issues must be addressed in order to create better CRM programs which include gender-related differences.

Research Questions

This study explored three basic questions: (1) how do male and female learning and leadership styles differ? (2) what barriers to gender integration and crew teamwork are perceived by pilot crew members? (3) what recommendations can be made to support improved CRM training programs?

Learning and Leadership Styles

Women do not learn as men do. Tannen (1990) states that men prefer debate-like situations in which they pursue knowledge by ritual opposition, while women like to share and learn by interacting in a collegial manner. According to Gilligan (1982), authoritative systems are more important to men in defining relationships than to women and Belenky et al (1986) contend that women value affiliation and acceptance more then do men. Females tend to be more participatory in their learning styles and males are more independent (Emanuel and Potter, 1992). Gilligan differentiates men's and women's thinking with the metaphors of the web and the ladder. Women operate in a web, suggesting interconnectedness and relationship-building; men operate on a ladder, suggesting achievement orientation and hierarchical thinking (Bannister, 1990).

Women, according to Simeone (1987), are channeled by societal tradition and custom into roles which are less directive and more supportive. In terms of role anomalies, women are often first identified by sex rather than by career role. Role anomalies cause confusion and misunderstanding. Women are still assumed to be primarily responsible for family care. These kinds of assumptions generate doubts about women's professional role. If women appear to put their work first, there are some who consider them inappropriate.

Communication has different meaning for males and females. Sociolinguistic studies, reported by Weiss (1993), reveal actual gender differences in language, including vocabulary, intonation and sentence structure. Male language is direct and female language contains greater imagery. "Women use intensifiers (e.g. so, such, quite, very, etc.), modifiers, tag question (e.g. isn't it?), and mild expletives. There is a general notion of uncertainty or hesitancy in female speech. Male language is more absolute; female language more abstract and emotional. Men tend to dispel knowledge; women tend to seek consensus." (p.57)

Women excel in communication, according to Machado (1994). He agrees with Tannen that women are more inclined to "negotiate" in their communication style. Men speak to exchange information and establish status in a group; women talk to exchange information and establish cohesion. Men are more competitive and women are more collaborative.

Research Design

The methodology of the study included fifteen interviews with airline, military and corporate pilots of both genders in order to determine their perceptions concerning the three research questions addressed in the study. A committee, consisting of two airline pilots (one male and one female) and a researcher in women's leadership styles, validated the data, conclusions and recommendations.

Research Results:

A number of themes regarding learning and leadership styles emerged from the interview data.
- Men and women were reported to have different leadership styles.
- Men were reported to be more task oriented and to exhibit more confidence as members of a crew.
- Women were reported to be better communicators, to exhibit more sensitivity to people and to be good negotiators.
- Women were reported to work harder at learning technical information to compensate for a possible lack of background in mechanical training.

Barriers to women's integration in the crew team were reported by both males and females:
- Lack of understanding of gender differences
- "Macho" pilot image
- Males perceived as the leaders
- Stress on females to continually earn the respect of their male peers. Both males and females agreed that mistakes made by women become generalized and are perceived as gender weaknesses.
- Small number of female pilots-in-command
- Male beliefs that females have logged fewer flight hours
- Males who don't view female crew members as professionals. (taking care of women or making sexual advances)
- Language choices by both males and females

With regard to factors that improve crew teamwork, the following themes emerged from the interview data:
- Males and females reported that better teamwork emerges from better communication.
- Males and females agreed that all crew members should "do the job."
- Better situational awareness and the ability to listen and evaluate were considered by males to be important ingredients to cockpit teamwork.
- Females agreed that shared decision-making, conflict resolution and patience were factors which improve crew teamwork.
- Females believed they should behave in a confident manner, particularly toward males.

- Males reported favorable reactions to self-critiques of behavior in cockpit simulation situations

Discussion

The results of the study include the identification of a body of research which clearly demonstrates differences between males and females in learning and leadership styles. Yet, several individuals interviewed stated that they did not perceive differences in learning styles. This may be due to the sample size or lack of awareness of the emerging research regarding women's learning.

Pilots interviewed, however, generally expressed awareness of differences between men and women in leadership styles. Women were deemed to function more successfully than men in leadership areas such as communications skills and interpersonal skills.
The following statements are indicative:

- Women are more sensitive to others' feelings and have compassion.
- Women try to empower others to do the job.
- Women are more subtle, less domineering.
- Women are more adept at addressing issues and talking things out.
- Women are better negotiators.
- Communication is easier for women.

However, It was further observed by both sexes that women should strengthen their abilities to demonstrate confidence and forcefulness.

- Men are more direct; they give orders easily.
- Men are assumed to be the leaders by virtue of gender.
- A pilot needs to be an aggressive type - independent, self-reliant.
- The best women pilots are not feminine; they have male qualities.

Both females and males stressed the desirability of demonstrating confidence; however, a problematic area of misunderstanding and conflict arose when females were perceived to act in a manner that was ascribed to males. This included assertive behavior, strong language and a forceful demeanor. Areas of conflict are the issues of quota hiring, pregnancy, and attitudes that associate males with leadership roles.

Implications for CRM

Based on the information which emerged from the study, there is a need to provide training for crew members regarding differences between men and women in learning and leadership styles. Lack of understanding of these differences inhibits communication and continues to cause gender-related bias.

Some of the issues and attitudes revealed in the study cause blockages to effective crew teamwork. For example, people are perceived as strong and more confident when they are assertive. However, forceful behavior and language is considered masculine. Therefore, women, who exhibit this behavior are considered by some men to be inappropriate.

Women and men agreed that all individuals should be regarded as professionals first. However, both men and women continue to experience situations in which they are demeaned in their sexual identities.

Important Issues Which Emerged

The following important issues emerged from this study:
(1) cockpit crew effectiveness may be significantly reduced due to lack of crew insight regarding the ways in which men and women learn and exert leadership differently.
(2) CRM training should include instructional designs that target the increasingly diversified crew population.

In a cockpit where the focus ought to be on cooperation, not competition and where decision-making is based on developing agreement, the full participation of EVERY member of the crew is essential to increased situational awareness and reduced risk of calamity. To the extent that CRM training can address the "styles", characteristics and attitudes of a diverse population, it will fulfill its purpose.

The results of this study imply both real and potential conflicts within pilot crews; they imply attitudinal and behavioral barriers; they imply issues which have legal ramifications; and finally they imply the need for serious re-evaluation of CRM strategies.

Recommendations for New CRM Instructional Designs

Instructional Design Reassessment is needed to identify problems that may be related to gender differences.

Focus Groups should be formed, offering crew members credit and incentives to study and discuss current research regarding gender differences.

External Assessment - CRM training programs should be periodically assessed by an external evaluator regarding the appropriateness of material included in training.

Discussion Groups - Frank discussion sessions during recurrency training should be provided for pilot crews. These sessions should be facilitated by an individual with expertise in group process. Of greatest importance is informality and freedom from penalty.

Crew Surveys should be conducted periodically to identify sensitive issues and developing interpersonal concerns.

Leadership Training Workshops should be offered to encourage pilot crews to acquire the kind of leadership skills required in today's aviation environment. These skills are very different from those required just a decade ago.

Check Pilot and Instructor Training Sessions - Instructors are key personnel in leading an effective CRM program. These individuals should receive careful training in current research regarding gender and multicultural issues. Bell (1992) found that training for instructor personnel should include awareness of small inequities that may have a cumulative effect. Instructors, for example, must consciously encourage both males and females to succeed; they must elicit responses equally; they must be conscious of attitudes, tone of voice and choice of language. They should dispel stereotypes and select anecdotal material with which both females and males can relate. Expertise in interpersonal relationships has become as crucial as recurrent training on aircraft systems.

De-briefing Sessions offer pilots excellent opportunity at the completion of a flight to expand their communication skills. Practice in positive critiquing is essential if de-briefing is to be effective. Critiquing skills, however, must be taught.

Peer Led Workshops provide opportunity for crew involvement in CRM training. If individual pilots or voluntary teams were encouraged to offer interactive workshops for their peers, it would provide an opportunity for each gender to share assets. In addition, direct participation by individuals affected by the CRM training would provide ownership and pertinent updating. CRM programs would become more flexible and focused on current needs.

Rewards and Incentives for participation in the development of activities that improve CRM is a strong asset to a training program which is committed to involving those who are most affected in the training process itself. The enthusiasm with which the pilots interviewed in this study responded to questions about interpersonal factors is an indication of the level of willingness to be involved.

Role-modeling is a key factor in any student's learning process. Female instructors should teach technical and operational training sessions at all levels.

Simulation exercises in which authority is used to delegate responsibility would permit more traditional crew personnel to experiment with a new paradigm in shared decision-making without threatening the autonomy of any individual.

Since the findings of this study cannot be generalized in all settings, a periodic survey of crew personnel is an appropriate means of assessing particular needs and problem areas that may be related to gender differences.

Conclusion

We cannot afford to let the different ways of seeing remain isolated from one another according to Antler (1990). We each have much to learn from the way our counterparts approach the world. The same energy that goes into aircraft systems training ought to go into carefully developing all the interpersonal skills that make successful teamwork. Human systems, in fact, are truly much more complex than mechanical systems.- a reality which we cannot afford to neglect if we are to prevent even a single aircraft tragedy.

References

Adams, R. J. & Driskell, J. E. (1992). *Crew Resource Management: An Introductory Handbook.*. Washington, DC: US Department of Transportation: Federal Aviation Administration.

Antler, J. & Bikley, S. K. (1990). Educating women students for the future. *Changing Education.* 21-24.

Belenky, M., Clinchy, B., Goldberger, J., & Tarule, J. (1986). *Women's ways of knowing: the development of self, voice, and mind.* NY: Basic Books.

Bannister, L. (1990, October). Women's rhetoric as literature. Salt Lake City, UT: Report presented at the Annual Meeting of the Rocky Mountain Modern Language Association. (ERIC Document Reproduction Service No. ED 325 846).

Bell, S. R. (1992). *Gender influences in the college classroom: optimizing the learning environment for women.* Unpublished MARP. NOVA University, Ft. Lauderdale, Florida.

Charles, M. M. (1991, May). Teamwork in the cockpit. *Flying.* **118.** 108-109.

Emanuel, R. C. & Potter, W. J. (1992). Do Students' style preferences differ by grade level, orientation toward college, and academic major *Research in Higher Education,* **33.** 395-414.

Gallos, J. V. (1991, April). *Educating Men and Women in the 21st Century: Opportunities for Real Leadership.* Boston, MA: ACHE Northeast Regional Conference.

Gilligan, C. (1982). *In a different voice.* MA: Harvard University Press.

Gilmartin, P. A. (1992, January). Women pilots' performance in desert storm helps lift barriers in military, civilian market. *Aviation Week and Space Technology.* **136.** 62-63.

Helgesen, S. (1992, April). The female advantage: women's ways of leadership. *Campus Activities Programming.* 68-69.

Lehrer, H. R. & Weitzel, T. R. (1992, Fall). A turning point in Aviation Training: the AQP mandates crew resource. *The Journal of Aviation and Aerospace Research.* **3.** 14-19.

Machado, R. (1994, January). A Happy Cockpit: Reducing Cockpit Stress Between the Sexes. *Flight Training.* **5.** 50-52.

Merrifield, J. T. (1986, June). Technical conference offers cockpit management guidelines. *Aviation Week and Space Technology.* **124.** 39-45.

Nagal, D. C. & Wiener, E. L. (1988). *Human Factors In Aviation.* San Diego: Academic Press Inc.

Simeone, A. (1987). *Academic women:working toward equality.* South Hadley, MA: Bergin and Garvey.

Tannen, D. (1990). *You just don't understand: women and men in conversation.* NY: Ballentine Books.

Weiss, M. J.; (1993, Fall) Integrating Communication and Gender In The Medical Setting. *Proteus, A Journal of Ideas.* **10.** 55-59.

41 Transfer of the CRM concept into operative medicine

H.G. Schaefer, MD FRCA
Department of Anaesthesia, University of Basel, Switzerland

The transfer of human factors research into the operating room (OR) adds a new aspect to the health care debate arising from the need to contain or reduce health care costs. Unfortunately this occurs at a time when treatment modalities are becoming more expensive and staff intensive serving patients, whose number, age and severity and complexity of disease continuously increase.

One approach to combat rising health care costs has been the introduction of quality control, total quality programs or clinical audit (Donabedian, Smith). However, many of these programs are heavily criticised by doctors and nursing staff concerned with the potential of using them to discipline health care workers, thus achieving an outcome opposite to that desired (Black et al). A newer and richer research focus is proposed by defining the OR team consisting of surgeons, scrub nurses, anesthesiologists and anesthesia nurses as a functional unit. Addressing this entire group of highly qualified people working together in a confined space for a limited time to treat patients is a promising perspective which allows study of the determinants of performance as related to quality and cost efficiency in real life and simulated settings.

A group dynamic model employed in aviation was adapted to develop an instrument for measuring values and attitudes regarding OR management among anesthesiologsts, surgeons, anesthetic and scrub nurses (Helmreich and Schaefer). Both organizational and national cultures can influence work values that individuals bring to their professions and the nature of group dynamics. Hackman has described the organizational shell within which flight crews function and the influences that impinge on work groups in organizations, while Hofstede's four-factor model of culture values is of considerable heuristic value in defining cultural boundaries.

Preliminary results, which will be presented, show strong differences and distinct subcultures related to specialities in the OR. Theoretically, a team composed of subgroups with sharply differing cultural values is unlikely to perform optimally.

Transfer of CRM concepts into operative medicine is feasible because the underlying theoretical model can be adapted and expanded to describe OR performance, and simulation technology in anesthesia and surgery has advanced to a standard comparable to that in aviation. Simulators have been shown to be particularly powerful tools in human factors research. High fidelity anesthesia and surgical simulators have now become available which duplicate the work environment of the OR team.

The concept of human factors training (CRM), successfully validated in aviation, appears to be the ideal paradigm to address issues of operating room performance. This human factors approach to quality and cost issues in health care provides concrete guidelines for intervention unlike quality programs which only identify problems.

References

Black, N., Thompson, E. (1993) Obstacles to medical audit: British doctors speak *Soc. Sci. Med.*, **36**, 849-856.

Donabedia, A. (1988), Quality assessment and assurance: unity of purpose, diversity of means. *Inquiry,* **25**, 173-192.

Hackman, J.R. (1993), New directions for crew-oriented flight training, in Wiener, B., Kanki, B., Helmreich, R.L. (eds), *Cockpit Resource Management.* New York Academic Press.

Helmreich, R.L., Schaefer, H.G. (1994), Team performance in the operating room, in Bogner, M.S. (ed), *Human error in medicine.* Livingstone, NJ: Lawrence Erlbaum. in press.

Hofsted, G. (1991), *Cultures and organizations: software of the mind.* Maidenhead, England: McGraw-Hill.

Schaefer, H.G., Helmreich, R.L. (1993), *The Operating Room Management Attitudes Questionnaire* (ORMAQ). NASA/ University of Texas Technical Report.

Smith R. (1993), *Rationing in action.* BMJ Publishing Group, London.

42 Crossing the cultural boundary

J.M. Davis
Department of Anaesthesia, Foothills Hospital and the University of Calgary

The journey between two seemingly disparate professions, aviation and medicine, can be illustrated by examining closely one specific branch of medicine - anaesthetics. In addition, comparing aviation and anaesthetics demonstrates how analogous the two systems are. This analogy may be demonstrated by a description of two specific areas: the work and the incidents/accidents, with an outline of these shown in Table 1. Details of each of these areas, with examples from both aviation and anaesthetics, are given. In addition, culture differences within anaesthesia, i.e. those based on socio-politico-geographical factors, are noted. Finally, viewing of one's own system, through the perspective of another, should lead to better comprehension and understanding of the problems, and of possible areas for their solution.

References

Eagle, C.J., Davies, J.M. and Reason, J. (1992), 'Accident analysis of large-scale technological disasters applied to an anaesthetic complication', *Canadian Journal of Anaesthesia*, **39**, 118-122.
Lee, R.B. (1991), 'Why accidents happen', *Canadian Journal of Anaesthesia* 38, 1030-1031.
Reason, J. (1990), 'The contribution of latent human failures to the breakdown of complex systems', Philosophical Transactions of the Royal Society of London, B.327, 475-484.

Table 1

Outline of two areas of analogy between aviation and anaesthetics

Work

- system components
- man/machine interaction
- tasks
- personnel

Incidents/accidents

- historical aspects
- nature
- incident
- objectives of investigation
- contributory factors
- prevention

Part 7
AUTOMATION

43 Automation and accountability

Kathleen L. Mosier
NASA Ames Research Center and San Jose State University Foundation
Linda J. Skitka
Southern Illinois University at Edwardsville

The motivation behind the introduction of most automation and automated aids is to enhance and supplement human capabilities. Although the enhancing effects of automation, such as increased fuel efficiency, ability to operate in poor weather, or protection from some types of human error have been well documented, other potentially negative or erosive effects have only begun to be defined. Among these is the evolution of what may be called an "automation bias" in crews, i.e., specific types of errors resulting from reliance on automated feedback as a heuristic replacement for vigilant information seeking and processing. In this paper, the nature and implications of this bias, as well as factors that might promote or exacerbate it, and the possibility of reducing this bias through reinforcing crew accountability will be discussed.

Automated warning systems

The history and development of automated warning systems foreshadows a tendency to rely heavily on automated aids. Many of these systems, such as the Traffic Alert and Collision Avoidance System (TCAS II) were created in direct response to specific needs. In the case of these automated warning systems, the straightforward notion of system accuracy, in terms of confidence that a "signal" is a true indication of an event, rather than "noise," i.e., a false or misleading indication, will be the primary determinant of system use. Because high reliability is a prerequisite to system certification, and because the costs of not attending to true signals is high, crews will depend heavily upon these aids, and the presence--or absence--of a signal will be treated as a reliable indicator of when events occur. In fact, reliance on automated warning systems has led at times to what Wiener and Curry (1980) have termed "primary-backup inversion," the utilization of warning systems as primary indicators of problems, rather than as secondary checks.

Automated decision aids

As automated aids become more sophisticated, and geared toward higher-level cognitive processes, such as situation assessment, problem solving, or decision making, other cognitive and social psychological factors will come into play. In particular, a psychological factor in the use of automated aids can be described in terms of the use of heuristic strategies to reduce cognitive effort.

Heuristics

Heuristics are simple decision-making rules often used to make inferences or draw conclusions quickly and easily. Their success depends upon their capacity to strike a balance between speed (or simplicity) and accuracy. The "rules of thumb" that crewmembers develop in the cockpit serve as useful short-cuts that reduce the time and mental work involved in assessing situations and making decisions. Because these rules are grounded in training, knowledge, and expertise, they are reasonably accurate most of the time.

The advent of automated decision aids, however, physically changes the array of diagnostic cues in the cockpit, introduces new, highly salient cues that are further removed from the raw data, and may cause the crew to question its role and responsibility in decision-making situations. The tendency to rely on these automated cues heavily and indiscriminately is rooted in part in the crew's perception of the authority or expertise of the automation. Additionally, the facts that the opaqueness of the automation interface makes it difficult to trace it s reasoning, and that automated cues are easier to use create a new, potentially inappropriate heuristic: Do what the automation says. The potential danger inherent in this heuristic is what we are labelling an "automation bias" in crews, and is manifested in two types of errors: (1) *omission* errors, and (2) *commission* errors.

Omission errors. Crews commit errors of omission when they fail to perform tasks or detect imminent problems because they have relied upon automated devices to do so for them. Parasuraman, Molloy, & Singh (1993) have described this phenomenon as "automation-induced complacency." A review of 166 ASRS (Aviation Safety Reporting System) reports involving automated control systems in conjunction with some kind of error revealed that the majority of errors resulted from crewmembers missing events or discrepancies because of complacency or non-vigilance (Mosier, Skitka, & Korte, in press). Omission errors can also occur when automation is compensating for some abnormality, but doesn't let the crew know, as was the case for China Airlines in 1985. Their Boeing-747 autopilot attempted to compensate for loss of one of the four engines, masking the approaching onset of loss of control of the airplane.

Commission errors. Errors of commission have been surfacing more recently as byproducts of automated systems, and result when crews act upon erroneous automated information or directives. Examples of these errors can be found in TCAS II incident reports, in which "ghost" or "phantom" radar images have led to erroneous advisories, resulting in airborne incursions and conflicts. Also, preliminary experimental data on commission errors has been cited in a NASA electronic checklist study (Mosier, Palmer, & Degani, 1992). Crews in this simulation study received conflicting indications from engine parameter readings and an electronic checklist. Over 50% (5 out of 8) of the crews using the electronic checklist followed its directives, shut down one engine inappropriately, and set themselves up to execute a go-around maneuver with one marginally operative engine.

The tendency toward automation bias will be exacerbated by at least three factors: 1) the extent to which airline organizations encourage the use of automated systems (organizational pressure); 2) the extent to which compliance with automated decision aids is mandated (legal or regulatory pressure); and 3) the extent to which automation is seen as "an expert" in the cockpit, and one that is perceived to yield more accurate or reliable outcomes than crew members' own judgment ("authority" pressure, or the need to be right).

Mitigating automation bias: Accountability

One potential strategy for ameliorating automation bias has its roots in social psychology. A wide body of social psychological research has found that many cognitive biases or errors can be attenuated by imposing great "accountability" on the decision maker. Accountability in this context refers to the need to justify one's judgments to and be evaluated by important others. The theoretical rationale is straightforward: Accountability demands sensitize decision makers to the need to construct compelling justifications for their choices. Therefore, decision makers employ more multidimensional, self-critical, and complex information processing and put more effort into identifying an appropriate response (Tetlock, 1983). Accountability demands have been shown to reduce cognitive "freezing" or premature closure on judgmental problems (Kruglanski & Freund, 1983), and to lead decision makers to employ more consistent patterns of cue utilization (Hagafors & Brehmer, 1983).

When applying accountability pressures as a check against automation bias, important considerations are to whom crews would be accountable, and when these demands are introduced (Tetlock, Skitka, & Boettger, 1989). Only when decision makers know <u>ahead</u> of time that they will have to justify their decisions to an audience with mixed or unknown views will shifts toward more vigilant decision making occur. In this case, we would expect crewmembers to engage in *preemptive self criticism* - a cognitive strategy that involves engaging in thoughts that increase one's understanding of the arguments on all sides of a decision or course of action. We would expect crews to take into account more data and evaluate available information more carefully when they expect to have to justify their choices.

Accountability in the cockpit: Directions for research

The demonstrated effects of accountability demands have all been produced under controlled laboratory conditions. To determine whether the same shifts to more careful, data-based decision-making strategies occur in the cockpit, research must be conducted to demonstrate the psychological impact of automated decision aids on cockpit decision making under a wide variety of conditions and situations. For example, studies need to be designed that vary in the stress and time pressure involved in making a decision, factors which may influence the tendency toward automation bias. Additionally, potential negative effects of imposing accountability on crews need to be investigated. For example, asking crewmembers to justify their decisions post hoc may lead only to *defensive bolstering* of how they made their decisions in the first place. Also, if airline companies put strong pressure on their crews to use automation (e.g., to justify the cost of automated decision aids, for better fuel efficiency, or because they believe that the automation is more accurate), we would not expect to see an ameliorative effect of accountability on automation bias. Rather, we would expect automation bias to increase, because reliance on automated aids would be a strategy that would be more acceptable to management (the *acceptability heuristic*).

Virtually none of the accountability studies conducted to date have measured time to arrive at a decision. If pressures are placed on crewmembers to avoid early closure on decisions, and to increase vigilance and attention to competing sources of information, it seems quite probable that the decision-making process will simply take longer. Also, crews may try to take ALL information into account, whether it is relevant or not, or may jeopardize safety by delaying action too long. The trade-off between heuristic-driven reasoning and complex information analysis on cockpit decision making must be examined in order to make recommendations to maximize both speed and accuracy in cockpit decision management.

Further, the research on accountability offers no clues as to how high accountability pressures could be implemented in the day-to-day operations of airline crews. It is obvious that crews cannot be met before each flight to "impose accountability demands." However, it is becoming evident that the regulations making the pilot in command responsible for the safety of the flight are not enough to guarantee thoughtful, vigilant decision-making processes. If airline organizations do not want their crews to yield responsibility for decisions to automated aids, they must reinforce human accountability through training and procedural interventions.

Clearly, much research is needed if we are to be able to predict when automation bias is likely to occur in the cockpit, and exactly what the effects of imposing accountability will be on crew decision-making processes. We have begun to investigate the factors which may interact with automation bias and accountability demands, including the criticality of decisions, the reliability of the automation, the availability and ease of accessing other information, whether action or non-action is required, the level at which the automated aid intervenes (e.g., raw data vs. action directive), and the experience and expertise of the operator. Our subject populations include students as well as pilots, and the research plan is to sort out and narrow down the list of potential interactive variables in the laboratory before moving to field and full-mission simulation studies.

Finally, we are in no way suggesting that automated decision aids should be removed from the cockpit. Rather, we are proposing that the psychological impact of these aids on cockpit decision making, especially with respect to the fostering of an automation bias, be very carefully studied. The ultimate success or failure of decision aids in improving the quality of the decision-making process and outcome may be dependent upon whether they enhance or supplant crew decision making processes.

References

Hagafors, R., & Brehmer, B. (1983). Does having to justify one's decisions change the nature of the decision process? *Organizational Behavior and Human Performance, 31,* 223-232.

Kruglanski, A. W., & Freund, T. (1983). The freezing and unfreezing of lay inferences: Effects on impressional primacy, ethnic stereotyping, and numerical anchoring. *Journal of Experimental Social Psychology, 14,* 448-468.

Mosier, K. L., Palmer, E. A., & Degani, A. (1992). Electronic checklists: Implications for decision making. *Proceedings of the 36th Annual Meeting of the Human Factors Society.*

Mosier, K. L., Skitka, L. J., & Korte, K. J. (in press). Cognitive and social psychological issues in flight crew/automation interaction. *Proceedings of the Automation Technology and Human Performance Conference.*

Parasuraman, R., Molloy, R., & Singh, I. L. (1993). Performance consequences of automation-induced "complacency." *The International Journal of Aviation Psychology, 3(1),* 1-23.

Tetlock, P. E. (1983). Accountability and complexity of thought. *Journal of Personality and Social Psychology, 45,* 74-83.

Tetlock, P. E., Skitka, L. J., & Boettger, R. (1989). Social and cognitive strategies for coping with accountability: Conformity, complexity, and bolstering. *Journal of Personality and Social Psychology, 57,* 632-640.

Wiener, E. L., & Curry, R. E. (1980). Flight-deck automation: Promises and problems. *Ergonomics, 23,* 995-1011.

44 Studying automation in the lab – can you? should you?

Clint A. Bowers, PhD
Florian Jentsch, University of Central Florida, Orlando, Florida
Eduardo Salas, PhD
Naval Air Warfare Center Training Systems Division, Orlando, Florida

Automated systems are playing an increasingly critical role in aviation. Therefore, it is important to understand the effects of these systems on human performance. Research in this area, however, has been limited and often presents unclear, sometimes contradictory results. In large part, this can be attributed to the lack of simulators available for this type of research and the large differences between them.

There have only been relatively few simulator studies investigating the effects of automation on crew coordination and communication. This might be attributed to the fact that, so far, adequately studying automation effects was thought to require technologically advanced simulators of high technical fidelity (Ruffel-Smith, 1979). These simulators are few in numbers and are often needed for the training of flight crews. Also, advanced simulators are seldom equipped for research and available to scientists (e.g., Hüttig, 1991).

Since most research facilities do not have access to such simulators, there is a need to identify other strategies for deriving data for cockpit automation research. One such approach might be to utilize simulations of low technical fidelity (see Bowers, Salas, Prince, & Brannick, 1992, for a discussion). This methodology usually employs PC-based simulations or games that are often capable of recreating many functions of actual aircraft, although they are not capable of replicating the "feel" of flying.

We would argue that the shortcomings of PC-based computer simulations in emulating the flight characteristics can be tolerated if the psychological fidelity of these devices is high (Caro, 1977). That is, the tasks simulated shall require the same cognitive resources and processes as those in the actual aircraft. In particular, crew coordination processes, such as communication, leadership, analytical, and other skills, can be sufficiently modeled in PC-based flight simulations if care is taken in developing the mission scenarios. Several studies investigating crew coordination issues used this methodology quite successfully (e.g., Smith, Baker, & Salas, 1994). To assess the feasibility of this approach, the present paper describes a taxonomic scheme for considering automation effects and discusses the degree to which low-fidelity simulations provide a valid test-bed for automation effects.

A system to conceptualize automation

In order to assess the feasibility of low-fidelity simulators for automation research, we must first develop a comprehensive definition of automation. Unfortunately, such a definition is not currently available. For example, when attempting to conceptualize automation, we think that it is rarely useful to consider automation as a dichotomous variable (i.e., present vs. absent). The majority of advanced aircraft contain at least one automated system, so the definition of automation by its presence or absence would not yield a useful discrimination for most studies. Researchers such as Wickens (1984) have, therefore, suggested that automation be considered along a continuum, with manual (human) control at one extreme, and totally automated systems (complete control by a machine) at the other. Using this approach, discrete points along the continuum could be identified to represent the capabilities of the system of interest. Sheridan (1991), for example, described ten such points to classify computerized decision aiding.

For the purposes of aviation psychology, we suggest that the capabilities of current automation systems should be captured at a minimum of five discrete points along the manual to automated control continuum: (a) no automated systems present; (b) a system offers advice but performs no active function; (c) a system performs an action, but only when specifically requested by the operator; (d) a system performs a function unless the operator intervenes but informs the human about the operation; and (e) a fully automated system without operator notification or interference.

Although using this system of classifying each system and function in an aircraft along the manual to automated control continuum would help in better describing different aircraft, it still would fail to discriminate effectively among the levels of automation present in today's advanced aircraft. Systems in these aircraft automate very similar functions using very similar technology, yet pilots feel able to distinguish "better" systems from "worse" (Wise, Abbott, Tilden, Dyck, Guide, & Ryan, 1993). Also, there have been occasional examples where automation may have been confused with other advanced (i.e., "glass cockpit") technology. Although automation and other advanced technologies are often cohorts, it must be noted that changing a display type does not change the level of automation. Indeed, because these technological changes are so frequently linked, it is vital to ensure proper experimental control when assessing the specific effects of either variable. Otherwise, the effects of automation and other advanced technologies could become hopelessly confounded.

Due to these various threats to the generalizability of research findings, a system to conceptualize automation must adopt a multi-dimensional appraoch when considering the automation capabilities of various systems and their components. Table 1 presents such a taxonomic approach. The four main criteria to assess automation capabilities that we suggest are flight planning, flight control, status monitoring, and systems management. Within each criterion, sub-divisions can be made to adequately describe the capabilities of the system, leading to high discrimination between different advanced technologies. The sub-criteria are flexible and reflect the changing needs and capabilities of automated systems.

Table 1
Taxonomy of automation levels

Criterion	Description
Automation Levels	
Flight Planning	Within each category, the system capabilities
Data Storage	can be described along the manual to fully automated
Route Planning	continuum using five discrete points:
Time/Dist. Calc.	
Comm. Plan	(a) complete manual (human) control
Flight Control	
Altitude Hold	(b) a system with advisory capabilities
Vertical Flight Path	
Heading Hold	(c) a system that performs functions only on demand
Horiz. Flight Path	
Speed Control	(d) an automated system that provides feedback
Status Monitoring	to the operator and can be switched off
Engines	
Electrical System	(e) a fully automated system that neither informs
Systems Management	the operator nor can be switched off
System Capabilities	
Emergency Checklist	

*more functional categories are optional

The use of low-fidelity simulators in automation research: Can you?

With respect to the study of automation, the system to conceptualize automation that was suggested in the previous part of this chapter serves as the framework for the use of low-fidelity simulations. Based on the classification shown in Table 1, the independent variables and the task characteristics of a psychologically valid task can be determined. Using the performance characteristics of the automated system under study, tasks can be specifically built to reflect the taskwork and teamwork characteristics of the system. Consider, for example, that system management in a particular aircraft involves the choice between advisory functions and automation on demand for the management of information (e.g., decision making). In this case, a valid manipulation investigating automation effects should offer just those two levels of automation; all other system components should stay unaltered. Although a full flight simulator may allow to emulate the exact layout of the devices, their spatial arrangement and interaction, it would be difficult to determine which confounding factor affected human behavior.

PC-based simulations, on the other hand, are unique in that they allow to manipulate several variables that are usually beyond the control of the experimenter, even in high-fidelity, full-mission simulators. It is, for example, relative difficult (or even impossible) to change the level of automation across a wide variety of functions in a full-mission simulator. Yet, in a PC-based, low-fidelity simulation, a few keystrokes allow to do just that (Table 2). The spatial layout and crew interdependencies of low-fidelity simulations can be changed easily, allowing to decompose possible effects further than in relatively rigid full-mission simulators.

The use of low-fidelity simulators in automation research: Should you?

Based on the discussion above, we conclude that it is possible to create manipulations of automation in low fidelity simulations which possess sufficient psychological fidelity to allow useful research. However, there are several other factors that should be considered in assessing the construct validity of these manipulations. The first of these is that the validity of low fidelity simulations is determined by the scenarios for which they are used. Clearly, the characteristics of these simulators are such that they require experimental scenarios designed specifically for that purpose (see Prince, Oser, Salas, & Woodruff, 1993 for a review).

A second concern regards the limited generalizability of low fidelity simulations. Despite the flexibility for cockpit emulation or the care used in creating experimental scenarios, the results obtained from these simulations may not generalize to particular aircraft. Additionally, automation studies using low fidelity systems tend to occur in relatively "sterile" environments. In operational systems which impose environmental stressors such as noise, vibration, and so forth, performance might differ.

In summary, we contend that low fidelity simulations offer promise for automation research, and can be used as a valid test-bed in some situations. However, the more appropriate, and perhaps more useful, application of this approach is to serve as method for developing hypotheses and conducting preliminary testing of variables, training technologies and so forth. In this fashion, the technique can be used to direct and optimize research conducted in expensive high-fidelity simulations.

Table 2
Taxonomy of capabilities of a low-fidelity simulator
(Microsoft® Flight Simulator™ Version 5.0)

Criterion	Description
Methodology	Laboratory experiment
Scenario	Unlimited (generic or realistic with expanded database)
Aircraft Type	Four base models, unlimited with expanded database
Design	Numerous (e.g., within, between, mixed)
Automation Levels	
Flight Planning	
Data Storage	Manual to automatic with additional equipment
Route Planning	Manual to automatic with additional equipment
Time/Dist. Calc.	Manual to automatic with additional equipment
Comm. Plan	Manual to automatic with additional equipment
Flight Control	
Altitude Hold	Manual to fully automated
Vertical Flight Path	Manual to semi-automated
Heading Hold	Manual to fully automated
Horiz. Flight Path	Manual to fully automated
Speed Control	Manual to semi-automated
Status Monitoring	
Engines	Manual to fully automated
Electrical System	Manual to fully automated
Systems Management	
System Capabilities	Manual to fully automated
Emergency Checklist	Manual, automated with additional computers
Moderator Variables	
Task-related	Numerous (e.g., clouds, wind, turbulence, temperature, time, equipment realism and reliability, traffic)
Team-related	Numerous (e.g., crew background, hierarchy)

Notes

1. The opinions expressed herein are those of the authors and do not necessarily reflect those of the institutions they are affiliated with.
2. This work was supported in part by Naval Air Warfare Center Training Systems Division Contract No. N61339-93-C-0101.
3. The Naval Air Warfare Center Training Systems Division was formerly the Naval Training Systems Center.

References

Bowers, C., Salas, E., Prince, C. and Brannick, M. (1992), Games teams play: A method for investigating team coordination and performance, *Behavior Research Methods, Instruments, & Computers*, **24** (4), 503-506.

Caro, P.W. (1977), *Factors influencing air force simulator training effectiveness* (Report No. HumRRO-TR-77-2), Human Resources Research Organization, Alexandria, Virginia.

Hüttig, G. (1991), Centre for flight simulation technology Berlin - Airbus A340 simulator for research and training, in Jensen, R. (ed.), *Proceedings of the Sixth International Symposium on Aviation Psychology*, 847-850, Ohio State University, Columbus, Ohio.

Prince, C., Oser, R.L., Salas, E., and Woodruff, W. (1993), Increasing hits and reducing misses in CRM/LOS scenarios: Guidelines for simulator scenario development, *International Journal of Aviation Psychology*, **3** (1), 69-82.

Ruffell-Smith, H.P. (1979), *A simulator study of the interaction of pilot workload with errors, vigilance, and decisions* (NASA TM-78482), NASA-Ames Research Center, Moffett Field, California.

Sheridan, T.B. (1991), Automation, authority and angst - revisited, in *Proceedings of the Human Factors Society 35th Annual Meeting*, 2-6, Human Factors Society, Santa Monica, California.

Smith, K., Baker, D. and Salas, E. (1994), *Training assertiveness for team environments* (Manuscript submitted for publication).

Wickens, C.D. (1984), *Engineering psychology and human performance*, Charles E. Merrill, Columbus, Ohio.

Wise, J.A., Abbott, D.W., Tilden, D., Dyck, J.L., Guide, P.C. and Ryan, L. (1993), *Automation in corporate aviation: Human factors issues*, Embry-Riddle Aeronautical University, Daytona Beach, Florida.

45 Automation and the corporate aviation environment

John A. Wise*, David W. Abbott**, Donald S. Tilden*, Patrick C. Guide*, Jennifer L. Dyck**
*Center for Aviation/Aerospace Research, Embry-Riddle Aeronautical University
**Department of Psychology, University of Central Florida

INTRODUCTION

Corporate aviation[1] is growing in its use of automation, with some corporate aircraft having greater sophistication than air carrier aircraft. Previous studies (Wiener & Curry, 1980; Wiener, 1989) have identified a number of safety concerns associated with automation in the airline industry. The problems identified were often associated with periods of change (e.g., amendments in flight plan, vectors for traffic). Because the *raison d'être* of corporate aviation is flexibility and change, it would appear to follow that the corporate aviation industry may be more susceptible to some of the negative effects of automation. As a matter of fact, NASA's Aviation Safety Reporting System (ASRS) identified 84 self-reported incidents between 1986 and 1991 (Aviation Safety Reporting System, 1992) that involved advanced automated corporate aircraft.

Corporate aviation by its nature describes a very wide range of activities and sophistication. Operations vary from a business where the owner flies herself to business meetings to dispersed fleets of large aircraft. As a result, the levels of automation vary from a simple two axis autopilot to sophisticated computer based flight management systems capable of flying the aircraft from lift-off to touch down while maintaining optimum performance throughout. It was therefore necessary to limit the scope of this study to only a those aircraft with both CRT-based displays and computer-based flight management systems. However, the study did include observations of flight departments that varied

---
[1] Corporate aviation is the part of general aviation that supports the travel of businesses and corporations, particularity the upper management of those organizations.

from dispersed multiple location operations to an operation where one person acted as manager, maintainer, and pilot (the aircraft used was approved for single-pilot operation).

Another area that makes corporate aviation unique is that its pilots are usually type-rated in more than one aircraft. While this was a challenge in the days of conventional controls and displays — where the pilots had to learn basic systems and flight characteristics of the various aircraft — the new world of automation *also* makes it necessary that they essentially learn different computer operating systems. This problem is exacerbated by the fact that the interface for most of the computer based systems are essentially patterned after programming languages developed two decades ago.

Finally, manufactures of corporate aircraft tend to be smaller operations that the typical airline manufacturer. As a result, few if any have a professional human factors presence in the design team. Most "human factors" work is often the result of input from the flight test staff.

Corporate aviation is thus a theoretically interesting domain for the study of aviation automation because it operates where the problems are thought to exist and because it uses the highest technology available. Corporate aviation is also an area that has received a very low level of attention from human factors researchers. Therefore, corporate aviation is both ripe for study and the members of the community are very appreciative of the work.

This paper provides a discussion of some of the results of a two year study of automation in corporate aviation. It involved 1) collecting opinion data from the pilots via questionnaires and workshops, 2) riding in the jumpseat on actual corporate missions, and 3) observing initial and recurrency training. The effort relied to a great extent on the work of Wiener (1987) and his colleagues, who have identified a wide range of both problems and advantages associated with automation technologies in air carrier operations. As they have done a outstanding job of describing them, no attempt will be made to summarize them here. Rather, it will be noted that the issues raised above make the application of high quality interfaces very important.

It also relied on the significant literature in human-computer interaction that provides a significant data base of criteria for the evaluation of such interfaces. Issues such as coding, data density, use of color, menus, and command languages, while far from solved, have an adequate level of empirical data from which one can perform sound design decisions and evaluations. Likewise, the traditional "knobs and dials" data base provides the basic human factors criteria that is applicable to all interfaces, automated or not.

Last, all the investigators were rated commercial pilots who had flight experience in a wide variety of aircraft types and missions. This experience played a significant role in the ability to collect data (e.g., the subject pilots were comfortable telling "war stories" to other pilots) and the interpretation of the data in light of the operating environment.

APPROACH

This two year study involved data collected via: 1) two questionnaires sent to pilots currently flying automated corporate aircraft, 2) flight observations of 62 corporate missions, 3) over 160 hours of observation during initial and recurrency training in flight simulators, and 4) two pilot workshops.

DISCUSSION

There is a lot that is still unknown about the *optimal* relationship between the human and automation in aviation. However, the research accomplished to date has generated a strong basis for the effective — if not optimal — integration of automation. It is within these intellectual boundaries that the following discussion takes place. There is no intent on the part of the authors to imply that unequivocal answers are available for all of the problems identified, but there is enough evidence that good initial directions can be chosen.

Software Interface

The human-machine interface of the current automated systems needs considerable work to improve usability and reduce probability of error. One anecdotal piece of evidence of the complexity of the interface was a remark by a pilot undergoing recurrency training in the simulator. He noted, in discussions with the investigator, that, during recurrency, he only used about thirty percent of the automation he normally used because he knew there would be emergencies and he did not have time to "mess with the automation."

One particular flight provided a good example of the possible difficulties with the use of an FMS system under high workload and frequent ATC route change conditions. This was a single pilot flight in an FMS/EFIS aircraft. Clearance delivery provided a revised clearance which included a waypoint defined by DME distance out on a given radial from a VOR. Since the flight plan was filed /R (RNAV equipped aircraft with altitude encoding transponder), this was an acceptable waypoint for ATC to assign, but was not included in the original flight plan that the pilot had filed. The pilot spent 10 minutes on the ramp — in increasing frustration trying — to enter such a waypoint into the FMS. He finally gave up and departed without a complete flight plan in the FMS. As the flight progressed, severe weather with hail and thunderstorms caused the pilot to request frequent course changes and vectors. Upon arrival at the destination airport, the pilot did not have clearance to land or hold. The pilot stayed outside controlled airspace until he was able to break in on a congested approach control frequency. He obtained further clearance instructions and landed without incident. A simpler way to make programming changes would have been a great help. Although weather was a factor, the incomplete flight plan confounded the tasks with air traffic control. In this case a "*" or a "/" might have called up a hidden menu page to allow the sort of waypoint definition needed to create the assigned waypoint.

With an "easier to use" system, the automation could have been a great aid to a single pilot operation under difficult circumstances. As it turned out for this pilot with his level of proficiency, the *FMS was part of the workload problem* rather than part of the solution. It could appear that this is simply a problem of inadequate training. The observer who rode on this flight asked many other pilots on subsequent flights what they thought about single pilot operation of this FMS/EFIS equipped aircraft. They all said the same thing, although many of them were very proficient with the FMS, "We only fly single pilot when delivering an empty aircraft for service." With two proficient pilots, one will have time to overcome the awkward interface programming demands and thus use the FMS as a workload reducer for the two pilot crew. This poor interface/programming logic in the FMS is evidently too great for a single pilot to effectively use while concurrently flying the airplane.

Many pilots told us during discussion and during flight that the FMS sometimes surprised them and that they had limited understanding of the full features available in the system. Compared to modern computer interfaces for application programs the FMS is not "user friendly."

All of the pilots who participated in this research requested standardization of the interface. Most admitted that they did not care if the interface was bad, as long as it was standardized. That statement was heard numerous times. From a human factors point-of-view, there is some considerable doubt that the current state of the art in human-computer interface knowledge is such that a final set of standards could be written. Also, because the technology is young and rapidly developing it may be inappropriate to set restrictive standards. At this time many of the applications are near copies of old electro-mechanical designs, and it may be some time until familiarity with the systems and creativity mix to allow the creation of a truly superior interface.

But that is not to argue that nothing should be done. Rather, we would like to propose that a set of very basic standards be developed that would allow reasonable standardization of basic operations while allowing for future improvements and product differentiation between vendors. As mentioned above, some standardization could be implemented as Apple Computer has done with the Macintosh interface. Such a standard would improve the performance of pilots who must fly a variety of aircraft types.

Beyond the need for standardization is the critical need for a dramatic improvement in the quality of the interface from a human factors engineering perspective. All of the current FMS interfaces are basically an extension of the old interactive programming languages that were developed in the late '60s. They were all developed assuming a computer science professional with formal programming training and experience. Such languages were designed assuming the operator would be a programmer at a desk who could debug the software as it was developed. It was not intended for the non-programmer, who is interested only in using the application and who works in a time critical environment, such as aviation. A more effective, user-friendly interface is desperately needed.

Coding

Coding of data is a critical issue in effective human-machine interaction. There exists a set of basic standards (e.g., color coding of airspeed indicators), but they were drawn up assuming a steam gauge era cockpit. Standards need to be developed based on high quality empirical data relating coding techniques and human-machine performance. This total laissez faire attitude toward coding is nowhere better seen than with color coding.

This is the area where automated systems are most criticized by corporate pilots. Poor training and awkward interface design can be overcome eventually, but the corporate pilot's task is to fly more than one type of aircraft. For example, when applying what is correct action in one aircraft to a second aircraft, the pilot may unwittingly commit an error in the second aircraft. Negative transfer of this type increases the likelihood of the pilot making a potentially serious operational error.

The color coding that was observed was primarily being used as a marketing tool and generally did not follow basic design principles related to human perception of color. Most color codes are placed at the whim of the designer and accepted by an equally naive test pilot, usually based on previous experience (e.g., in the C-47 it looked like this). From a purely human factors point of view, much of the color coding would be expected to inhibit performance rather than improve it. The coding rules appear to be based on some cultural stereotypes, such as red represents danger, and little else. While cultural stereotypes are important, they are far from the most important considerations when using such a salient stimulus such as color. Finally, many of the color coding techniques used were not multimodal, i.e., if the color was lost, all of the coding would be lost. This can be dangerous for any pilot.

Research needs to be done to support the development of effective coding of information in advanced cockpits, not just the color issue discussed here, but symbology in general. For example, what basic set of symbology should be defined as standard across all cockpits? What type of variance is acceptable?

The fact that corporate pilots typically fly more than one type of aircraft creates a much greater problem in the area of nonstandard systems than for the air carriers. Some flight departments limit their pilots to only one type of aircraft to avoid these problems, but this is exception rather than the norm. The need for flexibility may require maximum pilot utilization.

Knobs and Dials Human Factors

A quick review of the cockpits of the multi-million dollar aircraft have a significant number of basic design errors identified by human factors research programs in the 1940s and 1950s. The placement of controls that operate dramatically different aspects of the aircraft (e.g., heading, altitude) and cursors knobs which are located adjacent to each other with exactly the same shapes, causes many problems, such as altitude busts. It was also noted that, on some series of the same aircraft, the relative position of knobs changed, again causing problems for pilots who flew both aircraft. Likewise, the direction of movement of tape, and other type, displays was studied and specified in the 1950s, yet examples of design errors are still being created and sold.

On one aircraft, the communication radio selection is located on a side panel up front of the cockpit while radio tuning takes place elsewhere. We observed the pilots spending a considerable amount of time tuning and attempting to activate a frequency. It was later discovered that it was not the appropriate radio.

The cockpit layouts seemed better in the physically larger aircraft. Fewer inputs or monitoring activities require the pilot to turn to the side or back. In aircraft where the FMS is located at the extreme back part of the center console, data entry into the FMS requires great physical dexterity.

The keyboards used to enter data are another significant cause of problems. Not only does the design vary from system to system, but their use often forces simple tasks to become very difficult, e.g., typing in a list of locations to create a flight plan as opposed to pointing to those places on a map. Not only do standards need to be developed for keyboards, different methods for inputting data need to be explored. The Military, for example, have used "coolie hat" switches on top of control sticks and yokes to provide continuous cursor control.

Check Ride Requirements

As it currently stands, a person in the U.S. can get a type rating on a highly automated corporate aircraft with all of the automation turned off. There is currently no requirement to demonstrate skill at operating the aircraft the way it is designed to be used, i.e., in the highly automated mode. The authors recognize the need for the requirement that a pilot demonstrate the skill to fly an aircraft in a manual mode. But because the automated mode is the normal mode of operation and because there are parts of the automation that can induce serious consequences, it would appear to make sense that one should demonstrate the skill to use the automated equipment.

This is especially critical in aircraft that can come equipped with a variety of FMSs and yet require one type rating. Flying the same airframe with a different FMS can be drastically different in many ways. It would seem that some consideration must be given to at least studying the proposal that type rating be made FMS-specific using some criteria similar to those that are used to determine whether different airframes need different type ratings.

The spirit of the approach would be much the same as some airlines operate: pilots must demonstrate the capability to use all flight-related equipment during check rides, but have the authority and responsibility to use their own techniques during normal operations.

ACKNOWLEDGEMENTS

This research was sponsored by the Federal Aviation Administration under contract DTFA01-91-C-00042. The opinions expressed are solely the authors, and do not necessarily reflect those of the sponsor. The authors would like to thank the FAA Technical Officer, Mr. John Zalenchak III, for his assistance and support. Requests for copies of the final report of this project should be sent to Mr. John Zalenchak III, ARD-210, Federal Aviation Administration, 800 Independence Ave. SW, Washington, DC 20591.

REFERENCES

Aviation Safety Reporting System. (1992). *Corporate Advanced Cockpit Incidents* (Search Request No. 2407). Mountain View, CA: Author.

Wiener, E. L (1987). Fallible humans and vulnerable systems: Lessons learned from aviation. In J. A. Wise and A. Debons (Eds), *Information systems: Failure analysis.* (pp. 162-181). Springer-Verlag, Berlin.

Wiener, E. L. (1989). Human factors of advanced technology ("Glass Cockpit") transport aircraft. (NASA Contractor report 177528. Contract NCC2-377). June.

Wiener, E. L., & Curry, R.E. (1980). Flight deck automation: Promises and Problems. *Ergonomics*, 23, 995-1001. Also published in R. Hurst and L. Hurst. (1982). *Pilot Error: The Human Factors.* London: Granada.

Part 8
INDIVIDUAL FACTORS

Section A
ALCOHOL

46 Early intervention of alcohol problems among pilots

Dr Fanny Duckert, The University of Oslo

Introduction

There are strict rules regulating alcohol use in aviation. Registrations of fatal flight accidents in U.S.A. have shown that the dead pilots have not had detectable blood alcohol concentrations (BAC), since 1964, except for a non-American crash in Alaska in 1977, where the pilot had a BAC of 1.2 o/oo, and a crash in 1986, where the pilot had a BAC of 1.6 o/oo However, in 1990 three pilots were arrested, after landing a B-727, belonging to Northwest Airlines. They all had high levels of BAC. Surveys have shown that a considerable number of pilots are regular alcohol users, and that 10-15 per cent must be considered as heavy drinkers, drinking more than 5 drinks at a minimum of two times a month, or had a daily intake of more than two drinks (Agelii, 1991).

Because of the high level of responsibility among pilots, and the transparent milieu in cockpit, there are reason to believe that the frequency of traditional alcoholism is rather low. However, there are other forms of hazardous drinking that may be more frequent, and that may represent a threat to safety in aviation. More typical may for example be episodic heavy drinking, or periodic, continuous use of alcohol.

Individual differences in drinking patterns are of importance. For instance, a regular heavy consumption will result in an increased tolerance, which implies that the person may appear quite sober, while having a high BAC. This person will change relatively little during intoxication, but will be in danger of suffering serious withdrawal symptoms for prolonged periods after end of drinking. He will for instance be in danger of suffering seizures or having hallucinations even after several days of abstinence. Another hazardous drinking pattern may be irregular, episodic heavy drinking. This pattern usually will imply stronger behavioral acting out during intoxication, and a more acute feeling of hangover during withdrawal, even if the withdrawal period will be shorter than in the first example.

Both groups will be in the danger of starting a working period while still being under the influence, since the phenomena "acute tolerance" which appear during a drinking episode, may result in a misjudgment of one's own level of intoxication (The day-after effect).

Studies have shown that hangover effects are a very serious threat to safety in aviation ((Flight Safety Bulletin, 1989). Even with a demand on 24 hours of abstinence before going on duty, a heavy drinker may go on duty, in the middle of, or just having entered the phase of withdrawal. This means that he will have no detectable BAC, but will still perform poorly for several hours. Withdrawal effects include for example impaired perceptual capacity, and impaired capacity for handling unforeseen events.

Even if existing studies of aviation accidents in the majority of cases have failed to detect alcohol in the blood of the pilots, no existing studies can safely eliminate the possible effects of withdrawal as one causal factor in aviation accidents!

Special attention should also be given to the use of alcohol as a sleeping drug, or as self-medication in periods of stress and depression (Simons 1990). Many pilots experience problems connected with stress and sleeping disturbances. Alcohol is easily available and seemingly effective in making the user relaxed and sleepy. However, the harmful, long-term effects are often overlooked. The quality of sleep is changed (most obvious is the decrease in REM-sleep, i.e. dream-sleep, which is essential for restitution of normal brain activities). In addition the ability to fall asleep in its self will be disturbed. Thus the long-term effects of using alcohol as a sleeping drug is an increase in sleep difficulties. The same effect has been found when alcohol has been used as self-medication for anxiety or depression.

The above hazardous uses of alcohol are not limited to the drinking patterns of the so called "alcoholics", but may be part of "normal" alcohol users drinking patterns. Situational hazardous drinking may be a much more predominant threat to safety than "alcoholism". Traditional beliefs and assumptions about alcoholism and alcoholics may easily become an hindrance to early detection and treatment of problem drinking in pilots. Traditionally, the problem drinking has been going on much too long before intervention has been started. The airline industry, the CAAs, and the aircrew unions must increase their awareness of early signs of problem drinking. This implies investing more resources on non-moralistic information, and awareness raising activities among aircrews and managers. Also self-help guides for changing harmful drinking patterns should be distributed to all aircrews. These should both include guidelines for assessing hazardous and harmful drinking, and advices about how to change drinking patterns.

Up to now, one method of identifying problem drinkers has been to take blood tests, especially of liver functions, hoping to detect heavy drinkers that way. However, most tests in use have low sensitivity. Also, these tests will be most useful, discovering continuous heavy drinking, but will miss out persons with low over all consumption, but episodic binge drinking. Thus, medical examinations will only be of modest usefulness for detecting early problem drinking (Duckert, 1993). The most important source of identification is peers' observations. However, the consequences for the pilot of being identified as an alcohol addict, usually have been quite serious, including immediate loss of licence and a demand for extensive treatment. Therefore many pilots have hesitated to report a colleague, misbehaving himself. Covering up for peers are common, delaying the possibility for early intervention.

Treatment programs aimed at early detection and intervention of hazardous drinking and early problem drinkers should be developed. According to the U.S. Institute of Medicine (1990) In-patient treatment of early problem-drinking is more expensive, but not more effective than out-patient treatment. Early intervention programs therefore should be based on outpatient treatment.

Early intervention, will imply that the pilot in question, not automatically should loose his licence, but might continue flying during treatment. Of course with adequate surveillance arrangements. This would make it easier for peers to report a colleague with a hazardous drinking pattern, and it would make it easier for the pilot in question to admit his problem and accept help.

For an early intervention program to be successful, it is necessary with a commitment and co-operation between the management, the helping agency, the pilot in question and his trade union representative. A contract must be made out, clarifying the responsibilities and tasks of each person involved. Also unambiguous criteria for success and failure should be made out in the contract.

Continuous evaluation is of utmost importance. This may take form of regular meetings, involving the relevant parties, including the problem drinker himself. Also if there is doubt about anyone fulfilling his part of the contract, anyone involved should be licensed to claim a meeting to discuss the situation. Regular medical check-ups may also be part of the evaluation procedure.

A Norwegian Program for Early Intervention

The program in question is based upon newer knowledge about alcohol problems and treatment, and recommendations from WHO, and the National Health Authorities of Norway. It was developed for problems drinkers in usual and has been run about ten years (Duckert, 1993).

We were contacted in 1989 by representatives from the pilots' union in Norway. They were concerned about several suicides among pilots that had followed after treatment in Minnesota institutions, and wanted assistance in giving an alternative treatment offer to pilots with alcohol problems. During the next two years, we had six pilots through the program. Of these five were successfully rehabilitated.

The program is based upon the assumption that problem drinking is a lifestyle problem, caused by the learning of destructive drinking habits. The traditional beliefs about "alcoholism" and "alcoholics" are looked upon as unsuitable to early intervention. Alcohol problems are varied and changing, and it is possible to have drinking problems in certain situations and some phases in life, but not in others. Problem drinkers are just as different as anyone else. These individual differences must be taken into consideration when intervening in their drinking patterns. Problematic drinking is amendable and responsive to therapeutic techniques in the same way as with other human behaviours.

Admission to the program was through a referral from a social committee, with members from the pilots trade union and the management. The medical doctor of the company also participated in the committee. Reports about pilots usually had been given by pilot colleagues. In one case, the spouse had taken the initiative and in one case, the pilot himself had asked for assistance.

First, a meeting, involving the relevant parties, including the therapist and the pilot in question, was held, discussing the problems, needs for change and wishes of the pilot himself. A contract was made out and details of the future arrangement decided upon.

Thereafter a medical examination was done. If the pilot showed no signs of ill health, he was allowed to resume his work tasks. But he had to be under some kind of peer surveillance for one year.

The treatment started with a thorough examination of the drinking pattern and problems connected with drinking. Also the pilot's personal and social situation was mapped. Treatment was aimed at both the drinking pattern in itself, giving training in control techniques, and at the general life situation, and personal problems of the pilot. When relevant, family members were included in the therapy. The duration of the program was one year. Therapeutic sessions were held once a week the first six months. Thereafter once or twice a month.

With regular intervals, follow-up meetings were held, discussing the progress of the treatment, and handling eventual problems or doubts. These meetings were arranged every second month the first half year, and every third month thereafter. If an unforeseen problem appeared between meetings, anyone in the group was licensed to call a meeting, including the pilot in question, handling the problem as soon as possible.

Concluding Remarks

Even if the experiences with this kind of program so far is somewhat limited, the preliminary results have turned out to be promising. There are several elements of the program that may be of importance:

* The program is flexible and non-bureaucratic
* It is based upon a reciprocal commitment and co-operation between the management and the pilots' trade union
* Adequate follow-up procedures are looked upon as vital
* It does not stigmatize the problem drinker
* The problem drinker can go on with a normal life while in treatment
* Early detection and intervention are more likely

This is a program, which has an humanistic approach, without minimizing the importance of safety. When some of the stigmatization, connected with the traditional AA-oriented approaches is removed, it will be easier to make persons recognize potential harmful drinking, and to participate in an intervention program, than before.

References

Agelii, M.: Alkohol. *Flygposten, Svensk Pilotforening,* nr. 3, 1991

Duckert, F.: *Alcohol Problems and Treatment,* National Institute of Alcohol and Drug Research, Oslo, 1993.

Simons, M.: Environmental factors influencing flight crew performance. Paper presented at the *ICAO Human Factors Seminar,* Leningrad, 1990.

U.S. Institute of Medicine: *Broadening the Base of Treatment for Alcohol Problems,* The National Academy Press, Washington, 1990.

47 A program to treat alcoholic airline pilots and return them to work

Richard B. Stone
Program Manager, HIMS II, Denver, Colorado

In the early 1970's, the US Air Line Pilots Association (ALPA) recognized that pilot members who suffered from alcoholism were either being fired or retired for medical reasons. Unfortunately, other alcoholic pilots who were able to continue drinking during their time off died prematurely.

At the 1972 ALPA Board of Directors meeting, the board held a closed session to consider finding a remedy to the hardships and devastation suffered by members who were alcoholics. A grant from the US Government helped establish a method of dealing successfully with these pilots. Three airlines were to be used as test cases for the program, but the concept quickly spread and soon many airlines were involved. The grant began in 1974 and lasted for eight years. Today the program has helped establish Employee Assistance Departments at many airlines and almost all airline employees are able to receive assistance with dependency problems.

The Human Intervention Motivation Study, or HIMS, as the grant program came to be known, was based on the concept that alcoholism was a detectable disease, characterized by denial but amenable to treatment. HIMS required changes in Federal Air Regulations (FAA regulations); supervisor, peer, and physician training; and a procedure to ensure abstinence by recertified pilots. These were not all developed overnight but took years to perfect. Other changes were required, such as company policies and an attitude reorientation by individuals working with alcoholics.

In 1976, soon after the establishment of the HIMS program, the FAA (1976) changed its definition of alcoholism and became an advocate for rehabilitation. Current FAA regulations state: "As used in this section, 'alcoholism' means a condition in which a person's intake of alcohol is great enough to damage physical health or personal or social functioning, or when alcohol has become a prerequisite to normal functioning."

On August 26, 1992, the Journal of the American Medical Association published a new definition of alcoholism as constructed by a multidisciplinary committee of the National Council on Alcoholism and Drug Dependence and the American Society of Addiction Medicine. The committee found: "Alcoholism is a primary disease with genetic, psychosocial, and environmental factors influencing its development and manifestations.

The disease is often progressive and fatal. It is characterized by impaired control over drinking, preoccupation with the drug alcohol, use of alcohol despite adverse consequences, and distortions of thinking, most notably denial. Each of these symptoms may be continuous or periodic." Historically, airlines and government have been reluctant to allow pilots to continue flight duties if they showed any signs of less than excellent health or normal behavior. Some modifications of this philosophy began to appear in the 1950's when it became apparent that medical standards were too conservative and were hurting individual pilots without an accompanying increase in flight safety.

Today, the liberalization of medical standards continues in many areas where experience has led the FAA to allow airmen to fly despite the use of previously disallowed medications, surgical procedures, or other medical conditions that have little impact on flight safety.

From 1960 to 1971 (Pakull, 1979) eight airline pilots petitioned the FAA for an exemption to the mandatory deniable condition of alcoholism. No petitioners were granted relief from this standard during this period. Between 1972 and 1975, 21 airline pilots filed petitions, with 18 exemptions granted. The first real impact of increased exemptions showed in the statistics in 1976. Both HIMS and some company Employee Assistance Plans (EAP's) were now in effect and working together. Figure 1 delineates that change

Years	Number
1976-1977	96
1978-1979	163
1980-1981	121
1982-1983	124
1984-1985	174
1986-1987	163
1988-1989	168
1990-1991	221

Figure 1. Aeromedical Certification Exemptions/Special Issuances (Pakull)

Between 1974 and 1982, HIMS operated with moneys from the US Government as well as the support of the ALPA and companies dedicated to changing the old way of doing things. Training sessions were held for management, peers, and physicians. Each management and pilot group developed it own style, but consistent in all programs were training, cooperation, and compassion. The FAA was closely involved in training and also streamlined it own procedures for the recertification of airmen who were considered alcoholics. What evolved out of this eight-year government-supported program is still substantially unchanged. The technique consists of identification, intervention, treatment, continuing care, and monitoring.

The first requirements for embarking on this program are an enlightened company policy statement and an agreement between labor and management. Not all the T's have to be crossed, but senior managers must understand the realities of the disease and peers have to be ready to work cooperatively with management in the pilots' best interest. The training of supervisors and peers really starts the program. We believe it is important to do this training together because it forges greater trust between managers and peers.

A variety of persons close to the alcoholic pilot may provide the initial identification. Family, peers, and supervisors provide the bulk of the data needed to progress to an intervention. The sharing of confidential information between managers and peer committee workers begins slowly as trust is gradually gained. Experience shows that the labor-management barrier disappears more rapidly than might be thought. Even an aggressively hostile relationship between management and pilots can be put aside when the need to help another employee is at stake.

Interventions are intended to break down the pilots' denial so that they will seek treatment. An intervention is conducted in a carefully controlled and previously rehearsed atmosphere. It is normally held on company property and may consist of family members or other pilots who can recount actual instances where drinking caused problems. A trained alcoholism counsellor, chief pilot, and peer representative provide strength and guidance in the intervention. A successful intervention results in the pilot agreeing to an evaluation and treatment, if appropriate.

Evaluation and treatment usually consists of a 28-day in-patient regime. Treatment centers are selected for the quality of their in-patient treatment as well as the post-treatment care, now commonly referred to as continuing care. Centers who tie their continuing care to Alcoholics Anonymous are preferred.

If the pilot has made suitable progress throughout the treatment phase and continuing care phase, the pilot may be recertified within two to six months. A psychiatric evaluation must accompany the applications for recertification, and the physician who will monitor the pilot during the monitoring phase must support the pilot's recertification. Of course, the physician must also have been trained, as were the managers and peers. We call these trained physicians "independent medical sponsors".

The monitoring of pilots continues for no less than two years following recertification. These monitoring sessions are conducted monthly by the trained manager, peer, and medical sponsor, usually independently. Written reports are forwarded to the pilot's independent medical sponsor.

Between 1982 and 1992, ALPA sponsored frequent training sessions and some airlines developed their own training programs. However, by 1992 the FAA wanted to take a more proactive part in the continuation and expansion of the program. Thus in 1992 the FAA published a request for proposals to stimulate and expand the HIMS Program. ALPA applied for and was successful in obtaining a two-and-one-half-year contract for the support of HIMS (now with the new title, "HIMS II"). The contract requires that assistance be given to all sectors of the US airline industry. Just over one year of that contract has concluded. The contract calls for periodic training sessions and the development and distribution of educational and training materials. The training sessions are in two forms. One is a three-day session, intended for managers, peers, or physicians. The second is a one-day training session specifically for regional airline personnel who cannot attend the three-day sessions. These one-day sessions are numerous and conducted in different areas of the country. Figure 2 describes the curriculum of the three-day training session.

> The Disease Concept of Alcoholism
> Identification of Potential Cases
> Physiology of Alcohol and Drug Abuse
> Behavioral Indicators of Pilot Problems
> Intervention I - Methodology
> Intervention II - In Practice
> Treatment
> FAA Overview of Medical Certification Issues
> Preparing Cases for Medical Certification
> FAA Certification Standards for Successful Recovery From Alcohol and Drug Abuse
> Continuing Care Concepts
> The Monitoring Interview and Reports
> Legal Issues in Addictive Disorders
> SPECIALTY WORKSHOP FOR MEDICAL SPONSORS Physicians Only
> Medical Monitoring and Relapses
> Initiating a Program
> Elements of a Model Program

Figure 2. The HIMS II three-day seminar

There are other critical parts of the HIMS II contract with the FAA. A video describing the HIMS process was produced and distributed and is intended for pilot recurrent training. The video attempts to portray how HIMS works and the average line pilot's role in the process. Three educational brochures will be distributed to the pilots' homes. The families are the first victims of alcoholism but often are the least capable of knowing what to do. They need to know help exists without jeopardizing the career and income of the pilot. Finally, the contract will produce a manual that describes a model program for airlines who wish to introduce a new program or evaluate an existing program.

As of late in 1993, the FAA had recertified almost 2000 airline pilots who have been diagnosed as alcoholics. The success rate has been approximately 92%. Relapses occur at the rate of just under 10% within the first two years. A cost-benefit analysis of this program shows a savings of four to five times the investment when returning experienced, expensively training and qualified pilots to the cockpit.

Alcoholism can affect flight safety. An untreated alcoholic who decides to quit drinking may suffer a seizure disorder. At the wrong time that can spell disaster in an airplane. We now know that many pilots (including alcoholics) drink only during their time off. Drinking while on duty is usually the province of the late stage alcoholic.

We are hopeful that the days of considering alcoholism a character weakness are behind us. Genetic predisposition and environmental factors have been identified as playing a large role in alcoholism. The strength of the HIMS program lies in its method, cooperation between management and the pilot group, and in the airline pilot's desire to continue to fly.

References

FAA (1976) Alcoholism and Airline Flight Crew members. Federal Aviation Administration letter.

Pakull, B (1979). Improving the Prognosis for Successful Rehabilitation. Fourth Southeastern Conference on Alcohol and Drug Abuse. December 16, 1979, Atlanta, Georgia.

Pakull, B. Unpublished data

Section B
PERSONALITY

48 Personality on the flight deck

Greg Stead
Managing Consultant, Saville and Holdsworth Australia

What is personality?

The word "personality" is derived from the Latin "persona". A persona we are told was originally a mask used by actors in Greek theatre to portray different stage parts. Gradually the word came to mean the character being portrayed rather than just the mask itself. The origin of "persona" meaning mask is significant in that some psychologists see personality as a series of assumed roles which we act out in different circumstances.

Because we behave differently depending on the particular circumstances in which we find ourselves it begs the question whether it is possible to establish any general truth about what an individual's personality really is. Research suggests, however, that although we are able to adapt our behaviour to particular circumstances, there is nevertheless a good degree of consistency in our behaviour.

Whilst there are a number of definitions of personality, the one that I suggest as being appropriate is; *personality is that which is concerned with a person's typical or preferred way of behaving, thinking and feeling*.

People vary in their personality. That is to say there are demonstrable individual differences between people. Whilst these differences in human behaviour are consistent to a great extent, it should be recognised that personality is not a rigid, fixed characteristic, it is capable of change but will still show certain stabilities. This recognises the day to day variations we see in individual behaviours. Despite these variations there will be certain behaviour styles which some individuals are likely to find difficult to adopt. In this regard the desired personality for given job activities can be difficult for some individuals to maintain. Personality in the occupational context, then, may be seen as an ability as much as an emotional construct.

That we often behave differently in different situations begs the question of whether it is possible to establish any general truth about what an individual's personality really is. Research suggests, however, that although we are able to adapt our behaviour to particular circumstances, there is nevertheless considerable consistency in our behaviour across situations and over time.

There are many influences that can impinge upon our attempts to control and modulate our behaviour. These include, biological, cultural, situational, and environmental influences that will affect each of us differently and, in a work context, can influence the quality of our performance.

The relevance of personality at work

Personality characteristics are often key attributes which differentiate between people's effectiveness in a job. It is reasonable to suggest that approximately 70% of attributes which are associated with success at work are dimensions of personality rather than ability. In aviation, especially in a multi-crew flying role some of these attributes may include:

- *Influence/Leadership* - Able to take charge and control a team towards an objective, making their presence felt, motivating subordinates, delegating effectively and monitoring performance.
- *Communication Skills* - Able to comprehend and express ideas and opinions accurately and persuasively.
- *Organising/Planning* - Able to think ahead, prioritise and organise.
- *Motivation/Energy* - Shows energy, drive and enthusiasm. Maintain high work output, is proactive rather than reactive.
- *Analytical* - Reasons objectively and critically with both verbal and numerical problems, comprehends and processes information at a high level of complexity.
- *Empathy* - Able to understand the strengths, weaknesses, views and feelings of others, supports others and is a good crew member.
- *Emotional Maturity* - Responds well to criticism, is frank and open and able to take pressure.
- *Decision Making* - Having the confidence to take own decisions but is prepared to listen to the views and inputs of others.

Whilst the above criteria may not be applicable to all aviation organisations, they do highlight the fact that personality can be an integral component leading to job success. Despite this fact, promotion or important responsibilities are often given on the basis of technical qualifications or status.

Personality and attitudes

Personality traits (characteristics) and attitudes are interwoven and have a fundamental influence on the way we conduct our lives, both in our private lives and our work lives (Hawkins 1987). Basically, attitudes describe our likes and dislikes. An attitude then, is **"that state of mind which pre-determines and governs our approach to people and situations"** (Qantas CRM 1989).

It is not unreasonable to suggest that many of our attitudes and beliefs are deeply seated in the personality of the individuals holding these attitudes and that they often lie in our early life experiences and in our work and social settings. Some of these attitudes become firmly internalised while others are more superficial and can more easily be subject to change or modification.

Attitudes can be both positive and negative and the stronger the attitude the more the potential for distortion of "reality". In flight deck situations where the focus must be continually on monitoring and evaluating factual data, strong attitudes, either positive or negative are not appropriate. They can affect performance significantly (Qantas CRM 1989). Attitudes have an effect on such things as *Decision Making, Communications, Team Work and Leadership*.

An example where the attitude of one pilot adversely affecting communication, team work and indeed leadership responsibility can be found in the following example:

> "Air Traffic Control had issued a speed restriction which was repeatedly ignored by the captain. After several attempts had been made by the co-pilot to convey the information, the captain responded by saying, 'I'll do what I want.' Air Traffic Control enquired as to why the aircraft had not been slowed, advised the crew that they almost collided with another aircraft and issued a new clearance which was also disregarded by the captain despite repeated clarification by the co-pilot. Following the last advisory from the co-pilot the captain responded by telling the co-pilot 'just look out the damn window'" (Foushee and Helmreich 1988).

There is considerable evidence available which highlights those aircrew involved in most incidents and accidents, which are attributable to poor human performance, had at the time of the incident or accident, the capacity and skills to have performed effectively, yet appeared not able to do so. Thus, performance was influenced by factors other than the possession of technical skills, medical fitness, or cognitive reasoning abilities. Where human performance has significantly decreased, all such situations and behaviours involve personality or attitudes, which in aviation not only has an effect on efficiency but also on safety. In fact, personality and attitude differences have been cited in many surveys of pilots as being a cause of problems on the flight deck.

Can attitudes be changed?

The simple answer is yes, although, the process of change is not all that easy to achieve. Many attitudes tend to be enduring and quite resistant to change. Our attitudes towards seniority, duty schedules and pay are examples of those attitudes that tend to be very resistant to change. However, not all attitudes are so resistant. Those which are not central to a belief or an essential part of one's basic perception of life and living may be changed more easily (Hawkins 1987)

Many airlines both large and small have been attempting, through such courses/programs as *crew resource management* (CRM) to heighten pilot awareness of the dangers of holding entrenched attitudes that run counter to crew cohesiveness, communication, decision making and leadership. These programs which focus, in the main, on group interaction and team work have, as an outcome, operating effectiveness and safety. The effectiveness of such training programs in changing an attitude will, of course, depend on the strength of individually held attitudes. There is evidence to date that suggests these programs are effective, although there will always be some pilots who will be resistant to change for many different reasons.

What about personality?

It is unrealistic to imagine that routine training within the aviation industry in general, or in airline captaincy or management training in particular, can have a significant influence on personality traits. These are deep-seated characteristics which are not easily amenable to change. In the aviation industry, and particularly in flying, undesirable personality traits must be detected during the initial screening and selection process and appropriate action taken at the time (Hawkins 1987). This is not as easy as it sounds, and is not without its difficulties. Given that we can determine a person's personality style, there is still a requirement to identify the criteria to be used and the desirable and undesirable personality characteristics relating to particular flying roles. It is not unrealistic to assume that there will be differing requirements for different organisations and for different flying operations.

The pilot role has been evolving since the Wright brothers first took to the air. The early pilots had no crew to manage and no computer to program and many of these early pilots were strong individualists, pioneers and adventurers. A personality problem may have led to their own demise but it was unlikely to have made the headlines as a major international disaster.

Today's pilot has responsibility for a more complex aircraft that includes computers and automatic flight guidance systems on the flight-deck. These aircraft, more often than not, are multi-crewed. The required personality characteristics of the pilot of today and, indeed tomorrow are not only different from early pilots, but is arguably quite different from those pilots of only a generation ago. Even into the 50's and 60's, many airlines and charter operators did not discourage individualism on the flight-deck. The 1952 guidelines for pilot proficiency checks at a major airline explicitly stated that the first officer should not correct errors made by the captain. Even today, aviation regulations covering pilot qualifications deal almost exclusively with the acquisition and maintenance of individual pilot proficiency (Foushee and Helmreich 1988), although we are seeing the introduction of Human Factor, Crew Resource Management, and Team Building type programs into commercial and/or ATPL license courses.

Personality and team work

Much of the work most of us undertake includes interacting or directly working with other people. Even single pilot operations are dependent to some degree, on others, eg ATC, Company Management and staff, refuellers etc. The safe and efficient operations of the aircraft, whilst primarily in the hands of the pilot, are also dependent upon the direct or indirect co-operation and support of others.

Team work can however, be best illustrated by multi-crew operations. The Australian pocket Oxford Dictionary (1976) defines cockpit as *"a place of many battles; space for pilot in aircraft"*. It is not surprising that many interpersonal phenomena can affect flying operations - thus the words "a place of many battles", while not specifically referring to an aircraft cockpit, can be reflective of the actual working environment. A cockpit crew is a highly structured small group where a number of social, organisational and personality factors are directly relevant to flight efficiency and safety.

Airline crews are task teams that are more structured and less voluntary than social groups. Task teams are usually characterised by:

- Individuals who must interact in order to accomplish some specific task;
- Relationships in the team which are usually defined by the organisation and involve members holding different of authority and responsibility;
- Individuals working in close proximity to each other;
- The duration of the team being dependent upon the nature and achievement of the task (Qantas CRM 1989).

It can be assumed that the development of a strong group norm (group behaviour) will increase the probability that subordinate crew members will function more effectively in critical instances. Obviously, the captain's leadership style and indeed personality, is an important component for the establishment of such a norm, but it is by no means the only component (Foushee and Helmreich 1988). However, it should be recognised that an over commitment to team conformity or group thinking characteristics can and will have a strong negative influence on team behaviour and overall performance where members of the team (crew) go out of their way to avoid even soft criticism of the ideas, actions and decisions of other team members. This is often done to avoid disrupting the very cosy, comfortable, amicable team environment that exists not only in performing their flight-deck duties but also in the time spend socialising together. It is important to emphasise, however, that group norms are more than just standard operating procedures (SOP's). They include how crew interact generally both on and off the flight deck.

To achieve effective team work, all members of the team have to work at it. A group of highly qualified individuals does not necessarily constitute an effective team. How we react to other members of the team, our own personality, the personality of other team members, our biases, prejudices, our attitudes and many other group and environmental influences can all lead to substantial performance differences when we are required to work closely with many different types of people.

By no means does all inefficient crew work lead to unsafe operations. However, inefficient crew work has been a clausal factor in many accidents and incidents. It is important for pilots, and indeed other company staff to have some understanding of team dynamics and to have at least some basic understanding of human behaviour and how it directly relates to human performance. Although there is no one singular personality type that will make one person a better pilot than another, there are many individual behaviours, or characteristics, that can help or hinder pilots in the performance of their work.

Summary

Attitudes can, albeit with difficulty, be changed and many aviation organisations have initiated programs to bring this about. The techniques used are found in such programs as CRM, Air Crew Awareness, Loft, various types of seminars and feedback sessions. These programs are, primarily, aimed at increasing the skills of pilots in relation to small group functioning. Some pilots are willing to change their attitudes as they can see the benefits of enhanced crew performance.

Others change more reluctantly and it is often the peer pressure that helps to facilitate change amongst those pilots who are initially resistant to change. Of course, there is also another group that is completely resistant to change no matter how much pressure is placed upon them.

Personality on the other hand is far more enduring and less susceptible to major change. This is not to say that we will not see some change within the personality of an individual over a period of time. Changes in personality are likely to be quite subtle and influenced largely by what is happening around us. These changes will usually occur over longer rather than shorter time frames. There is considerable evidence to support the view that personality is an important factor in many incidents and accidents and that it plays a significant role in the overall maintenance of flight safety, be it single pilot or multi-crew flying.

The operation of a sophisticated multi-crew aircraft is, as has been mentioned, a highly structured team performance situation where there exists many individual interpersonal factors relevant to air-crew effectiveness. The personality of each individual in a flight-deck crew can have a direct bearing on overall crew efficiency and personality and its relationship to team dynamics is often not easily understood and have been too easily overlooked by many operators.

Personality is not a dirty eleven letter word. Arguably, personality variables do account for large differences that occur in the quality of work performance between individuals, given those individuals have similar levels of skills and abilities. The assessment of personality criteria to be used during selection, be it for a small or large aviation organisations, must not only take into account the role of a pilot as it exists today, but also as it may evolve over the next generation of pilots. Personality is assessable and there are various techniques for doing this, but it is important that our selection criteria be consistent with operational and training needs and there should be a focus on identifying those pilot candidates who are congruent with CRM type objectives.

References

Foushee H.C., and Helmreich, R.L. (1988) 'Group Interaction and Flight Crew Performance', in Weiner, E.L. and Nagel, D.C. (eds), *Human Factors in Aviation,* Academic Press, San Diego

Hawkins, F.H. (1987)*Human Factors in Flight,* Gower Technical Press, Aldershot

Qantas CRM (1989)*Qantas Cockpit Resource Management,* Qantas Airways Ltd, Sydney

Saville, P. and Holdsworth, R.(1992) *Occupational Personality Questionnaire Course Notes,* London

49 A comparison of personality characteristics for freshmen entering a university professional pilot program with third-year students and airline pilots

Joseph H. Dunlap and Maureen A. Pettitt PhD
Western Michigan University

Introduction

With the decreasing number of pilots being produced by a down-sized military and a declining general aviation sector, the U. S. airline industry will be looking to other sources of qualified pilots. Certainly as we approach the next decade, collegiate aviation programs will increasingly be called upon to educate the future pilot population. It is also likely that this educational shift will be accompanied by a reevaluation of the methods presently used for pilot selection and training.

Pilot selection procedures in the airline industry have traditionally emphasized psychomotor and technical skills. Personality assessment has been used primarily to screen out undesirable candidates rather than to select optimal candidates. For example, the U.S. airline industry has relied on clinical personality assessment tools, such as the Minnesota Multiphasic Personality Inventory (MMPI). While these instruments may be appropriate for the clinical diagnosis required for therapy, most pilot applicants do not suffer from behavioral disorders.

The authors believe a better approach would be the use of a personality instrument that discriminates within the normal range of behavior--one that reveals information about critical work-related traits and can, in turn, be linked to academic and operational performance. Especially significant to this theoretical foundation is the evidence indicating that the effectiveness of airline crews is a product of not only technical skills and attitudes, but also the more stable personality traits of the crew members (Chidester, Helmreich, Gregorich & Geis, 1991; Hormann & Maschke, 1993).

The NEO Personality Inventory

The NEO-PI was developed to operationalize the five-factor model of personality. Factors are defined by groups of intercorrelated traits. Specific traits are referred to as facets and each cluster of facets is termed a domain. The NEO-PI has five domain scales: Neuroticism, Angry Hostility, Depression, Self-Consciousness, Impulsiveness, and Vulnerability. Within each domain there are six facet scales. The NEO-PI personality inventory was selected for use in this study because of the focus on normal behavioral traits and the predictive value of several NEO scales with occupational performance (Barrick and Mount, 1991).

Purpose of the study

This study represents the first phase of a multi-phase project to develop a model to select professional pilot applicants into a university aviation flight program. The research presented here has two objectives. The first is to determine if the personality profile of freshmen enrolled in an introductory aviation course is significantly different from the personality profile of persistors, those students enrolled in third-year flight courses. The second objective is to determine if there are any significant differences between the university students and a selected sample of 20 pilots employed by a major U.S. carrier.

The researchers were also interested in analyzing differences in the student population based on demographic factors, such as gender and degree objective, and examining the relationship between the NEO-PI scales and academic success.

Method

The self-report version of the Revised NEO Personality Inventory (NEO-PI-R) was administered to 142 students who were enrolled in four-year aviation degree programs at a U.S. university. The degree programs included professional pilot, aviation maintenance management, aircraft maintenance engineering technology, and aviation technical management. The first student group consisted of 92 aviation majors enrolled in the freshman introductory aviation course. Of this group, the majority--69 students--were professional pilot majors. The second student group consisted of 50 professional pilot majors enrolled in one of three third-year (junior) flight courses. The third group in this study was a selected sample of 20 pilots employed by a major U.S. carrier.

Results

The scores of the 142 aviation students were plotted on the NEO profile form to get a general sense of these students relative to the normative groups by gender. Male and female scores were plotted on the corresponding profile sheet. Both male and female students were higher than the normative group on Extraversion. This can be accounted for primarily by the higher score on Excitement Seeking facet of this dimension for both groups. Interestingly, in the Conscientiousness domain, both male and female students scored slightly lower on the Dutifulness facet than the normative group and the males also scored lower in the Self-Discipline facet in this domain.

The t-test for independent samples was used to compare the scores of students enrolled in the freshman course with students enrolled in the junior flight courses. We have used the term persistors to describe the latter group since these students have persisted in their academic career. Significant differences were found in three domains: Neuroticism, Extraversion, and Conscientiousness. The greatest differences were found in the Neuroticism domain. Students enrolled in the freshman course are more prone to feelings of guilt and sadness (Depression), inferiority (Self-Consciousness), and less able to cope with stress (Vulnerability) than students enrolled in the junior course. The persistors were significantly more forceful and dominant (Assertiveness) and feel more capable and effective (Competence) than the first-year students.

When the professional pilot majors enrolled in both the freshman and junior courses were compared, the only significant differences were in the Neuroticism domain. The persistors scored lower on the Depression, Self-Consciousness, and Vulnerability scales.

While there were only 23 non-pilot majors in the sample, the scores between the professional pilot and non-pilot majors were compared. The non-pilot majors were more self-conscious and, interestingly, their scores suggested this group is less friendly and affectionate, less assertive, and less likely to experience positive emotions than the pilot group.

The authors were also interested in the differences in scores based on gender. The 23 female aviation students--16 of whom are professional pilot majors--are significantly more anxious than their male counterparts and more prone to feelings of guilt, hopelessness, and loneliness. However, these women also have a deeper appreciation for art and beauty (Aesthetics), are more willing to try different activities or new experiences (Actions), and more readily reexamine social, political, and religious values (Values) than the male students.

In addition, there were significant differences between the male and female students in the Agreeableness domain. The significantly low scores on the Straightforwardness facet suggest that male students are more willing to manipulate others through flattery, craftiness, or deception than are female students. The lower scores on the Tender-Mindedness facet indicate that the male students are both more hardheaded and hardhearted than the female students.

Because there is some evidence to suggest that a relationship exists between academic and occupational success and the traits associated with Openness (McCrae, 1987) and traits associated with Conscientiousness (McCrae & Costa, 1987), the correlations between the grade point average of the persistors and the NEO-PI scales were analyzed. The highest correlations--in number and significance--are between grade point average and the Conscientiousness domain and all six facets in this domain: Competence, Order, Dutifulness, Achievement Striving, Self-Discipline, and Deliberation. Moderately high positive correlations were also found between grade point average and both Trust and Straightforwardness in the Agreeableness domain. There are moderately high negative correlations between two facets in the Neuroticism domain, Depression and Impulsiveness, and the Aesthetics facet in Openness.

The t-test for independent samples was used to compare the scores of the students who were professional pilot majors with the airline pilots. There were significant differences between these groups in the Neuroticism domain and in all six facets in this domain, the students scoring higher than the pilots on Anxiety, Angry Hostility, Depression, Self-Consciousness, Impulsiveness, and Vulnerability. The students also scored significantly higher on the Excitement-Seeking facet in the Extraversion domain. The students also scored significantly lower on the Agreeableness dimension and on Trust, Straightforwardness, and Compliance in that domain. They were significantly lower on Conscientiousness and five of the six facets in that domain: Competence, Dutifulness, Achievement Striving, Self-Discipline and Deliberation.

Conclusions and discussion

Overall, the aviation students included in the study scored higher on Excitement-Seeking than the normative group. Professional Pilot majors who had persisted to their junior year of course work scored lower on Neuroticism and on the Depression, Self-Consciousness, and Vulnerability facets within that domain than students in the freshman course. The female students scored higher on Anxiety and Depression, higher on Openness and several facets within that domain, and higher on both Straightforwardness and Tendermindedness than the male students.

Barrick and Mount's (1991) meta-analysis of 117 criterion-related validity studies examined the relation of the five personality factors to job proficiency, training proficiency, and personnel data for a wide range of occupational groups. Since the ultimate goal of our larger research project is to be able to better predict the academic and occupational success of pilot candidates, Barrick and Mount's findings provide an interesting comparison.

Barrick and Mount found the Conscientiousness dimension to be a consistently valid predictor of training proficiency and job proficiency across the wide range of occupational groups included in their study. Our research supports their findings--grade point average was highly correlated with the Conscientiousness domain and with all six facets in this domain.

Another finding in Barrick and Mount's meta-analysis was that Openness to Experience was a valid predictor of training proficiency but not job proficiency. They theorize that individuals with high scores on this dimension have a more positive attitude toward learning experiences. It is also this dimension which has the highest correlation of any of the personality dimensions with measures of cognitive ability (McCrae & Costa, 1987). It is interesting, then, that in the present study there is little relation between grade point average and the Openness domain or any of the facets within Openness. More surprising, with the exception of Values, the relationships are negative.

Extraversion was also found to be a predictor of training proficiency. This scale, Barrick and Mount suggest, may in fact differentiate between active and passive learners. While in the present study the correlations between Extraversion and grade point average were relatively low, it is worth noting that the persistors scored significantly higher on Extraversion than the students enrolled in the freshman course.

This study has potentially important implications for pilot selection and training. First, our findings support the notion that there is a strong relationship between the Conscientiousness personality dimension and academic success, as measured by grade point average. Second, the finding that persistors scored significantly higher on Extraversion than students enrolled in the freshman course may also provide additional insight into the personality dimensions associated with academic persistence.

Another intriguing finding is the significant differences between the students and airline pilots. More research is needed to explain these differences. The next phase of this research project is to identify multiple measures of cockpit performance which can then be correlated with the personality dimensions used in the NEO-PI.

References

Barrick, M. P., and Mount, M. K. (1991), 'The big five personality dimensions and job performance: A meta-analysis', *Personnel Psychology,* **44**, 1-26.

Chidester, T., Helmreich, R., Gregorich, S., and Geis, C. (1991), 'Pilot personality and crew coordination: Implications for training and selection', *The International Journal of Aviation Psychology,* **1**, 25-44.

Hormann, H. and Maschke, P. (1993), 'Personality scales as predictors for job success of airline pilots', *Proceedings of the Seventh International Symposium on Aviation Psychology,* Ohio State University, Columbus, Ohio.

McCrae, R. R. (1987), 'Creativity, divergent thinking, and openness to experience', *Journal of Personality and Social Psychology,* **52**, 1258-1265.

McCrae, R. R., and Costa, P. T. Jr. (1987), 'Validation of the five-factor model of personality across instruments and observers', *Journal of Personality and Social Psychology,* **52**, 81-90.

Section C
PSYCHOPATHOLOGY

50 Flying, depression and social disruption

Oscar Quintero MD
Aviateca Airlines, Medical and Industrial Relationships Managing Department, Guatemala

Introduction

Despite an apparently totally healthy state and consequent productiveness in daily work, depression, as an always potentially present entity in human emotional and psychological spheres, adopts light or masked forms in those persons who are constantly involved in extreme or high stress situations. In so many cases however, this is not the main reason for the referred pathology to show up, it is merely due to the consequences of this kind of living for the person affected. This paper refers specially to the alterations that the psycho-socio-sentimental status (marriages, friendships, unions, alliances, etc.) suffers throughout a "vicious" cycle, in which emotional alterations affect both personal and working life (e.g.with the couple at home or in work showing a defiance for authority, or showing a lack of a real interest, showing lack of concentration and difficulties in relationships with work mates). Logically, this starts and ends with the individual's personality. And though these are elements that in no way can be considered new in psychopathology; rather they receive a new focus.

Hypothesis

At least a 40% of flying personnel actually suffer some kind of covert or hidden form of depression, associated with disruption of psycho-socio-sentimental states.

Background

Within the terms of reference of the study, it is very important to establish as a fact that people involved in flight activities might be identified with the stereotype of persons with psycho-affective disorders, principally because of the over-control of their emotions and specifically the material and time elements in life. Some persons in this group also have shown a constant adventure seeking mood, that makes them very fond, but not deeply bonded and real, in the sentimental area. They have been recognized throughout history as glamorous and likely to prefer and to execute, what are for most people rather non-normal activities,but certainly usual for them, such as flying, constant travelling, facing one or another risk, changing location, or meeting new people.

The study

Personnel included in this study (20 pilots and 20 flight attendants) were chosen at random from a group of volunteers to whom the purposes of the study were all explained, except for the home relationship, so that disposition could not invalidate the answers. Conditions for the study were, as follows:

a- Flight attendants:

10 female, 10 male, not under 20 years old, having a minimum of 3 years working in the job area. Not specifically from any particular airline, but from Guatemala

b- Pilots:

20 male, with a minimum of 1 year working for an airline company (in Central America); minimum experience time of 5 years in airliners, 10 with military background, 10 with civilian training

Tools

In the main, clinical interviewing was used to detect elements of depression. As well as this, a scale designed by the author in which different depressive symptoms and facts were graded,was used with each person. Scores were as follows:
a- depression absent: 0-3
b- hidden and mild depressive states: 4-6
c- depressed (but still mild): 7-10

Results

Results were distributed in groups. The first is related to age. Second is the findings of depressive indexes and their relation with the integration of homes. Finally, the results of anxiety, anguish, fears, guilt and the rest of the symptoms related to various depressive states are included in the other table. Codes for reading all tables, are:

    a = age in years
    p = pilots
    paf= former air force pilots
    cp = civilian trained pilots
    W = flight attendants, women
    M = flight attendants, men

Table 1
Age distribution

a	paf	cp	W	M	frequency
20-23	0	1	2	2	5
24-27	0	1	4	1	6
28-31	1	2	3	7	13
32-35	6	4	1	0	11
36-39	1	2	0	0	3
40-43	2	0	0	0	2
Totals	**10**	**10**	**10**	**10**	**40**

Table 2

Parents and actual home conditions, and current depressive indexes comparisons

Condition	Parents home	Actual home	Depression
Married	13	13	7
L.Together	2	6	
Divorced	8	10	5
Abandoned	4	2	1
Single P.	1	5	1
Widows	9		7
New wedd.	1	2	1
Others	1	2	
Totals	**39**	**40**	**22**

Table 3

Events in persons with depressive mood

Events	paf	cp	W	M
Anxiety	1	3	5	2
Guilt	6	2	4	1
Remorse	1	0	1	1
Anguish	1	3	4	0
Occ. Sadness	2	3	2	1
Self harm ideas	1	0	0	1
Fears	3	4	1	2
Psy. som.	7	5	9	6
Totals	**22**	**20**	**26**	**14**

Discussion

As in all activities dictated by emotions, in life the real psychological and social base for the existence of mature and real feelings in adulthood is located in childhood and some particular home characteristics. Sixty three percent of persons (25) in the group have family antecedents in which the nucleus of the family has suffered some disruption, either voluntarily or forced by circumstances. In those cases, mainly related to mourning, and not only with deceased parents but also in those in which daily living has been altered (e.g. a broken relationship of a couple, divorces, separations, unfaithful behavior, high pitched constant discussions, and constant differences of criteria led to the breakdown of the stable familial reference frame). This non-resolved situation urges the need to chase an ever running, adventurous and changing life, so it can compensate for the absence and the consequent lack of that cherished and lost love. This situation will not allow a real and easy solution in a very high number of cases; not even in those in which the parents and close relatives are yet alive, if a social disruption has prevailed. Similar are those too, in which the circumstances of working force an individual to abandon his activities and presence at home (it must be noted, that it is not purely economical or financial presence, because at any time, in most cases, he or she will be able to give the needed amount). The individual thus starts to confront not only the belonging but also the feelings of compunction, created fundamentally by anxiety and guilt born from "sadness" of not being able (depending on the productive stage of life) to give the family not only enough time but also the right kind of time, that, in one way or another, could be a compensation for that absence.

Conclusions

1. In this very particular case, the psycho-social cultural role determines a special and important place for manifestations of depression mainly because Latin American people are very prone to miss home easily. Some years ago the Boeing Company conducted a study in which through the "Power Distance Index", they got to measure, among other cultural influences, the "homesick" elements among pilots of various countries. For this study it is the highest one.
2. Principal and important manifestations of depressive mood occurred in 47.5% of the sample. Of those who are married (n = 13) 7 showed hidden depression (17.5% of the sample). Of those who are divorced 5 exhibited depressive mood (12.5%) of the widows with family (of both sexes) 6 showed a hidden depressive mood (15%) and one with a mild presentation (2.5%).
3. Of the persons (26 in all) with a depressive mood, a total of 16 presented some psychosomatic manifestation (65%), being the most frequent, followed by gastrointestinal disturbances, respiratory tract irregularities and finally skin and respiratory tract allergic manifestations.
4. The largest frequency of age in this study is in the range from 24 to 35 years, a very productive age.
5. Factors mentioned in this paper are another element to be taken into account for flight security considerations, in the particular geographic and socio-cultural area of study, as well as in others, where some of these manifestations could be present, but yet unnoticed.
6. Consideration of particularly difficult themes, such as use and abuse of some medicinal drugs and substances (anxiolitics, opiates, barbiturates, alcohol), private matters concerning promiscuity, sexual conduct, as well as pathological or other personality factors necessarily involved with aviation and flying shall be open to further and deeper studies.

Solution strategies

1. Establishing and improving periodic evaluations of emotional aspects of personnel will further help to avoid incidents.
2. Assembly of counselling groups, among the different work teams will help in learning how to deal with and manage these situations.
3. It is important to think about the creation of prophylactic methods to prevent incapacitation, and learning methods, e.g. stress managing techniques, sports activities, and family involvement in art practices and games.

References

The Boeing Company, Flight Safety Trends, Culture & Accident Relationships. U.S.A.